ƒP

MARKETING STRATEGY

Customers and Competition

SECOND REVISED AND UPDATED EDITION

STEVEN P. SCHNAARS

THE FREE PRESS

NEW YORK LONDON TORONTO SYDNEY SINGAPORE

*f*P

THE FREE PRESS
A Division of Simon & Schuster Inc.
1230 Avenue of the Americas
New York, N.Y. 10020

THE FREE PRESS and colophon are trademarks
of Simon & Schuster Inc.

Designed by Michael Mendelsohn of MM Design 2000, Inc.

Manufactured in the United States of America

10   9   8   7   6   5   4   3   2   1

Library of Congress Cataloging-in-Publication Data

Schnaars, Steven P.
    Marketing strategy: a customer-driven approach /
Steven P. Schnaars.—2nd rev. and updated ed.
        p.   cm.
    Includes bibliographical references and index.
    1. Marketing—Management. 2. Strategic planning. 3. Competition
I. Title.
HF5415.13.S345   1998
658.8'02—DC21   97–21554
                                                        CIP

ISBN 0–684–83191–0

This book is dedicated to Francis Connelly,
a Dean who gave so much and died too young.

CONTENTS

CHAPTER 1

MARKETING'S INFLUENCE ON STRATEGIC THINKING

Business strategy has always relied heavily on marketing ideas, but in recent years the influence of marketing on strategy has grown greatly. Today, more than ever, strategy is dominated by ideas that sink their roots deeply into the discipline of marketing. Customer satisfaction, the idea of getting close to customers, creating a customer-driven company, the profit impact of new product introductions, and an explosion of product variety are among the ideas that now dominate strategic thinking. They supplement market share, market growth, and myriad other ideas that have previously been mainstays in strategy.

The reasons for this newfound interest are many. Competition is more intense and global in scope while product quality and customer expectations have risen steadily in the past decade. Firms must do more to compete. They must run faster merely to keep up.

But the most important reason for the ascendancy of marketing ideas in strategy is the realization that the most elegantly drawn strategic plans are worthless if the firm is unable to create satisfied customers willing to pay for the firm's products and services. Without that foundation the firm has virtually no chance of long-term success.

Marketing bywords such as "customer," "product," and "market" reverberate loudly throughout the study of strategy. Knowing your business, your customers, your markets, and your products are the essential ingredients for strategic success. Gone are the days when strategists thought they could manage diversified businesses like portfolios of stocks. With the benefit of hindsight it seems ridiculous to think that it did not matter what products the firm sold as long as the firm's position in that business was dominant. Today, customers are widely viewed as the cornerstone of a firm's very existence. It is for those reasons that firms scramble to create a customer orientation.

CONSUMER ORIENTATION

In recent years, there has been a virtual stampede to become customer oriented. Firms now strive to place customers at the center of all the firm's actions. They seek to form lasting relationships with customers, track customer expectations and satisfaction with products and services, and become more cognizant and responsive to changes in the marketplace. Such actions are a recognition that it is customers who will ultimately determine whether the firm's strategy was brilliantly conceived or blindly concocted.

THE MARKETING CONCEPT

Marketing has a long history of placing customers at the center of all marketing actions. Typical of that orientation is the series of imbedded boxes shown in Exhibit 1.1. As the exhibit illustrates, the customer-oriented firm centers its actions on serving consumer needs, wants, and desires. At the heart of this orientation is the marketing concept.

The marketing concept is the most fundamental precept in the discipline of marketing. It holds that firms should try to discover what consumers want and make products to satisfy those wants. It is based on the "market-pull" model of marketing, a commonsensical notion that consumers will demand products that meet their needs and pull them through the channel of distribu-

Exhibit 1.1
The Customer Is King

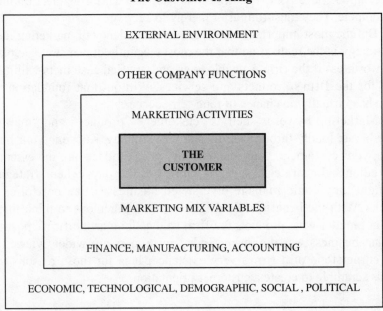

tion. When implemented correctly, a firm that employs the marketing concept will not have to rely on hard-sell campaigns to persuade consumers to buy the goods it produces. At the extreme, the marketing concept can be defined as that condition where selling is unnecessary.

The origin of the marketing concept lies with three prominent authors in the 1950s: (1) Peter Drucker in his landmark book *The Practice of Management,* (2) John B. McKitterick of General Electric (a firm that also pioneered many strategic planning techniques), and (3) Ted Levitt, the noted Harvard professor and author of the seminal article "Marketing Myopia." All three agree that the very purpose of business is to create satisfied customers. Most important, the marketing concept was conceived as, and remains, a long-term business orientation rather than a short-term, quarter-to-quarter, financial fix.

The marketing concept held sway throughout most of the 1950s and 1960s, a time when American business dominated world markets. By the 1970s, however, times had changed. Many of the newer strategic formulations ignored consumers and focused, instead, almost solely on the task of outfoxing competitors. With the orientation toward competitors during that decade, the importance of consumers was lost.

But a switchback in trend started to occur in the mid-1980s when Fredrick Webster, the noted marketing scholar, observed that many firms started "coming back to the basic marketing concept articulated in the mid-1950s."[1] He foresaw a marketing renaissance. Firms began to recognize that the fundamental purpose of business is customer satisfaction and the reward is profit. That was the essence of Peter Drucker's original statement about the marketing concept. He believed that financial goals were merely the results and rewards of customer satisfaction, not the primary purpose of business. The move toward creating a customer-oriented firm almost perfectly mirrors the disillusionment of corporate America with formal strategic planning tools based on financial analogies.

Fredrick Gluck, an expert on strategic planning, agrees with Webster's assessment. He concludes that newer strategic planning techniques are aimed at better understanding customers. The shift is long overdue. He notes: "The same kind of diligent information gathering some managers reserve for their competition should be focused on getting 'closer' to their customers."[2] Once again, strategy is reaffirming the marketing concept after a bout of philandering in the 1970s.

CRITICISMS OF THE MARKETING CONCEPT

The marketing concept is not without its critics. Some argue that the concept hurts rather than helps the competitive performance of firms that embrace it. Roger Bennett and Robert Cooper, for example, in two strongly worded articles, argue that the marketing concept has diverted attention away from a long-term emphasis on product development and quality manufacturing to a short-term emphasis on superfluous advertising, selling, and promotion.[3] As a result, product value has suffered. As evidence they point to the automobile and television industries, where American firms once dominated, but which are now dominated by imports. They blame the marketing concept for those industries' problems. While American firms stressed short-term promotions, these authors argue, foreign firms offered superior product value.

The marketing concept is flawed, they contend, because of its overreliance on the "market-pull" model, where marketing research is used to discover what consumers want. According to the "market-pull" model of innovation, marketing asks customers what kinds of new products and services they want, listens intently, then tells R&D which products to develop. Since consumers can only speak in terms of the familiar, they cannot express a need for radically different innovations with which they have no experience. Imagine consumers trying to tell a market researcher about their need for a compact disc player or a microwave oven before those products were introduced. It would be very unlikely. As a result, firms that rely on the "market-pull" model miss truly innovative products and instead focus on products billed as "new and improved" but that are really nothing more than minor product modifications and incidental line extensions. Those firms are then forced to rely on heavy promotion to catch up with firms that introduced truly innovative products. This is the tragedy of the marketing concept according to Bennett and Cooper.

Another influential article, published at about the same time by Robert Hayes and William Abernathy, voiced similar criticisms.[4] It argues that three trends have conspired to decimate the competitiveness of American business: (1) an overreliance on financial controls (management by the numbers), (2) portfolio management (managing a business like a portfolio of stocks), and (3) the marketing concept. They too belittle the "market-pull" model. The essence of their argument is that it has given us newfangled potato chips, deodorants, and pet rocks, but missed the truly creative innovations of our time, such as lasers, instant photography, xerography, and the transistor. In short, with the marketing concept, we are managing our way to economic decline.

SHOULD YOU IGNORE YOUR CUSTOMERS?

In more recent years, there has been an increasing call to ignore your customers! Consumers are said to be unimaginative, anchored to past practices, and the ultimate conformists. They are unwilling and unable to consider radically new ideas. Asking them what kinds of new products and services they want not only can't help but it can actually lead firms in the wrong direction. When Chrysler first tested its minivan, for instance, which turned out to be one of the most successful new cars introduced in a generation, consumers were troubled by its odd design and the fact that it was neither a passenger car nor a station wagon. They expressed little interest in the product. Had the firm listened to those customers it might have canceled the whole project. But Chrysler desperately needed a new product hit and decided to introduce the radical new van anyway. It turned out to be one of the best moves the company ever made. Market research might have argued for slight variations on existing models, but such a choice would surely have been far less successful than the bold move the company actually made.

Critics also argue that consumers often say one thing, then do another. Surveys show, for example, more interest in new low-fat foods than actual sales once those products are introduced. McDonald's McLean sandwich debuted to great fanfare but consumers stuck with the fat-laden burgers, which tasted better. Such results suggest that you cannot trust what consumers say about their own future behavior.

TECHNOLOGY-DRIVEN COMPANIES

Many companies gain competitive advantage and roar past rivals by creating breakthrough innovations. They do not listen to customers and are distrustful of marketing research and the marketing concept. These companies are technology driven rather than customer oriented. They understand that breakthrough innovations are not the result of marketing research or the market-pull model of innovation. Such innovations almost always come, instead, from the creativity and insight of scientists and engineers, who make technological discoveries and then work them into radically new products. Those new products are then put onto the market where they are either adopted or rejected by consumers. This "technology-push" model of innovation pushes the product toward consumers rather than allowing consumers to pull new products through the distribution pipeline. It is in this way, proponents argue, that truly new products such as fax machines, personal computers, and even mountain bikes work their way to market.

Technology-driven companies embrace an orientation toward markets akin to what is called the "product concept" in introductory marketing textbooks. It holds that consumers will demand products of the highest quality. Most of the stunning innovations of our time, including the videocassette recorder, the microwave oven, the cellular phone and the compact disc player, have been the result of the product concept, not the marketing concept.

FAITH, INSTINCT, AND DETERMINATION

The competitive strategy of technologically driven firms begins with the ingenuity and inventiveness of scientists rather than the needs and wants of consumers. Listening to customers plays only a limited role in the process. Technology-driven strategies eschew focus groups and endless rounds of consumer surveys and opt, instead, for bold moves based on faith, instinct, and determination. Technology-driven companies create change, shake people up, and sometimes cause excitement. They are usually led by a charismatic champion who is more concerned with convincing customers that they need what the company has developed, or wowing them with the wonder of new product development, than listening to customers and then making products to satisfy their current needs. Terms like vision, commitment, and conviction are typically used in descriptions of such individuals and the companies they run. Marketing research is not.

ACTION VERSUS ANALYSIS PARALYSIS

Critics contend that some firms are so intent on listening to their customers that they are unable to make any decisions without first conducting consumer surveys and focus groups. They argue that this has two negative effects. First, it slows down the rate of reaction to opportunities and threats that present themselves. In the most severe cases, such firms become paralyzed by consumer analysis and are unable to act in a timely fashion. Second, endless rounds of consumer studies dull the instinctive senses. They replace the spirit of entrepreneurs with the oftentimes mistaken view of consumers. Firms, as a result, miss breakthrough innovations and bold strategic moves and instead focus on the bland and the ordinary.

PLANNING VERSUS DOING

A variation on this theme occurred in the 1970s when overly formal strategic planning practices led to lots of study and very little action. During that decade, armies of professional planners produced ever-thicker plans to guide firms into the future. These plans worshiped calculation and abhorred action. Vision was replaced with a false sense of precision.

The result was that plans and planners became more and more removed from the real world. Firms became paralyzed by the process of planning. They cautiously avoided risk but in the process avoided opportunities as well.

Operational personnel, those involved in the day-to-day running of the firm, came to view planning as an arcane art of little practical value. Many elegant plans ended up relegated to file cabinets, read by no one but those who drew them up. Disillusionment with the entire process led directly to drastic cutbacks and outright disbanding of strategic planning departments in the early 1980s. Planning seemed dead.

Recognizing these changes, a *Business Week* cover story called for an expanded role for marketing in the planning process. It noted that firms no longer want "bean counters" who will foster further study and promote analysis paralysis, but look for hands-on managers who will not only develop, but also implement product strategies.[5]

The debate between acting versus planning continues to this day. Some consultants argue that firms should forget about formal planning and simply move quickly to take advantage of a fast-changing world. Tom Peters is a central proponent of that position. He argues that markets are so disorganized that any attempt to plan for the long term is doomed to failure. He opts, instead, for the "Pete Rose" strategy, where a firm hustles to meet opportunities, trying to get on base rather than always swinging for the deep outfield.

Bureaucracy is the enemy of a hustle strategy. Its sole function is to slow things down. It should be cut ruthlessly and the resulting "lean-and-mean" firm should strive to move more quickly. Planning, according to this view, has three fatal flaws: (1) it is designed for an age of stability that no longer exists, (2) it serves only to slow things down, and (3) it make obvious to competitors what you intend to do. It is better to respond randomly than to respond with a detailed plan.

STRATEGY'S RESPONSE

Proponents of strategy contend that responding randomly to an ever-changing environment confuses not only a firm's competitors but its customers, employees, and suppliers as well. It creates an army without a general. While some companies succeed by moving quickly to attack opportunities as they present themselves, other very successful firms excel while relentlessly pursuing the same strategic path year after year. Wal-Mart, for example, stresses low-cost retailing. It is known for that skill and inculcates that competitive advantage among all its employees and suppliers. Likewise, sellers of prestige luxury goods would be mistaken to race willy-nilly toward any business opportunity. They should carefully restrict the markets and products they pursue so as to protect the value of their brand. In the 1980s many sellers of prestige brands diluted the value of their brand equity by carelessly pursuing short-term opportunities. It would have been better for those firms to focus on one aspect of their business and try to excel at it.

IN DEFENSE OF THE MARKETING CONCEPT

Proponents argue that much of the criticism against the marketing concept is misplaced. They argue that seemingly alternative approaches, such as the product concept and acting rather than strategy, must ultimately be subservient to the marketing concept if they are to be successful. Scientists and engineers, rather than consumers, may well be the source of new product ideas in technology-driven companies, but the products that arise from those ideas must satisfy customer needs or they will end up serving no market at all. It is important to remember that the technology-push model of innovation often leads to product failure. It produced the Nimslo three-dimensional camera, AT&T's picturephone, tilt-rotor aircraft, and numerous other high-quality products that no one wanted. As McGee and Spiro put it: the product concept is really just "synonymous with customer satisfaction as described by the marketing philosophy."[6]

PRODUCTION-ORIENTED FIRMS

Some firms focus on low-cost, efficient manufacturing. They emphasize low costs and low prices in an attempt to reach large numbers of mass-market consumers. Such producers seem unconcerned with studying consumers' needs and wants and strive, instead, to fulfill a widespread need with very low prices. In virtually every sector of the economy there are firms that succeed by following an efficient-producer model. Wal-Mart in retailing, Goldstar and Samsung in consumer electronics, and discounters of every ilk excel in this way.

Production-based strategies seem to follow a variant of the production concept found in most introductory marketing texts. The concept hypothesizes that consumers will desire products that are priced low. Throughout past decades, many strategy formulations have embraced variations of the production concept as viable ways to compete. Experience curve analysis, for example, which holds that firms should keep costs falling by continually expanding cumulative production, was popular during the 1970s.

Marketers have historically ridiculed the production concept as old-fashioned and obsolete. To them, it describes how business was conducted in the late 1800s and shows how times have changed over the past century. In short, marketers abhorred what many strategists embraced.

In reality, however, low-cost producer strategies are neither old-fashioned nor uncompetitive. Many consumers favor products that are widely available at the lowest possible prices. But, once again, efficient product must be subservient to the needs and wants of large numbers of consumers. The efficient production of 8mm movie projectors in the age of VCRs, for example, would be folly. The emphasis still must be placed on consumers before production, even if low-cost producers wait for others to discern those needs and wants. Only then can companies gain from efficient production.

A COMPETITOR FOCUS

Most of the popular strategic planning formulations of the past two decades have focused on competitors rather than customers. The premise of almost all formulations has been that firms can succeed by gaining competitive advantage with strong brand names, distribution strongholds, promotional muscle, cost efficiencies, and countless other advantages that allow some firms to prevail over less well endowed rivals.

What all competitor-oriented formulations share in common is their attempt to avoid (or change) markets characterized by the economists' model of perfect competition. Competitive strategy seeks to destroy the assumption that all products are the same, all competitors are equal, there are no barriers to entry, and no one firm dominates. Competitive advantage is often a codeword for a way in which to create imperfect competition.

Interest in a competitor orientation moved even farther to the forefront of strategic thinking with the publication of Michael Porter's landmark book, *Competitive Strategy,* in 1980. It became increasingly clear that the purpose of strategy is coping with competition.

Competitive strategy also implies a sense of warfare. You fight your competitors, whereas you serve your customers. Military analogies are commonly applied in business marketing strategy. In their book *Marketing Warfare,* for example, Ries and Trout argue that the strategies of famous military generals can be directly applied to marketing.[7] They contend that marketing is no different than warfare. Their analogy is controversial, but it points up the importance and ferocity of competition in today's markets.

The motivation for military strategy lies with the results of competitors' actions. Many companies have created innovative new products only to have them copied by lower-cost or higher-quality competitors with advantages in manufacturing or distribution. In many instances, American marketers have won the battle of discovering consumer needs only to lose the competitive war to keep the markets they pioneered. It is important to understand what consumers want but it is equally important to protect your discoveries from competitive response.

The power of competitive reaction has caused many marketing scholars to argue that a marketing concept needs to be empowered with a sense of competition, maybe even warfare, that is missing from an orientation that focuses solely on consumer needs. That orientation contrasts greatly with what has actually happened in past decades, when marketers focused mostly on consumers and ignored the effects of competition.

The marketing concept, by itself, provides an incomplete view of business. By ignoring competition, it has painted only part of the picture. While marketers have sought to satisfy consumers' needs, competitors have outmaneuvered them in the marketplace. As Jack Trout noted in *Business Week:* "Knowing what the customer wants isn't too helpful if a dozen other companies are already serving the customer's wants."[8]

Some marketing experts have argued forcefully that marketers should switch from a traditional customer-oriented approach to a stance that stresses competition.[9] Such a focus allows firms to exploit competitors' vulnerabilities and defend their own flanks against attack. George Day and Robin Wensley have gone even further. They contend that a "paradigm shift" is underway in marketing.[10] Marketing has moved away from its traditional focus on consumer decision making. In the authors' own words: "another set of priorities has emerged, with the emphasis on the development of sustainable competitive positions in product-markets." It is clear that paying attention to competitors is at least as important as paying attention to customers.

DUAL CONSUMER AND COMPETITOR ORIENTATIONS TOWARD MARKETS

The essence of marketing strategy is to attract and keep customers while keeping competitors at bay. One element of strategy without the other is simply incomplete. History is replete with examples of firms that attracted customers with stunning innovations only to lose their early lead in the ensuing competitive battle. Many other companies have concocted elegant strategic plans designed to outfox the competition but forgot that their ultimate mission was to provide value to paying customers. In each instance, the result was failure.

MINI-CASE: GATORADE

Some companies have successfully managed the balance between customers and competition. Consider the case of Gatorade, an immensely successful product that single-handedly created the entire new product category of sports drinks. It all started in the early 1960s when researchers at the University of Florida were searching for a liquid to rapidly replace fluids lost to the hot tropical sun. In 1965, the fruits of their labor were tested on ten members of the University of Florida's Gator football team. As a result, the test drink acquired the name Gatorade. The Gators had a winning season that year. More important, they acquired a reputation as a team that excelled during the second half of play. Observers attributed the superior performance to Gatorade. Its coveted reputation spread solely through word-of-mouth advertising and unpaid publicity. The crowning plug came when the Gators beat Georgia Tech in the Orange Bowl on January 1, 1967. After the 27-to-11 loss the Georgia coach was quoted in *Sports Illustrated:* "We didn't have Gatorade. That made the difference." From that point on, coaches all over the country clamored for the new product in order to negate the Gators' competitive advantage.

In 1967, Stokely–Van Camp, the canned fruit and vegetable company, bought the exclusive rights to make and market Gatorade in the United States. It contracted with the National Football League to become the league's official sports drink. The picture of professional athletes swilling Gatorade on the sidelines created a national market for sports drinks among ordinary consumers. Sales soared as Gatorade acquired the cult status of a magical elixir. Armchair athletes felt empowered by the image of superior athletic performance. Gatorade seemed good for you, while soda was not.

Stokely–Van Camp was acquired by Quaker Oats in 1983. At the time sports drink sales were a substantial business of $85 million per year. But Quaker Oats had the money to create an even larger market. With heavy spending for popular promotional figures such as basketball's Michael Jordan and the savvy to become the official sports drink of the National Football League, Gatorade sales soared to $1 billion a year by 1993, representing an astonishing 22 percent of Quaker Oats profits. Quaker Oats reaped the rewards of its successful implementation of a consumer orientation. It had figured out the first half of the equation.

But competitors sought to gain a share of what by the early 1990s was the fasting growing segment of the soft drink industry. By 1992, there were at least twenty-seven separate competitors in the U.S. market alone. Coke and Pepsi, due to their sheer market power, seemed most threatening. Coke introduced Powerade in four markets in 1992. Following Gatorade's lead, Powerade became the official sports drink of both the 1992 and 1996 Olympic games and World Cup Soccer. Deion Sanders, the prominent football player, was signed to appear in ads. Coke used its overwhelming advantage in distribution to muscle market share from the market leader.

Pepsi followed a similar tack. Its All Sport debuted in test market in 1992 then quickly went national. Pepsi hired basketball's Shaquille O'Neal as spokesperson and allied its entry with college basketball. Published reports claimed that Pepsi offered some retailers twenty free cases for every twenty cases purchased, meaning All Sport sold for 25 percent less than Gatorade in some retail outlets.

But Gatorade managed the competitor half of the equation superbly. Even with the onslaught of the soft drink giants, by 1995 it still held over 80 percent of the sports drink market while Coke's Powerade and Pepsi's All Sport limped along with less than 4 percent each. Quaker Oats had figured out how to use its potent brand name to attract customers and keep them to itself, even in the face of intense competition from powerful rivals with a history of successfully dominating product categories pioneered by others. Gatorade, in short, figured out both halves of the strategic equation.

MINI-CASE: DIET RITE COLA VERSUS COKE AND DIET PEPSI

Over the past three decades, Royal Crown has been responsible for most of the major innovations in the soft drink industry. Royal Crown did not invent diet soft drinks. Smaller, regional rivals, such as Brooklyn-based Kirsch, sold sugar-free soft drinks long before Royal Crown. But Royal Crown created the first truly successful brand once the trend toward calorie consciousness caught hold in the early 1960s.

Royal Crown introduced Diet Rite Cola in early 1962. Basically, Royal Crown's innovation was to sell diet soft drinks as a mass market alternative to regular soft drinks. It brought the product category into the mainstream by (1) reducing the price to match that of regular soft drinks, (2) putting it in returnable bottles like regular soft drinks, (3) placing it on the same supermarket shelves as regular soft drinks, and (4) heavily promoting it to calorie-conscious consumers with an aggressive advertising campaign. All of those actions gave Diet Rite Cola the imprimatur of a regular soft drink and removed the stigma attached to consuming a product designed for the chronically ill.

Sales and market share skyrocketed. In 1962, sales of diet soft drinks doubled to fifty million cases and their share of all soft drinks soared to 4 percent. By 1963, 7 percent of all soft drinks sold were dietetic. Royal Crown Cola dominated the fast-growing market for diet soft drinks through the mid-1960s. Like Gatorade, it owned a seemingly immutable 50 percent share of the market. Also like Gatorade, Royal Crown was the first to figure out the consumer part of the equation.

But Royal Crown did less well when it came to the competitor side of the equation. Its product was aimed straight at the heart of Coke and Pepsi drinkers. Diet Rite tried to switch regular cola drinkers to diet cola. Since Royal Crown held only a minuscule share of the regular cola business it had little to lose if consumers switched. Coke and Pepsi would lose plenty since most of their sales came from regular colas. Both had to follow Royal Crown to market.

Within a year, by 1963, both Coke and Pepsi had diet brands in limited test market. Both firms were reluctant to put their flagship brand names on the new unproved products. Coke entered with "Tab" while Pepsi entered with "Patio Diet Cola." Sales of Patio Diet Cola were disappointing, so it was replaced with Diet Pepsi, a risky decision that entailed using the company's coveted flagship brand name. All three firms targeted calorie-conscious women.

Royal Crown's dominance started to erode once Coke and Pepsi entered. It was not a question of clear product superiority. Diet Rite Cola was as tasty as Tab or Diet Pepsi. Basically, Coke and Pepsi entered with parity products that had no overwhelming sensory advantages. Their success was due to two other key advantages. First, Coke and Pepsi dominated soft drink distribution channels, and as an expert quoted in *Forbes* remarked years later: "This is a distribution business. The bottler decides what goes on the shelf, and all the rest is just conversation."[11] In 1964, Coca-Cola had 1,120 franchised bottlers, Pepsi was a distant second with only 530 bottlers, and Royal Crown had a pitiful 370. Second, both Coke and Pepsi had the money to fund massive promotional programs that Royal Crown could not match. Throughout the second half of the 1960s, while Royal Crown held double the market share of Coke or Pepsi, the two soft drink giants spent three to four times as much as Royal Crown on advertising.

In 1982, twenty years after Royal Crown's entry, Coke introduced Diet Coke, which initially appealed to a growing market for men wishing to limit caloric intake. By the 1990s, Coke and Pepsi's victory was complete. Both brands dominated the top ten soft drinks overall, while Royal Crown hung near the bottom of the rating. Many experts are amazed that Royal Crown is still in business. It may have figured out the consumer part of the equation but it clearly failed the competitor part. Coke and Pepsi, in contrast, misread the initial promise of the diet soft drink market, but excelled at the competitor part of the equation.

Why, in your opinion, did Coke and Pepsi miss the diet soft drink market? Is there anything they could have done to recognize its true potential earlier than they did?

Is there anything that Royal Crown could have done to better manage the competitor part of the equation?

THE POWER OF EXTERNAL EVENTS

Most observers agree that it is essential to "worship" the external environment. That is because it is usually events outside the company's gates that affect the firm's products and markets. Exhibit 1.2 illustrates this component of marketing strategy along with the others.

External events stem from many sources. Changes in consumer tastes, demographic shifts, competitive challenges, legal and regulatory changes, economic factors, and technological developments can all conspire to create powerful market changes.

The external environment changes constantly. Furthermore, most changes are beyond the control of individual firms. Firms must react to, or anticipate, market changes. Overall, changing market conditions create opportunities for some firms and pose threats to others.

TECHNOLOGICAL CHANGE

The development of new technologies creates opportunities for some firms and destroys opportunities for others. Consider the development of videocassette recorders in the mid-1970s. Before that time home videos were made almost exclusively with 8mm home movie cameras and projectors. But the future of companies that sold that technology was forev-

Exhibit 1.2
The Four Factors Influencing Marketing Strategy

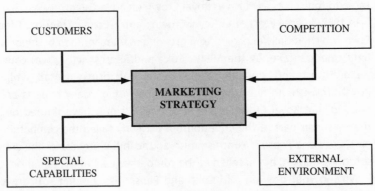

er changed by the development of the inexpensive VCR. No matter what the price, or how persuasive the salespeople, the makers of 8mm movie cameras were doomed. Change came quickly and from the outside. What had once been a viable product was made obsolete by a technological development outside the industry.

Likewise, consider the case of Keuffel & Esser, the leading seller of slide rules. Its premium-priced product was highly valued by engineering students of the 1960s. But when the electronic calculator hit the market in the early 1970s it took only a few short years for the firm's key product to be transformed from an industry mainstay to an obsolete curiosity.

DEMOGRAPHIC SHIFTS

Demographic shifts also change the need for products and services. An aging population, for example, creates a growing market for health care services while a bulge in the birth rate is usually followed by an increasing need for housing. More households bodes well for appliance sales while a surge in the number of young men aged eighteen to thirty-four often creates growth for sellers of motorcycles, but can also signal a surge in crime statistics. Few of these changes are controllable, but many are predictable, since they evolve more slowly than other aspects of the external environment.

SOCIAL CHANGES

Social changes can enhance or decimate the prospects for a product category as witnessed by the decline in sales of cigarettes and distilled spirits in the U.S. market. Scotch whiskey, for example, has been following a clear, long-term downward trend. Throughout the 1980s, distilleries in Scotland closed down in record numbers as demand dwindled. Creative marketers stemmed the decline in dollar sales if not overall volume by selling premium brands at premium prices.

GOVERNMENT DEREGULATION

The deregulatory trend that started in the United States in the 1980s created promising opportunities for new entrants and competitive challenges for industry incumbents. AT&T faced newfound competition from MCI and Sprint while the full-service brokerage firms found themselves competing with a horde of discounters led by Charles Schwab. The airline industry, long a bastion of protectionism, was deregulated and incumbents encumbered with high costs were forced to compete with low-cost airlines selling very similar products.

SPECIAL RESOURCES

Many firms possess something special that provides an edge against the competition. It may be an inimitable asset or unique skill. It might be a coveted brand name or a lockhold on distribution channels. Coke and Pepsi, for example, dominate "fountain" sales of soft drinks with exclusive distribution contracts. McDonald's sells Coke exclusively. Pepsi, which owns Taco Bell and Pizza Hut, sells its soft drinks through those captive establishments. Second-tier soft drink sellers have little chance of penetrating those outlets.

Some competitive advantages are sustainable while others are transitory. A leading brand name, for example, can dominate its product category for decades. In fact, one study found that twenty-three of the twenty-five top brands in 1923 still dominated their product categories in 1992.

Over the past few decades strategy scholars have focused on inward-looking concerns such as "core capabilities" and "competing on capabilities." A more recent variation argues for a "resource-based view of the firm."[12] It holds that companies should be viewed as a collection of tangible and intangible assets and capabilities. These might include assets such as a popular brand name, special skills and experiences which are built up over time, and unique organizational cultures. Key to the resource-based view of the firm is that firms should focus on resources that are hard for competitors to copy (like Disney's brand name), durable (retain a competitve advantage for a long time), and produce profits that cannot be appropriated or substituted by other members of the channel of distribution, such as when a powerful retailer bargains away a manufacturer's margins.

MARKETING AS A BOUNDARY-SPANNING FUNCTION

Overall, marketing is in a unique position among company functions to deal with customers, competition, and other external events because it is a boundary-spanning function. Most of the other business functions such as management, finance, accounting, research and development, and data processing face inward toward events that occur within the firm. That is probably why the influence of marketing on strategic thinking has grown greatly in recent years.

NOTES

[1]Frederick E. Webster, Jr., "The Rediscovery of the Marketing Concept," *Business Horizons,* May–June 1988, p. 37.

[2]Frederick W. Gluck, "Strategic Planning in a New Key," *McKinsey Quarterly,* Winter 1986, p. 33.

[3]Roger Bennett and Robert Cooper, "The Misuse of Marketing: An American Tragedy," *Business Horizons,* November–December 1981, pp. 51–60. And Roger Bennett and Robert Cooper, "Beyond the Marketing Concept," *Business Horizons,* June 1979, pp. 76–83.

[4]Robert Hayes and William Abernathy, "Managing Our Way to Economic Decline," *Harvard Business Review,* July–August 1980, pp. 67–78.

[5]"Marketing: The New Priority," *Business Week,* November 21, 1983, pp. 96–106.

[6]Lynn McGee and Rosann Spiro, "The Marketing Concept in Perspective," *Business Horizons,* May–June 1988, p. 44.

[7]Al Ries and Jack Trout, *Marketing Warfare,* New York: McGraw-Hill, 1986.

[8]"Forget Satisfying the Consumer—Just Outfox the Competition," *Business Week,* October 7, 1985, p. 55.

[9]Alfred Oxenfeldt and William Moore, "Customer or Competitor: Which Guideline for Marketing?" *Management Review,* August 1978, pp. 43–48.

[10]George Day and Robin Wensley, "Marketing Theory with a Strategic Orientation," *Journal of Marketing,* Fall 1983, pp. 79–89.

[11]Joshua Levine, "Affirmative Grunts," *Forbes,* March 2, 1992, p. 91.

[12]See, for example, David Collins and Cynthia Montgomery, "Competing on Resources: Strategy in the 1990s," *Harvard Business Review,* July–August 1995, pp. 118–28; Kathleen Conner, "A Historical Comparison of Resource-Based Theory and Five Schools of Thought Within Industrial Organization Economics: Do We Have a New Theory of the Firm?" *Journal of Management,* Vol. 17, No. 1, 1991, pp. 121–54; and Ingemar Dierickx and Karel Cool, "Of Competitive Advantage," *Management Science,* December 1989, pp. 1504–11.

CHAPTER 2

A BRIEF HISTORY OF MARKETING STRATEGY

The term "strategy" is widely used to describe a seemingly endless number of marketing activities. Today, everything in business seems to be "strategic." There is strategic pricing, strategic market entry, strategic advertising, and probably even strategic strategy. In recent years, the appellation has been appended to nearly every marketing action in order to make the ordinary sound modern and competitively inspired.

DEFINITION AND SCOPE OF MARKETING STRATEGY

There is no consensus as to what a marketing strategy actually is. Instead, there is a bewildering array of competing visions. The name "marketing strategy" is commonly used, but no one is really sure what it means.

One review of the history of marketing strategy found that the term "strategy" has been applied to at least three types of marketing issues, each at a different level of aggregation.[1]

1. At the most macro level, *marketing strategies* focus on manipulations of the marketing mix variables—product, price, place, and promotion. According to that definition, setting a strategy consists of selecting a price for a product, designing an advertising campaign, then deciding on a plan of distribution.
2. There are also *marketing element strategies,* a more narrow concept that applies to individual elements of the marketing mix. There are "push versus pull" promotional strategies, "intensive, selective, or exclusive" distribution strategies, and "skimming versus penetration" pricing strategies.
3. Finally, there are *product-market entry strategies,* which include strategies for building, defending, or harvesting market share.

Other authors prefer other definitions. Marketing textbooks often limit the scope and content of marketing strategy to two elements: (1) picking a target market, and (2) selecting a marketing mix to serve that market.

A more encompassing definition of marketing strategy, one more akin to corporate strategy, became popular in the 1970s. A popular text envisioned strategic market planning as a four-step process that entailed: (1) defining the business, (2) setting a mission, (3) selecting functional plans for marketing, production, and other areas, and (4) budgeting for those plans.[2]

Just as there is no consensus as to what constitutes a marketing strategy, nor is there one commonly accepted definition of corporate strategy. One study reviewed seventeen influential articles and books and found very different definitions of strategic management.[3] There were, however, three recurring themes throughout most discussions of strategy.

1. Most visions of corporate strategy include an *environmental analysis,* which looks outward toward the external environment and includes an analysis of the markets a firm must compete in.
2. A firm's *resources* or *special competencies,* and how those resources fit with the environment, are also prominent themes in strategic management.
3. Finally, setting *objectives and goals,* and how resources are to be deployed to achieve those goals, are essential parts of strategy.

Setting objectives that maximize the fit between a firm's resources and the environment it faces leads directly to one of the oldest and most basic formulations in strategy—the well-known SWOT analysis. SWOT is an acronym for strengths, weaknesses, opportunities, and threats. The idea is to identify a firm's strengths and weaknesses and then design a strategy that matches those strengths against market opportunities and a competitor's weakness. If done correctly a firm can highlight its strengths and minimize its weaknesses to pursue opportunities and avoid threats. Exhibit 2.1 illustrates the SWOT formulation.

Exhibit 2.1
SWOT Analysis

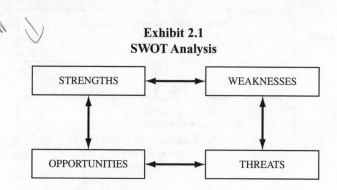

MILESTONES IN THE HISTORY
OF MARKETING STRATEGY

Strategy has been around at least as long as the ancient Greeks. But they were more interested in military applications than business competition. Even the word "strategy" conveys its militaristic bias. It is derived from the same word as the current Greek word "stratigiki," which means "art of the general." Strategy is what the general does. Like their military counterparts, marketers must marshal their forces to fight the competition.

One excellent historical review traced the first mentions of marketing strategy back to Leverett S. Lyon in 1926, who provided a very modern-sounding discussion of strategy.[4] Lyon talked explicitly about the ever-changing environment, and how marketers had to rearrange their product offerings to fit that environment. Said Lyon: "Marketing management . . . may be conceived of as the continuous task of re-planning

Exhibit 2.2
The History of Marketing Strategy

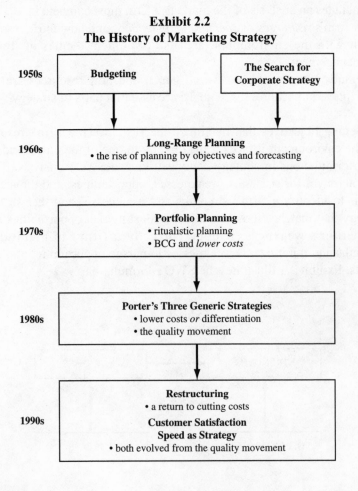

the marketing activities of a business to meet the constantly changing conditions both within and without the enterprise." That definition holds up pretty well after more than seventy years.

Another study traced the origins of the first "strategic management concept" back to Von Neumann and Morgenstern, who in 1947 (like Leverett Lyon) viewed strategy as a series of actions taken by a firm to deal with the environment it had to compete in.[5]

Most reviews of formal strategic planning trace its origins to the period just after World War II. As Exhibit 2.2 illustrates, strategy has evolved steadily over that fifty-year period. Each decade is described below.

1950s: BUDGETING AND THE SEARCH FOR OVERALL STRATEGY

Modern strategy began with two trends that emerged right after World War II: (1) the growth and sophistication of budgeting techniques, and (2) the search for a way to create an overall corporate strategy.

Strategy in the 1950s was little more than a gussied-up form of budgeting, the financial and accounting practice of allocating funds within a particular firm. There really was no explicit strategy. Instead, there were annual budgets that allocated funds to different projects within the organization. The emphasis was on control rather than strategic intent. Budgeting, which is sometimes called basic financial planning, evolved gradually into strategy as the 1950s grew into the 1960s.

At about the same time, there were attempts to create an overall, explicit corporate strategy by integrating the individual plans made up by each of the functional business disciplines—marketing, finance, production, research and development. Before the 1950s, most functional departments created their business plans without formal regard for the overall picture. The interest in creating an overall corporate strategy led directly to the rise of long-range planning.

1960s: THE DECADE OF LONG-RANGE PLANNING

The 1960s was the decade of long-range planning. The evolution of budgeting into long-range planning was motivated by three key factors.

1. *Long-Term Consequences of Annual Budgeting Decisions.* It became apparent that annual budgets had consequences far beyond a single year. If a firm funded a new product development project, for example, the expected payoff from that product would not be realized until many years later. That led to five-year plans, based on five-year forecasts of sales, profits, market share, and market growth. Annual budgeting evolved into longer-range planning.

2. *The Importance of Setting Objectives and Goals.* Interest in creating an overall corporate strategy for the firm focused on the setting of explicit objectives and goals for the *entire* firm. Top management would set those goals and then long-range plans would be drawn up to achieve them. One of the primary contributions of long-range planning was that it laid the foundation for objectives-driven strategies.

3. *Advances in Forecasting.* Coinciding with the widespread use of computers, there was also a pervasive belief that tremendous advances in planning and forecasting were being made that would allow firms to peer confidently into the future and take advantage of opportunities and avoid threats. George Steiner, who wrote one of the most influential texts on the topic, observed in 1969: "Great advances, for instance, have been made in the theory of qualitative methods in business planning. The theory of forecasting is growing stronger."[6]

Long-range planning in the 1960s was based squarely on long-range forecasting. In fact, it is sometimes called "forecast based-planning."[7] Forecasts were made, and plans were then set in light of those forecasts. As Steiner noted in 1969: "The forecast is the basic premise upon which planning proceeds."[8] Without accurate forecasts, planning could not proceed, or succeed.

The entire notion of long-range planning was infused with a sense of unbridled optimism. It was considered management for modern times. As a result, top management set about creating huge planning departments staffed by hordes of professional planners. The profession of long-range planning grew rapidly during the 1960s. An atmosphere of science and precision permeated the planning process. Missions, objectives, and goals would be set by top management and communicated to others in the organization. Plans would then be drawn up to achieve those objectives. As the decade unfolded professional planners provided ever-thicker plans that looked ever further into the future.

With long-range planning and long-range forecasting firms would be able to monitor the future and avoid the fate of the Baldwin Locomotive Works, an example often cited during those times. Baldwin was the largest producer of steam locomotives in the United States during the 1920s and 1930s. Then diesel locomotives challenged the old technology. The first diesel locomotive was built in Sweden in 1913. General Electric and Alcoa sold diesels in the 1920s. Diesel locomotives had many advantages over steam locomotives. But, like many market leaders, Baldwin did nothing. It did not sense the threat and did not see that its market was inevitably changing. As a result, it went bankrupt.

THE DECLINE OF LONG-RANGE PLANNING

By the mid-1970s, long-range planning had fallen out of favor. There were three key reasons for its decline.

1. *Long-range forecasts proved less accurate than expected.* Unforeseen changes in the environment made five-year forecasts obsolete after a single year. That directly affected the value of the five-year plans based on those forecasts. They, too, diminished in value after only a single year. In essence, long-range planning degenerated into a series of one-year plans, the very thing it sought to replace.
2. *Resource allocation became an important issue.* The "go-go" years of the late 1960s, when conglomeration was popular, produced widely flung businesses. Top management could not know the specifics of each business, yet they needed a reliable method of allocating resources among those businesses. Long-range planning proved deficient in that regard.
3. *Overall, long-range planning was oversold.* It simply could not live up to the incredibly high expectations that had been created for it. Planners were plagued by a false sense of what could actually be accomplished. The energy crisis of the mid-1970s proved to be the death knell of long-range planning. The crisis was not anticipated, and its effect on five-year plans was catastrophic. After the energy crisis it became abundantly clear that five-year planning was a thing of the past rather than a vision of the future. It had to be replaced.

1970s: THE DECADE OF PORTFOLIO PLANNING

If the 1960s was the decade of long-range planning, then the 1970s was surely the decade of what has come to be known as portfolio or formula planning. Portfolio planning proposed simple, easy-to-understand, conceptual schemes for allocating resources in diversified firms.

That proved appealing to top managers who faced an abundance of investment opportunities in their highly diversified firms but had little means of selecting which businesses to fund and which to deplete. There was no formal theory. At the end of every year, when budgets were allocated, it was difficult for managers to tell which opportunities were truly promising and which were merely the result of the best presentations for funds. That dilemma led to the devising of seemingly scientific schemes for making strategic decisions.

There were many versions of portfolio planning, each promoted by a prestigious consulting firm. What they all had in common was a simple, but powerful, set of strategic concepts that allowed management to guide their firms into the future. It was all very persuasive. Consultants thrived as firms rushed to have their businesses plotted strategically. It was during these years that dozens of strategy "boutiques" flourished.

The most popular version of portfolio planning was the Boston Consulting Group's growth-share matrix, which is covered in detail in a later chapter. It was one of the genre of planning methods that proposed managing a widely diversified business like an investment portfolio. You did not need to know the business itself, the consultants advised. You merely managed the parts of the portfolio for the overall good of the company. Top management embraced portfolio planning with enthusiasm. It sounded, once again, like science at work in management.

It was during the 1970s that planning grew fastest. The rise of professional strategic planners at corporate headquarters and the growth of strategic consulting firms accelerated. In many instances, planners gained control of companies. As planning staffs grew, so did the plans themselves. By the end of the decade it seemed that plans were judged more by weight and volume than content.

The power of operating managers waned as the power and prestige of strategic planners grew. Operating managers were often required to fill out forms aplenty. The plans were drawn by well-educated MBAs who were strong on theory but weak on actual business experience. The two groups clashed. The end was near for formula planning.

THE DECLINE OF FORMULA PLANNING

By the 1980s formula planning had fallen out of favor. It seemed to be attacked from every angle. Some of the more common criticisms are summarized below.

The High Priests of Planning. Plans were constructed by professional planners at corporate headquarters under the guidance of consultants. To be successful those plans had to be implemented by those who actually made and sold the firm's products. Since line personnel were not involved in writing the plans, they viewed them as a burden rather than a guide. More often than not, elaborate and elegant plans simply got filed away and forgotten. They were beautifully written but never implemented. As one Westinghouse Electric executive noted: "The notion that an effective strategy can be constructed by someone in an ivory tower is totally bankrupt."[9]

Ritual Rather Than Substance. Portfolio planning moved farther and farther away from customers and other business basics. The planning process itself became ritualistic and mechanistic. It desensitized people and became routine. Strategic planners ended up pursuing form over substance. They wrote plans in isolation from those who had to implement them, as well as from those who would eventually buy the products. By 1980, the errors of those ways were apparent.

Unidimensional Answers to Multivariate Problems. Portfolio planning also provided easy answers to very complex and interrelated problems. That approach proved unrealistic. Competing for customers entails more than merely plotting businesses in boxes and following the arrows around in a circle. Product quality, teamwork, commitment, and dozens of other important issues were ignored while managers focused exclusively on market share and market growth. The Boston Consulting Group's overreliance on experience effects proved especially limiting. Portfolio planning turned out to be easy to understand but grossly incomplete.

Grossly Optimistic Forecasts. A final criticism of formula planning is that it never really overcame the problems of forecasting that led to the demise of long-range planning. It often held unrealistic assumptions. Forecasts of market growth, sales, and profits were often based on "hockey-stick" financial projections (they looked like a hockey stick) that were destined to fail from the minute they were made.

Some critics even referred to the genre of formula planning as the "sea gull" method of strategy. The consultants flew in, crapped all over the place, then flew away, leaving others to clean up the mess.

Nearly thirty years ago, George Steiner recognized the pitfalls that would destroy formula planning. His insights proved remarkably prescient. He argued that planning would fail if it relied too heavily on the following:

- Extrapolating rather than thinking
- Developing such a reverence for numbers that irreverence for intuitive and value judgments predominates
- Seeking precision in numbers
- Developing a rigid structure
- Top management's assumption that it can delegate the planning function to a planner[10]

In spite of Steiner's advice, many of the popular planning formulations of the 1970s committed those very errors. In hindsight, formula planning offered magic bullets that promised an easy way to win the game of business. Beginning in the early 1980s, strategy departments began to shrink or be disbanded. Strategy fell on hard times.

1980s: PORTER'S GENERIC STRATEGIES

In 1979, Michael Porter published a landmark article in the *Harvard Business Review* that offered a way to analyze competitive intensity.[11] He followed in 1980 (and again in 1984) with two influential books that tied together many existing ideas about competitive strategy.[12] In particular, Porter expanded on the Boston Consulting Group's idea that lower costs were the only means to business success. Porter added differentiation (sometimes called the quality advantage) as an additional strategic option. He recognized that while some firms succeeded in the marketplace by cutting costs and keeping prices low, others succeeded by selling higher quality or status products at higher prices. Porter recognized that there is more than one option. His ideas became so influential that it is virtually impossible to discuss strategy in the 1980s without focusing on his work in detail. His influence continues to this day.

The later part of the 1980s was also characterized by the quality movement. In an attempt to profit by offering a quality advantage over competitors and as a reaction to the perceived quality advantage of imports, especially Japanese imports, firms embraced the quality craze with both arms. Everything from just-in-time inventory methods to product design for efficient production caught the attention of managers in the late 1980s.

1990s: RESTRUCTURING, CUSTOMER SATISFACTION, AND SPEED AS STRATEGY

The strategic ideas that dominated the first half of the 1990s have strong connections to what came before. Three powerful trends in particular have emerged.

The emphasis on cutting costs to stay competitive, which first captured the imagination of businesses in the 1970s, has reemerged in a new, more virulent form. Ruthless restructuring has dominated strategic actions in the 1990s. Rarely a week goes by without yet another announcement that ten thousand, twenty thousand, even forty thousand employees are being let go. "Lean and mean," in the hope of becoming more internationally competitive, became the bywords of the 1990s. Cutting costs by cutting employees became standard practice as firms downsized at an alarming rate.

Part of the reason for restructuring was to slim down bloated bureaucracies and quicken the speed of reaction to competitors' moves and environmental changes. Speed itself became a strategic thrust of the 1990s. Hurrying new products to market and speeding up the flow of goods through channels of distribution became goals for large and once-stodgy operators. Speed replaced size as a perceived competitive advantage.

The motivation for speed as strategy started with the Japanese, who were able to make model changes and bring new products to market more quickly than American firms. That was especially true in the auto industry where it took American automakers much longer to manage the flow of products. U.S. auto manufacturers began to adopt just-in-time inventory methods and kieretsu-like arrangements among members of the channels of distribution. Such productions were widely copied by other industries. By the 1990s, speed as strategy had acquired a cult-like status across a broad array of industries. Every aspect of a firm's business was studied in order to speed up the movement of goods from the seller to the customer, and information from the customer to channel members.

The customer satisfaction movement grew out of the quality movement. It started in the late 1980s with the idea of making products more durable and reliable and grew into the idea that if customers were happy, maybe even delighted, they might also remain loyal to the firm's products and services.

Customer satisfaction turned out to be one of the biggest trends of the 1990s. Part an antidote for lower-priced competition, and part a rediscovery of the marketing concept, customer satisfaction captured the imagination of large numbers of businesses. Many firms now routinely monitor customer satisfaction and the related concept of customer defections. Starting in the 1990s, many firms tied employee compensation to customer satisfaction ratings.

Customer satisfaction harkens back to the differentiation advantage proposed by Porter in 1980. It is based on the belief that price sensitivity can be minimized if the customer is catered to. It is a strategy that stresses performance rather than price. Marketers strive to form "relationships" with their best customers to keep them satisfied and loyal to the firm's products and services. The customer satisfaction craze continues to this day.

CURRENT TRENDS IN MARKETING STRATEGY

Other, more subtle, trends in strategy have been evident in the 1990s.

1. STRATEGIC THINKING: FROM ELITISM TO EGALITARIANISM

Strategic thinking is a way of thinking about consumers, competitors, and other aspects of the external environment that is inculcated into every member of the organization. It is the antithesis of planning conducted solely by an elite group of professional planners. Strategic thinking recognizes that front-line employees and operations personnel must participate in the implementation of plans. Strategic thinking goes hand-in-hand with the basic tenets of participatory management. Ideally, every member of the organization thinks strategically about consumers' needs, competitors, and competitive advantage.

2. FROM CALCULATION TO CREATIVITY

Like marketing itself, strategy formulation is more an art than a science. Henry Mintzberg has argued that strategies should be "crafted" rather than calculated.[13] The image of an artisan shaping a pot, he contends, is a more appropriate analogy than is the image of a engineer making calculations.

Strategy is emergent. Rarely are strategists smart enough to anticipate all of the outcomes that present themselves as the future unfolds. James Brian Quinn has argued that strategy formulation is not the rational-analytic process found in most textbooks.[14] Instead, it is a fragmented, intuitive, and evolutionary process, where initial decisions and external events flow together. In short, marketing strategy proceeds with the imprecision of an art rather than the exactitude of a science. You craft strategy: you do not calculate it.

3. FROM PRECISION IN PLANNING TO
LEARNING AND ADAPTATION

It is often said that change is the only certainty. That makes flexibility a desirable attribute. Learning, experimentation, and adaptation offer real advantages over the rigidity of previous strategic planning procedures. Quick response has replaced detailed long-range forecasts as the preferred approach to dealing with an uncertain environment. It is an approach that is more in sync with the times in which we live.

CONNECTIONS WITH THE PAST

The central premise of this book is that today's ideas about strategy are rooted deeply in the past. Over the decades marketing strategy has developed in a slow and steady evolution rather than a series of short-lived fads. The flow of this book follows the historical trends in marketing strategy. It begins with formula planning of the 1970s and ends with the currently popular practices of customer satisfaction and speed as strategy. The intent is not to dwell on old ideas, or to belittle past practices, but to show how strategy has evolved over the decades, culminating in today's seemingly brand-new ideas.

NOTES

[1]Harper Boyd and Jean-Claude Larreche, "The Foundations of Marketing Strategy," in *Review of Marketing,* Gerald Zaltman and Thomas Bonoma (eds.), Chicago: American Marketing Association, 1978, pp. 4–72.

[2]Derek Abell and John Hammond, *Strategic Market Planning,* New Jersey: Prentice-Hall, 1979.

[3]Jeffrey Bracker, "The Historical Development of the Strategic Management Concept," *Academy of Management Review,* Vol. 5, No. 2, 1980, pp. 219–24.

[4]David Gardner and Howard Thomas, "Strategic Marketing: History, Issues, and Emergent Themes," in *Strategic Marketing and Management,* H. Thomas and D. Gardner (eds.), Chichester, England: John Wiley & Sons, 1985.

[5]Bracker, "Historical Development," p. 220.

[6]George Steiner, *Top Management Planning,* New York: Macmillan, 1969, p. 718.

[7]Fredrick Gluck, Stephen Kaufman, and Steven Walleck, "Strategic Management for Competitive Advantage," *Harvard Business Review,* July–August 1980, pp. 154–60.

[8]Steiner, *Top Management Planning,* p. 17.

[9]"The New Breed of Strategic Planner," *Business Week,* September 17, 1984, p. 64.

[10]Steiner, *Top Management Planning,* pp. 720–21.

[11]Michael Porter, "How Competitive Forces Shape Strategy," *Harvard Business Review,* March–April 1979, pp. 137–45.

[12]Michael Porter, *Competitive Strategy,* New York: The Free Press, 1980; and *Competitive Advantage,* New York: The Free Press, 1984.

[13]Henry Mintzberg, "Crafting Strategy," *Harvard Business Review,* July–August, 1987, pp. 66–75.

[14]James Brian Quinn, "Strategic Change: Logical Incrementalism," *Sloan Management Review,* Fall 1978, pp. 7–21.

CHAPTER 3

ASSESSING COMPETITIVE INTENSITY

For decades, economists have recognized that excessive competition drives down prices and hurts profits. Governments may wish to promote perfectly competitive markets but firms seek to find or create markets where those mechanisms are not working perfectly. That allows them to earn higher profits than firms competing in markets where competition is cutthroat.

ECONOMIC MODELS OF COMPETITION

The intensity of competitive interaction is rooted in market structure. At its most basic level, there are three types of competitive markets—perfect competition, pure monopoly, and imperfect competition. Exhibit 3.1 arrays those types of competition along a continuum ranging from no control over prices to complete control. Consider each in turn.

Exhibit 3.1
Basic Economic Models of Competition

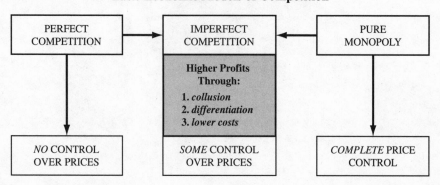

THE ASSUMPTIONS OF PERFECT COMPETITION

In the imaginary world of economic textbooks, firms compete in markets characterized by perfect competition. It exists when the following four conditions are present.

1. *Products are identical or homogeneous.* They are commodities, like wheat, eggs, and pork bellies, with no other difference between them—either real or imagined—but price. Price competition is fierce. Since all products are the same, consumers choose the one with the lowest price.

2. *All firms have perfect knowledge.* That is, in a perfectly competitive market they have equal access to production technologies and techniques. There are no patents, proprietary designs, or special skills that allow one firm to do the job better than competitors. Raw materials are available to all and available on similar terms. There is no such thing as competitive advantage in a market characterized by perfect knowledge.

3. *There are no entry or exit barriers.* Firms can enter and leave a perfectly competitive market at will. Supply expands (and contracts) quickly to meet surges (and declines) in demand. There are no brand names, capital expenses, or distribution strongholds to keep competitors out. Easy entry keeps strong downward pressure on prices. No one firm can make extraordinary profits. Instead, many firms make a modest profit slightly above the rate earned on U.S. treasury bills.

4. *There is atomistic competition.* There are many buyers and sellers, all roughly the same size. Market share leaders simply do not exist in a perfectly competitive market. As a result, neither buyers nor sellers have the power to influence prices. Both are at the mercy of efficient market mechanisms. There is no such thing as a large, important account demanding more favorable terms from the seller or an important seller dictating terms to a weak buyer. Buyers and sellers compete on an equal footing. Both are "price-takers." Like the farmer who sells his wheat at auction, sellers receive only what the market is willing to pay. There is no collusion, no industry cartels or other price-tampering mechanisms to interfere with perfectly competitive markets. All firms act independently.

Perfect competition makes for easy curve fitting and tidy economics lectures but it is an unrealistic view of almost all markets. Most markets deviate from the model of perfect competition in at least some respects. The more they deviate from that model, the less ruthless the price cutting.

MONOPOLY POWER IS RARE

A monopoly lies at the opposite end of the continuum from perfect competition. In a monopoly, there is no competition. There is only a single seller and that seller's product is unique. There is no substitute. A customer must pay what the monopolist demands or do without. There is no freedom of choice.

With the exception of electric utilities, and a few other highly regulated industries, pure monopolies are as rare as deviations from perfect competition are plentiful. And, when monopolies, or near monopolies, are found, their ability to control prices is usually thwarted by government oversight. Electric utilities, for example, cannot raise rates unilaterally. They must appeal to public utility commissions, which regulate their profits.

TYPES OF IMPERFECT COMPETITION

Most markets are neither entirely perfect nor purely monopolistic. They are imperfect—beset by a host of imperfections that lessen the intensity of competition and give sellers some control over price. The more imperfect the market, the more likely it is that some firms competing in that market will earn extraordinary profits.

Imperfect competition manifests itself in a number of distinct ways.

Collusion Among a Few Large Sellers. One way to exert control over prices is to collude. Adam Smith warned in *The Wealth of Nations* that when competitors gather, conversation inevitably turns to price fixing. Imagine turn-of-the-century "robber barons" fixing prices in a smoke-filled room and you have a vivid picture of how collusion worked in the past. But the past is not the present. Myriad laws have been passed outlawing explicit price-setting arrangements and antitrust actions. Given those laws, and the strong and lengthy history of "trust-busting" in the United States, it is easy to see why it would be foolish for modern-day companies to engage in such unethical, underhanded, and obviously illegal price-fixing activities. They would likely be caught and have simply too much to lose.

Implicit price fixing is a more subtle form of outright collusion. In some cases, there may be a tacit agreement among a few large sellers to keep prices high even though there is never a word mentioned among competitors. In a concentrated industry, there may be a willingness to act as a "good" competitor and play by the rules of the game. A gentlemen's agreement may exist not to break rank and cut prices on fellow competitors. Implicit price fixing is also illegal, but harder to prove.

Implicit arrangements are part of the larger issue of price signaling. Price signaling is a provocative practice that lies somewhere between explicit collusion and the First Amendment right to free speech. A commonly used practice is to publish current prices and tell of future price increases. Companies contend that they are merely informing customers. How, they ask, could they raise prices without first telling customers that they are going to do so? Critics are more cynical. They contend firms are really trying to convince competitors to raise prices as well. Price signaling, they argue, is merely a subtle form of collusion.

Legal challenges to price signaling have been mixed. In the mid-1980s, the U.S. Supreme Court ruled that American Hardwood Manufacturers Association (AHMA) violated antitrust laws when it collected and circulated price lists among member firms. The intent, the court ruled, was to fix prices. The airlines fared better in the early 1990s. Although they also published price changes on an industry-wide computer system, which critics argued was done to signal competitors, the argument that they had a duty to inform customers of impending price changes won the day.

The presence of a market leader can also serve to mimic collusive-like activities. The dominant firm may set prices which smaller firms follow in lockstep. Again, nary a word is spoken. Instead, competitors play by the unstated rules of the game. There is an implicit agreement.

Another way to fix prices is with cartels. Today, cartels exist in global markets for oil and diamonds. These modern-day cartels control supply and "administer" prices to world markets. OPEC, for example, the organization of oil-exporting nations, met and effectively set crude oil prices in the 1970s, although the resulting oversupply of the 1980s diminished their effectiveness. DeBeers, the South African diamond marketer, attempts to limit the supply, and therefore affect the price, of the world's diamonds by cajoling diamond-producing nations around the world to "market" through its organization for the collective good of the sellers.

Collusive activities usually occur in oligopolies, industries where there are only a few large sellers. They can erect barriers to entry, signal prices, and engage in other practices that create imperfect competition. What makes such actions special is that they control prices by "fixing" the market and violate the fourth assumption of perfectly competitive markets that all firms act independently. Collusion implies that competition is not at all "atomistic."

Government regulations can also be used to create imperfect competition and boost profits for individual firms. Firms can lobby Congress to grant federal tax breaks, direct agricultural subsidies, set quotas on imports, and award export subsidies and credit guarantees. Archer-Daniels-Midland (ADM), the agricultural products giant, was accused by critics of benefiting from such a system in 1996. The firm earned nearly $375 million in profits from corn sweeteners and ethanol, both of which are protected and subsidized by federal regulations. Critics claim the systems works as follows: ADM makes huge political contributions to candidates. In return, ADM gets regulations that constitute corporate welfare. Imports of sugar, for example, are severely limited by government edict. At the same time, price supports keep the price of domestically produced sugar about double that of foreign producers. That creates a huge market for ADM corn sweetener, which is widely used in soda, candy, and other sweetened products. One critic claimed: "We charge consumers more money through taxes, give the money to the company, and then charge consumers higher prices."[1]

Product Differentiation. A more subtle, more defensible, and maybe even more insidious way to exert control over prices is to create real or imagined differences among products. The result is a sort of "mini-monopoly," where a broadly defined mass market is *deliberately* splintered into narrowly defined market segments, each of which has a distinct and largely noncompetitive group of customers and competitors. Historically, such forms of imperfect competition have been called "monopolistic competition."

Monopolistic competition exists when firms operate their own little monopolies serving a distinct market segment. The most natural basis of monopolistic competition is geographic. In bottled waters, for example, where transportation costs are high, Arrowhead holds a large share of the West Coast market while in eastern markets Poland Spring is popular (although both brands are owned by the same parent firm). The basis of monopolistic competition can also include performance enhancements, design excellence, luxury goods, status and prestige products, exceptionally high quality, well-known brand names, product variety, exceptional service, convenience, and a host of other tangible and intangible factors that fall strictly within the purview of marketing.

In each instance, sellers minimize pure price competition by selling premium products at higher prices. It is a widespread practice. Almost every sector of the economy is populated with successful sellers that command higher prices by offering consumers products more closely tailored to their needs. It is price competition replaced with a quality competition.

Differentiation partially insulates sellers from ruinous cutthroat price competition. Tag Heuer, for example, the Swiss seller of upscale sports watches, does not tremble when Timex cuts prices on its sports watches. Neither does Nike, when faced with a price reduction in no-name, sell-them-out-of-bins sneakers. Differentiation exerts control over prices by reducing the direct substitutability of once-similar products. It violates the first assumption of perfectly competitive markets that all products are identical or homogeneous. The true beauty of differentiation is that it allows consumers to elect to pay higher prices. It thus avoids the illegality of explicit collusion, even though it often amounts to the same thing— less price competition.

Lower Costs. Firms can also create imperfect competition by lowering costs faster and farther than competitors. They can do so by sliding down the experience curve ahead of rivals and generating economies of scale or they can ruthlessly cut staff and functions deemed unnecessary to the firm's core operations as has happened so frequently and thoroughly in the 1990s. In either case, the earned cost advantage is usually passed along to consumers in the form of lower prices, which gives the firm its competitive edge.

FACTORS AFFECTING COMPETITIVE INTENSITY

Coping with cutthroat price competition is one of the central elements of a marketing strategy. Economists have identified the important factors affecting competitive intensity. Those factors were codified and popular-

Exhibit 3.2
Five Forces Driving Competition

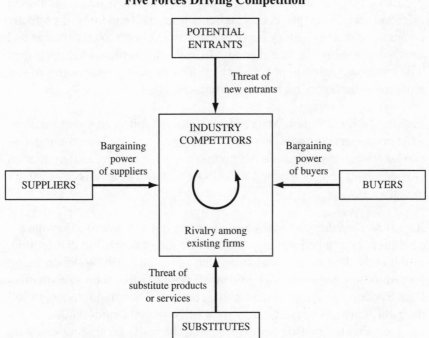

Reprinted with the permission of The Free Press, a division of Simon & Schuster, from *Competitive Strategy: Techniques for Analyzing Industries and Competitors* by Michael E. Porter, p. 4. Copyright © 1980 by The Free Press.

ized by Michael Porter in his influential 1979 *Harvard Business Review* article. He argued that "intense competition in an industry is neither coincidence nor bad luck."[2] In other words, firms can seek out markets where the mechanisms of perfect competition are not working perfectly or they can create the market conditions that violate the assumptions of perfect competition. In short, companies can influence the level of competitive intensity.

Porter describes five well-known forces that interact to influence the intensity of competition in an industry. Together those factors determine market attractiveness. Exhibit 3.2 presents the five factors graphically. Some markets have particularly unfortunate combinations of these five factors. As a result, competition is cutthroat and profits are poor. Other industries are more fortunate. The five factors combine in a manner that lessens the intensity of competition. As a result, firms earn higher profits. The five factors affecting competitive intensity are summarized here.

1. BARRIERS TO ENTRY

Incumbents want to keep other competitors out. If outsiders can easily enter a firm's home market then the profitability and the attractiveness of the market is diminished.

Entry barriers are the modern business equivalent of moats around medieval forts. They protect incumbents from the brutalities of perfectly competitive markets. Entry barriers allow incumbents to raise prices and earn substantial profit margins with a lessened likelihood that outsiders will enter, increase supply, and cut prices to gain share. Some of the more important entry barriers are discussed below.

Product Differentiation. Marketers use product differentiation to destroy what economists propose as perfect competition. It makes products dissimilar so that substitutes do not compete solely on price. Differentiation is widespread and, as detailed in a later chapter, it is an effective barrier to entry.

Access to Distribution. Many new entrants fail not because they have a poor product or a bad strategy but because they cannot find distribution. In the early days of personal computers—the early 1980s—distribution proved to be a potent barrier to entry. Smaller firms, such as Columbia Data Systems, produced fine products, but could not find retailers to sell their machines. As a result, many went belly up in the mid-1980s.

Incumbents often tie up distribution channels, precluding entry by others. They do so in two ways. Some rely heavily on long-term contracts that offer favorable terms for a lockhold on shelf space and promotional activities. That limits the space available to other entrants.

Consider the case of Hillenbrand Industries whose Batesville Casket division holds a 40 percent share of the coffin market while earning extraordinary profit margins. Batesville's strength lies in its hold on distribution. It builds strong relationships with funeral home directors by providing easy financing, overnight delivery of caskets, and, most important, a product that is marked up 200 to 400 percent in return for exclusive distribution. According to one analysis, discounters have made few inroads in this highly profitable market, even though they sell at much lower prices.[3]

The second way in which incumbents exert control over distribution is by proliferating their product lines, which means more shelf space for them and less shelf space for smaller, less powerful entrants. Coca-Cola, for example, now sells Diet Coke, caffeine-free Coke, caffeine-free Diet Coke, Cherry Coke, Diet Cherry Coke, and so on, in a nearly endless factorial of product combinations. Its increase in shelf space comes at the expense of lesser brands, which have been denied the opportunity to introduce their own myriad versions of cola.

Switching Costs. Incumbents often try to engineer switching costs into the buyer-seller relationship. They seek to offer something of value to the buyer in exchange for an implied promise to favor that seller. The intent is to make it expensive or inconvenient for the customer to switch to another seller. Long-term contracts and incompatible product designs are typical means of insuring brand loyalty. Much of the current interest in "relationship marketing" is about raising switching costs.

Patents and Intellectual Property Rights. Patents can protect products from copycats, giving the holder a near monopoly position for years. Polaroid successfully forced Kodak's instant camera off the market. NutraSweet also had a protected product. That gave it time to build a potent brand name before its patent expired in the early 1990s. The brand, though more expensive than generic aspartame, remains the artificial sweetener used in Coke and Pepsi.

The power of patents is greater in some industries than others. Pharmaceutical patents are very enforceable while patents for general product concepts and services are less so. Copying can be rampant.

Economies of Scale and Experience Effects. Smaller firms may simply not have the sales volume or experience to achieve the low-cost production of the industry giants. Auto producers, and other large-scale industrial operators, benefit from scale and experience effects that are unavailable to smaller-scale producers.

Scale effects also manifest themselves in distribution and advertising advantages. For example, large-scale food producers with broad product lines can carry many products into the supermarket, whereas small sellers are often forced to rely on outside brokers. Likewise, the large seller that distributes across the entire country can advertise nationally without wasting dollars to reach consumers in regions where the product is unavailable.

Capital Investment. Some industries require huge sums of money that can scare off smaller entrants. Capital can sometimes serve as a potent barrier to entry.

Expected Defense of Market Share. Some firms have cultivated a well-earned reputation for ruthless retaliation. If someone enters their markets they fight back hard to defend their position. Some incumbents spare no expense and set virtually no time limit on the effort they expend to repel invaders.

Consider the case of light beers, one of the fastest growing and largest segments of the otherwise stagnant beer market. Miller Lite was introduced in February 1975 with a $10 million advertising campaign, the most money ever spent on a new beer introduction up to that time. Lite, which was promoted with the tag line, "Everything you always wanted in a beer and less," was a stunning success that garnered a 60 percent share of the segment. The new product almost single-handedly pushed Miller beer from an also-ran to second place in the industry. Anheuser-Busch was incensed at the entry. It introduced its Bud Light nationally in the summer of 1982 with a $35 million ad budget. For the next decade, it unleashed an advertising and promotional barrage that not only sapped much of the profits from Miller Lite, but also sent a strong strategic signal to other potential entrants. The message seemed to be, "even though we initially misgauged the true potential of the light beer market, we will spare no expense, and set no time limit, for gaining back the dominant position lost to the new entrant." The sheer level of spending and threat of retaliation sends a clear signal to other competitors of Anheuser-Busch's commitment to its key markets.

2. INTENSITY OF RIVALRY

In some markets, competition is so intense that competitors employ nearly suicidal strategies that hurt themselves as well as their opponents. In other markets competition is more benign. Intense rivalry drives down prices, drives up promotional expenses, and otherwise affects profits negatively. That is especially true when competitors are fighting with price. Price cuts are so easily matched, and so utterly destructive to the bottom line, that unrestrained price rivalry is competition of the worst kind.

An industry with excess capacity is more likely to fight with price. One study found that competition in industries with high fixed costs and lots of excess capacity degenerates into "volume grubbing."[4] Competitors are forced to focus on sales volume at any price, rather than profits, in order to fill that capacity and keep cash flow up to pay the high fixed costs. Prices fall and rivalry increases as competitors fight for sales volume. Rivalry also tends to increase when a market is perceived to offer especially high rewards.

3. COMPETITION FROM SUBSTITUTES

Every product has a substitute. The question is not whether one exists but how closely related it is. Close substitutes allow consumers to switch sellers when prices are raised even slightly. That option is not possible when there are no close substitutes. A rise in the price of gasoline, for example, which has few substitutes, elicits loud protests to politicians but few other choices than to pay up or drive less. Clearly, sellers prefer industries where there are no close substitutes.

The "relatedness" of substitutes varies greatly. Sugar competes with the artificial sweeteners aspartame and saccharin in consumer markets. In commercial markets, it competes with corn syrups and other non-cane sweeteners. Network television competes with the more specialized fare that appears on cable, and both compete with video rentals. Soft drinks compete with fruit juices, fruit drinks, sports drinks, and bottled waters to quench consumers' thirsts. If prices rise too steeply in one category consumers may switch to another.

Substitute products can be defined broadly or narrowly. Bayer aspirin, for example, competes with less expensive private aspirin brands. It also competes with aspirin substitutes such as acetaminophen and ibuprofen. Tropical islands compete with cruises, lavish casinos, and ski resorts for the vacation dollars of some consumers. If the price of a European vacation climbs too steeply, consumers may decide to travel by car within the United States. Consumers may even decide to spend their discretionary income on a personal computer rather than a fancy vacation. Clearly, it is difficult to define substitutes precisely.

Technological changes can drastically alter competition among substitutes. Cable television, for example, used to have few substitutes. That is one possible reason why rates skyrocketed. Now, direct broadcast to home satellite dishes and the possible entry of the phone companies into consumer's homes through fiber optic cables threatens to increase the intensity of rivalry in that once nearly monopolistic industry.

Even if there are few close substitutes, consumers can reduce their consumption of a product when prices are raised too high. In 1995, the Association of Coffee Producing Countries, an industry cartel that covers roughly 80 percent of the world's production, tried to limit the supply of beans on world markets in order to prop up prices. Consumers rebelled. They cut back consumption of coffee, forcing some sellers to break ranks with the cartel and increase the supply from their particular country. Coffee prices fell in response.[5]

4. BARGAINING POWER OF CUSTOMERS

A market with powerful customers is less attractive than a market where customers are weak. That is because powerful customers can negotiate lower prices from a weakened seller. The seller has to acquiesce to the customers' demands or forego the sale. Powerful customers drive down sellers' prices and shift profits to themselves.

Consider, for example, the power a strong retailer like Toys 'R' Us exerts over toy manufacturers. More than 20 percent of all toys purchased in the United States are sold by Toys 'R' Us. That large share translates directly into immense power over toy manufacturers. If Toys 'R' Us dislikes a product, it may have to be withdrawn. As *Business Week* noted, "its decisions influence the whole industry."[6] Imagine yourself as a salesperson negotiating a deal to sell a large lot of toys to Toys 'R' Us. When the discussion turns to terms of the contract, who do you imagine holds the upper hand? In contrast, imagine the same set of negotiations between a major toy manufacturer and a small mom-and-pop retailer.

That market power has become so concentrated that Toys 'R' Us recently attracted the attention of the U.S. Justice Department, which has accused the giant retailer of antitrust violations. Specifically, in mid-1996 the government charged that Toys 'R' Us was refusing to buy toys from manufacturers that also sold to low-price warehouse clubs. The warehouse clubs, such as Price Costco, contend that the major toy manufacturers won't ship popular models for fear of losing Toys 'R' Us business. Toys 'R' Us contends that it has the legitimate right to buy from whomever it wants. It simply does not want to carry toys that are sold at lower prices at the warehouse clubs. The argument shows the fine line that sometimes separates competitive advantage from restraint of trade.

Changes can tilt the balance of power to, or away from, customers. Consider the case of prescription drug sales. In 1995, 55 percent of all sales were to customers enrolled in a drug benefit plan. Five years earlier, it was only 26 percent. Dispersed individual consumers have been replaced with powerful plans that decide what they are going to pay. Retail margins have gone down with the increased bargaining power of the consolidated buyers. According to one analysis, about one thousand independent pharmacies have gone out of business.[7]

Product variety can lessen the bargaining power of customers. It is difficult for consumers to compare prices when faced with myriad models and makes. Often, retailers carry only subsets of available models, and each retailer carries a different subset. In such situations, customers cannot easily play one seller off against the other.

Finally, a large body of research on consumer decision-making suggests that individual consumers rely on habit and simple decision rules when choosing a product rather than the rational optimization proposed by economists. Those shortcuts reduce the bargaining power of customers.

5. BARGAINING POWER OF SUPPLIERS

The bargaining power of suppliers is merely the reverse side of the coin as the power of customers. Powerful sellers can raise the price of raw materials, inventory, and supplies to the customers they serve. Powerful sellers can also dictate terms to the customer. Any one, or all, of those actions has the effect of shifting profits away from the buyer to the supplier. A firm squeezed between powerful sellers and powerful buyers competes in a very unattractive market.

Industry consolidation created by mergers and acquisitions has affected the competitive interplay between both suppliers and customers. If a major supplier merges with another supplier, then the power of the customer of those suppliers is diminished. Profits typically follow the flow of power. Conversely, if a customer for a firm's output combines with another customer, then the power (and the profits) shift to the newly empowered group.

USES OF COMPETITIVE ANALYSIS

The five forces affecting competitive intensity can be used in the following five ways.

1. FITTING THE CURRENT ENVIRONMENT

Firms can monitor the alignment of the five forces in order to match their strengths and weaknesses to the market's structure. A small firm, for example, with specialty products, may decide to avoid competition and focus on a segment of the market rather than trying to compete across a broad front.

2. ANTICIPATING MARKET CHANGES

Markets are constantly changing. Derek Abell has argued that such changes are like "strategic windows" that open and close creating opportunities for some firms while destroying opportunities for others.[8] Firms that monitor such changes are in a better position to change with the markets they seek to serve.

3. PICKING A MARKET TO ENTER

The alignment of the five forces can be used to identify diversification opportunities. Firms can seek out and enter markets where the economic mechanisms are not working perfectly and boost profitability.

4. RECONFIGURING THE RULES OF COMPETITION

Firms might enter a market and change the five forces in order to shift the balance of power in their favor. They might, for example, find a market where barriers to entry are low, then raise them. That might entail finding a product category where weak competitors spend little on advertising. The entrance of a large consumer products firm with marketing expertise might raise the level of spending, increasing the level of competitive intensity, raising entry barriers, and shifting competitive advantage to the large seller.

Firms can also reconfigure the five forces to their advantage in other ways. The creation of "big box" superstores, such as Toys 'R' Us, Home Depot, and Barnes & Noble bookstores, for example, weakens the bargaining power of suppliers, causing profits to flow to the retailer.

Mergers and consolidations among buyers, sellers, or both have shifted the balance of power (and profits) during the 1980s. Likewise, technological innovations and the creation of new channels of distribution have changed the rules of competition among the players.

5. PROTECTING THE STATUS QUO

Lastly, market leaders can manipulate the five forces defensively to ensure that their dominant position remains undiminished. Entry barriers can be kept high, customers and suppliers weak, and expected level of retaliation high in order to lower the attractiveness of the market to outsiders.

NOTES

[1]Tim Weiner, "Dwayne's World," *New York Times,* January 16, 1996, p. D4.

[2]Michael Porter, "How Competitive Forces Shape Strategy," *Harvard Business Review,* March–April 1979, pp. 137–45.

[3]Seth Lubove, "Dancing on Graves," *Forbes,* February 28, 1994, pp. 64–65.

[4]Sidney Schoeffler, "The Unprofitability of Modern Technology and What to Do About It?," *Pimsletter,* No. 2, Cambridge, MA: Strategic Planning Institute, 1983.

[5]Greg Burns, "At Last, Grounds for Celebration," *Business Week,* December 18, 1995, p. 48.

[6]Amy Dunkin, "How Toys 'R' Us Controls the Game Board," *Business Week,* December 19, 1988, pp. 58–60.

[7]Toddi Gutner Block, "We Need You, You Need Us," *Forbes,* May 8, 1995, p. 66.

[8]Derek Abell, "Strategic Windows," *Journal of Marketing,* July 1978, pp. 21–26.

CHAPTER 4

COMPETING ON COSTS

The Rise and Fall of Experience Effects
and the Growth-Share Matrix

Portfolio planning models dominated strategic thinking in the 1970s. Like the disco craze of the same decade, businesses bounced to the beat of "boxes and arrows" in an attempt to plot their strategic course to the future. No model was more popular than the Boston Consulting Group's growth-share matrix. It held that ever lower prices, driven by ever lower costs, was the path to strategic success.

Back in the mid-1960s the Westinghouse Corporation wanted to know why per unit costs declined every time it gained experience manufacturing products. Bruce Henderson, who worked for the firm, found the answer in the experience curve, a descendant of the learning curve that had been around for decades but was not widely used in business. The finding was then applied at other companies as well. Like an increasingly popular rock act, the growth-share matrix took the world of planning by storm. It literally defined strategic thought throughout the 1970s.

Experience effects and the growth-share matrix popularized the idea that strategy could be made universal. Managers of conglomerates could diversify risk and optimize the performance of their entire organizations by managing the parts of their business as though they were a portfolio of investments. It was management for modern times. The idea caught on big time.

But, like any craze, the matrix eventually fell out of fashion. The murmur of criticism started in the early 1980s and reached a crescendo by mid-decade. By 1990, the once modern matrix seemed hopelessly outdated.

The BCG matrix was only one of many matrix approaches to marketing strategy that became popular in the 1970s. They differed in some important respects but all reduced strategy to a series of boxes and arrows that prescribe the best strategy for a particular situation. Together, they fall under the rubric of "formula planning," "portfolio planning," or "matrix" planning.

This chapter details the rise and fall of experience effects and the Boston Consulting Group's growth-share matrix.

EXPERIENCE EFFECTS

Experience effects constitute the central theoretical basis of the Boston Consulting Group's growth-share matrix. The idea is that firms have an opportunity to lower costs as they gain experience producing a product. Experience is gained by increasing sales volume over time. The more experience gained, the lower the costs to produce each unit.

The concept is not new. As early as the 1920s, military manufacturers found that when they produced more planes, they produced them more efficiently and more economically. Planes produced later in the process were less expensive to manufacture than planes made earlier.

In 1954, Frank Andress argued that lower costs could be achieved as a firm gained experience making a product.[1] Ten years later, Hirschmann suggested that experience effects were more pervasive than previously thought.[2] They applied to *all* businesses, not just aircraft manufacturers. The Boston Consulting Group expanded the concept even further.

Costs do not decline automatically. In fact, they are more likely to rise than fall. The tendency is for staffs to expand, product lines to proliferate, and workers to earn higher wages as a business grows larger. According to the experience effects theory there is an *opportunity* to lower costs, but no guarantee. Only through a strict adherence to productivity goals, the adoption of new technologies to increase productivity, and a constant effort to cut unnecessary expenditures do costs decline. Experience effects come from the clever application of new procedures and methods. Winfred Hirschmann summed it up nicely a generation ago with three simple words: "Practice makes perfect."

EXPERIENCE EFFECTS VERSUS ECONOMIES OF SCALE

Cost declines due to size arise from scale effects or economies of scale. Experience effects accrue over time. It is the time dimension that makes them different. Scale effects arise from the size of the operation. Time is not a key factor. Doubling the capacity of an electric generating plant, for example, does not require twice the investment.

EXPERIENCE EFFECTS VERSUS LEARNING EFFECTS

Experience effects are more encompassing than learning effects, a popular concept in psychology. The learning curve captures the notion that productivity improvements are gained as a worker learns how to perform a task better (and faster). If you know how to type, you have observed the learning curve in action. If you plotted the number of keystrokes-per-minute from the first day you started typing to the present you would be plotting a learning curve. The curve would rise rapidly as you started to master the repetitive task. Your fingers literally learn to move faster.[3]

SOURCES OF EXPERIENCE EFFECTS

Experience effects include the learning curve, but capture other sources of productivity improvement as well.

1. *The learning curve* plays an important part, but not the only part, in experience effects.
2. *Specialization of labor* also improves the efficiency of an operation over time. When automobiles were first manufactured in the early 1900s each auto was virtually custom-made. As volume increased and experience accumulated the opportunities for specialization grew. Henry Ford dominated his contemporaries with worker specialization.
3. *Product innovations,* such as the development of a new type of magnetron, the key component in microwave ovens, can greatly reduce a product's cost.
4. *Process innovations* are developments made in the machinery and procedures used to produce the output of an industry. Disposable diapers, for example, are difficult to manufacture. It was not until the mid-1960s, when Proctor and Gamble perfected the production process, that costs declined and the market expanded for Pampers.
5. *New materials* often replace old materials as a market evolves. In autos, for example, plastics are now used to make parts once made exclusively of steel. Plastic is lighter, more durable, and often less expensive.
6. *Product standardization* occurs when an industry agrees on what form a product and its components will take. That allows for costs advantages.
7. *Product redesign for ease of assembly,* such as Hewlett-Packard's redesign of its printers to have the fewest possible parts, makes for easier and more efficient assembly.

THE EXPERIENCE CURVE

Experience effects are plotted on experience curves. A typical curve, as shown in Exhibit 4.1, shows that costs decline more slowly as experience accumulates. As a product category matures substantial cost declines

Exhibit 4.1
An Idealized Experience Curve

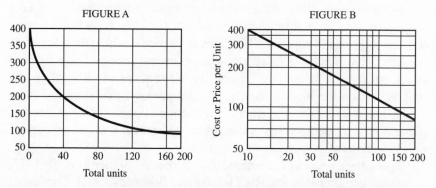

When prices or costs are plotted against cumulative volume, the resulting graph characteristically takes the form of a curve on a linear scale (Figure A). Although the smoothness of the curve suggests the regularity of the relationship, some of the particular aspects are obscured. As a result, it is more useful to plot C/V or P/V slopes on double logarithmic scales (Figure B).

Plots on a log-log scale have the unique property of showing percentage change as a constant distance, along either axis at any position on the grid. A straight line on log-log paper means, then, that a given percentage change in one factor results in a corresponding percentage change in the other, the nature of that relationship corresponding to the slope of the line, which can be read right off a log-log grid.

In the case of cost-volume or price-volume slopes, the plotting of observed data about costs or prices and accumulated experience for a product on log-log paper has always produced straight lines reflecting a consistent relationship between experience and prices and experience and costs.

Source: *Perspectives on Experience,* The Boston Consulting Group, 1968, p. 13. Reprinted by permission from The Boston Consulting Group, Inc., Boston, Mass. © Copyright 1968.

become more difficult to realize. Doubling sales of a mature product is less likely than doubling sales of a fast-growing new product. Substantial declines in the cost of manufacturing microwave ovens, for example, have already been realized.

Experience curves are usually described in terms of percentages. An 80 percent experience curve is considered typical. It is interpreted as follows: *as experience doubles costs per unit fall to 80 percent of their original value.* That is, costs decline by 20 percent. As sales rise from one thousand to two thousand units, for example, costs per unit decline from $100 to $80. Most experience curves decline at a rate of between 10 and 30 percent each time production doubles.

THE CASE OF POCKET CALCULATORS

Pocket calculators offer an excellent example of experience effects in action. It was the example often used in the 1970s, during the ascendency of experience curves, to illustrate the effect. In the mid-1960s, Texas Instrument (TI) engineers created a "calculator-on-a-chip," which made it possible to produce today's electronic pocket calculator. It turned out to be one of the most stunning inventions of the twentieth century.

In September 1971 the Bowmar Instrument Corporation of Fort Wayne, Indiana, started selling the "Bowmar Brain" at Saks Fifth Avenue in New York for a whopping $179. This for a model with only a few simple functions. Bowmar's calculator was an instant success that sold well as an expensive Christmas gift item. By the summer of 1972, after less than a year on the market, nearly 500,000 pocket calculators had been sold. That allowed for significant experience effects. Retail prices fell precipitously as competitors flooded into the market and gained experience. Declines of 40 percent were common.

Texas Instruments (TI) entered the market on September 20, 1972, exactly a year after Bowmar. Its TI-2500 and Bowmar's "901B" both sold at retail for $120. Prices declined further as the market expanded and the volume produced grew. By 1974, sales of pocket calculators reached more than 25 million units a year. Lower prices created additional demand.

Then came the shakeout. The ruthless price cutting made possible by experience effects caused many competitors to drop out of the market in the mid-1970s. Firms like Bowmar, that merely assembled parts made by others, had a tough time realizing further cost declines (since its suppliers controlled its costs) and were shaken out of the market.

Today, calculators can be had for a few dollars. What started out as a major purchase in the early 1970s transformed into an incidental item within a decade, all due to experience effects.

THE RELATIONSHIP BETWEEN COSTS AND PRICES

Experience curves can be used to plot costs to the firm and prices to the consumer. Prices sometimes run parallel to costs as a firm gains experience, but not always. As Exhibit 4.2 illustrates, prices sometimes behave as hypothesized by the product life cycle. Four stages are commonly observed.

1. In the *introductory stage,* prices are lower than costs. The firm loses money on each item sold. Volume is low. Inefficiencies are high. Experience effects have not yet kicked in.

2. In the growth stage of the product life cycle, labeled *price umbrella,* consumers clamor for the new product but the market leader feels no pressure to push prices downward in the face of tight supplies. Competitors have yet to enter in large numbers. As a result, prices do not fall as fast as costs. Costs, meanwhile, are declining rapidly as the benefits of experience effects are realized in full force. The market leader slides quickly down the steep slope of the experience curve. Volume doubles

Exhibit 4.2
The Cost-Price Relationship

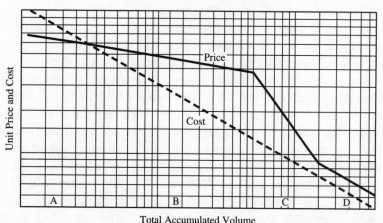

Total Accumulated Volume

Source: *Perspectives on Experience,* The Boston Consulting Group, 1968, p. 22. Reprinted by permission from The Boston Consulting Group, Inc., Boston, Mass. © Copyright 1968.

easily from a small starting base. Profit margins are highest during this stage of the product life cycle. But those higher margins attract new entrants seeking market share. At some point, competitors cut prices to gain market share and accumulate experience.

3. Then comes the dreaded *shakeout.* Vicious price cutting combined with an eventual slowing of demand as the market matures means that those competitors without the requisite experience effects have costs higher than the prevailing market price. They are forced out of the market. The ultimate goal of experience curve analysis is to survive this elimination stage. The near obsessive concern with this issue is based on the observation that when the shakeout is over only two or three major players remain. All others are forced to withdraw in the face of mounting losses.

4. The shakeout is followed by a *return to stability,* where prices stabilize at somewhere above the costs of the lowest-cost producer in the industry—the firm that has accumulated the most experience—and below the price at which other firms are attracted. From that point on, prices run parallel to costs. Stability reigns.

THE MERITS OF MARKET SHARE AND MARKET GROWTH

The strategic implications of experience effects are clear—a firm must gain experience at least as fast as the market leader if it is to survive the shakeout. Its costs must keep falling. If it does not increase sales volume fast enough, its costs will be higher than the industry price and it will not survive the shakeout.

Like children on a crowded playground slide, firms slide down the experience curve in order of entry. The only way to pass is by gaining market share faster than firms in front. But gaining market share, and hence accumulating experience, is easiest in the earliest stages of the product life cycle. The market is new and evolving, and no one competitor yet dominates. Brand switching is high and consumer loyalties are low. That makes share gains more likely than in a mature market where market share gains must come at the expense of entrenched competitors who are likely to fight vigorously to defend their turf. The basic strategic argument of the Boston Consulting Group is that firms should fight for market share in high-growth markets. That allows firms to accumulate experience faster than competitors, which leads to lower costs and higher profits. Exhibit 4.3 illustrates that sequence of events.

Exhibit 4.3
Logic of Growth-Share Matrix

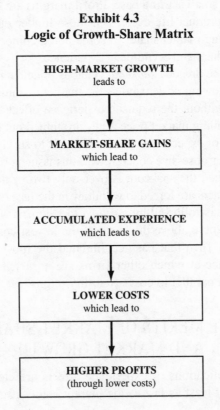

HIGH-MARKET GROWTH
leads to

MARKET-SHARE GAINS
which lead to

ACCUMULATED EXPERIENCE
which leads to

LOWER COSTS
which lead to

HIGHER PROFITS
(through lower costs)

Exhibit 4.4
The Growth-Share Matrix

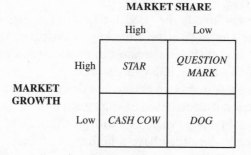

THE GROWTH-SHARE MATRIX

The growth-share matrix presented in Exhibit 4.4 is a simple two-by-two matrix that cross-classifies market share and market growth to yield four quadrants. Each of the firm's products (or businesses) is plotted on the matrix. Different strategies are designated for each quadrant based on the combination of market share and market growth.

In essence, the growth-share matrix is a strategic allocation model that shows how money can be transferred from areas of less opportunity to areas where the chances for success are greatest. Its purpose is to (1) optimize the performance of the *entire* portfolio of products or businesses, and (2) balance the cash flow among those products or businesses, designating some products as sources of funds and others as users of funds.

Neither market share nor market growth are dichotomous variables in reality, but the "high" and "low" labels have intuitive appeal and the two-by-two matrix makes for easy understanding. High-growth markets are defined as those growing by more than 10 percent per year. Markets growing by less than 10 percent are deemed low growth. High-share products (or businesses) are those that hold the largest share of their market. Otherwise, they are classified as low-share. The cutpoints are arbitrary but not unreasonable.

THE SOURCE AND USE OF FUNDS

Walter Kiechel writes in *Fortune* that the purpose of the growth-share matrix is "to show which businesses would throw off cash and which would wolf it up."[4] This colorful quote speaks clearly of the source and use of investment funds.

Market share affects the supply of funds available to the firm. Products with a high share usually earn more money. The reason is simple.

High-share firms have gained more experience. They have higher sales and lower costs than lower-share firms. Low-share firms have a weak incoming cash flow.

Market growth affects the need for funds. The chances of gaining share are greatest in high-growth markets. Consequently, the need for funds to "buy" market share is greatest in those cases. Low-growth markets are unattractive and need few funds.

The growth-share matrix gives cute, but descriptive, names to products in each of the four quadrants. Each product has a unique strategic profile.

Cash cows hold a large share of a low-growth market. They generate lots of excess cash since they have a high market share. Their need for cash is low because they compete in a low-growth market where competitors have already been shaken out. Market shares have stabilized. Consequently, cash cows are a source of funds for the firm. They are the only quadrant with a strong positive cash flow.

Question marks are the opposite of cash cows. They have a small share of a desirable high-growth market. They need a great deal of cash to gain market share but generate very little cash, since they possess only a small share of the market. Question marks need funds to fight for market share. They are sometimes called "problem children" or "wildcats."

Stars have a high share of a high-growth market. They generate significant amounts of cash because of that high share. But they require about as much cash as they earn to fend off firms trying to gain share in their high-growth market. A star must fight hard to maintain its position. On average, stars are said to be in cash balance.

Dogs occupy the least desirable position in the growth-share matrix. Their current position is poor and their future outlook is bleak. Dogs have a low share of a low-growth market. They are sometimes called "cash traps," an appellation that aptly captures their perceived value to the firm.

But, dogs can be controversial. They are in cash balance: they generate little cash, but they need little cash to maintain their position. Not all dogs are mangy mutts. Some can be faithful friends for years.

STRATEGIC PRESCRIPTIONS OF THE GROWTH-SHARE MATRIX

No market grows forever. Eventually, high-growth markets degenerate into low-growth markets as demand levels off. For the most part, market growth is uncontrollable or, at least, less controllable than market share. Share gains can be "bought" by spending heavily on advertising and promotion in new, fast-growing markets. As a result, the basic strategic advice of the growth-share matrix is to battle for market share in high-growth markets so that when maturation comes there will be funds to fight future battles.

THE PATH TO SUCCESS

The goal of the BCG matrix is to continuously generate future cash cows. That objective is accomplished by investing money earned by a cash cow in a question mark with the intent of gaining share. The hope is to turn that question mark into a star. As the market matures, and competition lessens, that star will then degenerate into a cash cow and the process will be repeated. New cash cows give the firm a steady source of funds to pursue future avenues of growth.

THREE PATHS TO FAILURE

Success is not assured. Disaster awaits the firm that does not follow the path to success outlined above. There are three paths to failure.

1. A firm may overinvest in a cash cow and underinvest in a question mark. As a result, the question mark becomes a dog rather than a star. When the cash cow becomes obsolete the firm is left with few funds to finance future ventures. The firm has traded future opportunity for present cash flow.
2. Similarly, a firm may underinvest in a star, which then becomes a question mark that eventually degenerates into a dog. For example, Adidas, the German athletic shoe seller, allowed Nike to gain share in the high-growth market for running shoes in the 1970s. Adidas never regained the loss of share. The firm followed the second path to failure.
3. The final path to failure occurs when a firm milks its cash cow too hard and the cow dies. It degenerates into a dog. Xerox, for example, milked its copier business too hard in the late 1970s and early 1980s to fund entry into the wild world of personal computers. The Japanese entered the market for copiers at the low end and Xerox never gained a dominant position in personal computers. Today, Canon is the world's leading seller of copy machines.

CRITICISMS OF THE GROWTH-SHARE MATRIX

No sooner did the growth-share matrix reach the pinnacle of its influence than it began to bear the brunt of vicious criticisms, thirteen of which are discussed on the following pages.

1. THE SUCCESS OF LOW-SHARE FIRMS

While the matrix argued that high share leads inexorably to higher profits and low share leads to disaster, critics found that many low-share firms are very successful. They succeed by avoiding competitive battles rather than seeking them out. A study by Hammermesh, Anderson, and Harris in 1978, for example, found that successful low-share firms compete only in segments where their strengths are most valued, they purposely stay small, and they try not to attract the attention of the larger competitors.[5]

A subsequent study by Woo and Cooper questioned the conventional wisdom "that companies with low market shares are doomed to marginal profits, at best, while market-share leaders show the best returns on investment."[6] The authors examined forty low-share firms and found that "many companies with low market shares survive and even prosper." Market leadership is important, but it is not the only path to business success.

2. THE FUTILITY OF MARKET SHARE GAINED

As early as 1972, studies found that market share wars were destructive. Would-be share gainers often ended up worse off than they started.[7] With many competitors trying to achieve the same goal, often by cutting price (which is easily matched), the result was a hollow victory for all involved. Entire industries were irreparably harmed by the devastating price wars that forever lowered margins on the business.

3. SUCCESS OF LOW-GROWTH MARKETS

Other critics argued that the BCG's obsession with high-growth markets was also overstated. Writing in *Fortune,* Jaclyn Fierman examined seven successful companies competing in stagnant or declining markets and found that many generated handsome profits.[8] They avoided battles for market share, emphasized quality, treated employees like family, used low-tech means to lower costs, and moved cautiously when it came to strategy.

Aaker and Day also questioned the assumption that high-growth markets are inherently more attractive than low-growth markets.[9] They argued: (1) that gaining share is not necessarily any easier or less costly in high-growth markets, (2) that share gains in high-growth markets do not necessarily give firms a head start down the experience curve, (3) the pressure to lower prices is not necessarily less in growth markets, and (4) that early entrants do not necessarily outperform later entrants.

4. SHOULD DOGS BE DIVESTED?

One of the most damning criticisms concerns the advice that question marks should be targeted for growth while dogs should be divested, ignored, or otherwise mistreated. A few simple calculations show the folly of such actions. Imagine a typical market. Assume that the market has five major competitors. One firm has the largest share. The other four firms are designated low-share competitors.

Then consider market growth. Imagine a simple economy made up of only twenty markets. Assume that 20 percent of those markets are growing by more than 10 percent. That means that four of those twenty markets (20%) are designated high growth while the remaining sixteen (80%) are deemed low-growth.

Combining the estimates of market share and market growth for this hypothetical economy yields a total of one hundred firms (five competitors in each of twenty markets) distributed as shown in Exhibit 4.5. Extrapolating these figures to the entire U.S. economy leads to the obvious conclusion that dogs are not a rare breed. Nearly two-thirds of all products and services are classified as dogs according to definitions typically used by the growth-share matrix (64 of 100). Does it make strategic sense to write off such a large sector of the economy? Critics contend that it might be better to treat dogs with love and affection rather than to routinely maltreat them, or, worse yet, put them to sleep.

An empirical study examined the performance of 418 dogs found that: "Dogs are not all mangy cash losers. In fact, some of them are handsome cash generators."[10] Successful dogs followed narrow product lines, avoided price competition with market leaders, and stressed product quality. Many dogs, it seems, are man's best friend.

Another study barked up the same tree. It argued persuasively that some dogs "might be viewed as bonds traditionally have been in a security portfolio, providing modest but relatively certain returns."[11] The study concludes that divesting dogs is often a mistake. Dogs can yield a steady, if small, return if managed correctly.

Exhibit 4.5
The Prevalence of "Dog" Markets

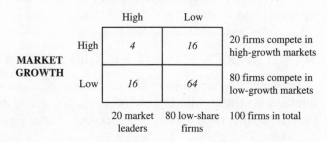

MARKET SHARE

		High	Low	
MARKET GROWTH	High	*4*	*16*	20 firms compete in high-growth markets
	Low	*16*	*64*	80 firms compete in low-growth markets
		20 market leaders	80 low-share firms	100 firms in total

5. HARVESTING BREAD-AND-BUTTER PRODUCTS

Another damning criticism leveled against the growth-share matrix concerns its advice to extract money from "bread-and-butter businesses" to fund entry into unproven markets. The result is often disaster. Firms may never build a viable position in the new market, and when they return to their core products, find that competitors have taken advantage of their inattention and gained the leading share.

That is what happened to the old Addressograph-Multigraph Corp. in the early 1980s. Executives were convinced that mechanical duplicating machines, the company's flagship product, were obsolete. Customers were switching to xerographic copiers. So they de-emphasized the mainstay product, changed the name of the firm to AM International, and set out to gain share in a host of exotic information technologies meant to serve the "office of the future." The firm ended up failing in virtually all of those markets. The old management departed and new managers divested the new businesses and returned to the company's core products. It was too late. As *Business Week* noted: "The resulting confusion caused the division to lose the lead position in its bread-and-butter product, mechanical offset duplicators."[12] An executive of the firm lamented: "We're now No. 2 and we have two Japanese competitors breathing down our necks." AM International filed for bankruptcy shortly after. Harvesting hurt them dearly.

6. IMPORTANCE OF BUSINESS "RELATEDNESS"

The popularity of the growth-share matrix is directly related to the growth of conglomerates during the "go-go" years of the late 1960s where firms found themselves competing in myriad markets about which they knew little. There was a belief that management skills could be readily transferred from one business to another, even if the businesses were completely unrelated. Managing real-world businesses was akin to managing a portfolio of stocks and bonds—hence the term portfolio planning. It did not seem to matter what the division made or sold, as long as it could be categorized into one of growth-share's quadrants. Today, such ideas seem foolish. The allure of conglomerates has been replaced with a desire to compete in a related set of businesses where the firm has experience and expertise.

7. PURSUING EXPERIENCE EFFECTS HINDERS INNOVATION

Abernathy and Wayne, writing in the *Harvard Business Review,* noted that "product innovation is the enemy of cost efficiency, and vice versa."[13] They argue that once a firm becomes locked into producing a standardized product very efficiently, and is constantly in search of lower costs, it is reluctant to embrace radically new products that, by their very nature, reduce efficiency and disrupt the ever-lower-costs trend.

8. THE CONFOUNDING EFFECTS OF SHARED EXPERIENCE

Shared experience occurs when a firm already has gained experience making a similar product. It is able to cut ahead of the first firm sliding down the experience curve. That happened with telephone answering machines where Code-A-Phone's early lead was quickly matched and surpassed by AT&T and Panasonic, which had vast experience in related areas. It also happened with CAT scanners. Once GE entered the fray, early producers such as EMI were history.

9. LOWER PRICES VERSUS MARKET SHARE: WHICH CAUSES WHICH?

William Alberts argues that the BCG has it backwards. Instead of market share allowing for accumulated experience, he persuasively argues that lowering prices (as a result of experience effects) leads to market share gains.[14] His argument points up the sometimes intractable problem of attributing causation to two correlated phenomena.

10. INTERNAL CASH FLOW

Another criticism of the growth-share matrix is that it allocates only internal cash flow. It doe not consider externally raised funds, even though during the 1980s many firms funded growth through capital markets.

11. A MECHANICAL RESPONSE INSTEAD OF A CREATIVE SOLUTION

The growth-share matrix offers a canned response to strategic problems that would be better solved by creative solutions. Such rigidness ensured that the matrix would fail when widely applied to many industries by all players. It is the unique move, which is often unexpected, that pays the greatest dividends.

12. NO CONSIDERATION OF PRODUCT DIFFERENTIATION

Another severe shortcoming of experience effects and the growth-share matrix is that they assume that all products are commodities that compete on price alone. That is simply not true. Many products sell on something other than the absolute lowest price. In fact, the very essence of marketing is that some sellers' offerings are special, and worthy of a higher price.

13. ONE WAY TO WIN: AN OBSESSION WITH LOW COSTS

The final criticism is that the growth-share matrix is predicated on the faulty assumption that there is only one way to win. On page one of the BCG's influential *Perspectives on Experience* the question is posed: "Are there basic rules for success?" The consulting firm answers: "There, indeed, appear to be rules for success, and they relate to the impact of accumulated experience on competitors' costs, industry prices, and the interrelation between to the two."[15]

That answer is only partially correct. Costs and prices are an important part of marketing strategy but they are not the only part. Just as every football team does not use the same play to win the game, neither do businesses succeed with a single strategy based solely on low costs and low prices. That obsession with a single strategic response limits the usefulness of experience effects and the growth-share matrix to some businesses in some industries sometimes.

THE RETURN OF COST COMPETITIVENESS

The great irony of experience effects and the growth-share matrix is that once both were totally trashed by critics, growing numbers of value-conscious consumers rediscovered the benefits of lower prices. That caused sellers to focus, once again, on cutting costs and prices to remain competitive. By the 1990s, the pendulum had swung back to a position close to that initially espoused by the BCG in the 1970s, although not to exactly the same place.

There has been a wholesale return to the belief that having a lower cost structure than competitors is essential to corporate survival. But the way in which those lower costs are achieved has expanded far beyond the basic premise of experience effects. In the 1990s, businesses have not only "learned" how to be more efficient through experience curve analysis, they have restructured from top to bottom, shedding jobs faster than a dog sheds his coat at the start of summer. The ruthless cost cutting and massive layoffs announced almost weekly during the first half of the 1990s went far beyond the form of cost cutting proposed by the experience effect. Even high-cost producers such as Procter & Gamble have gotten low-cost fever. Faced with severe price competition and a reluctance on the part of consumers to pay higher prices, *Business Week* reported in 1994 that the blue chip firm had "moved aggressively to cut costs, keep prices down, and improve customer service."[16]

In a sense, the current conception of cost cutting merely takes the next step in an expansive pattern set in place by the Boston Consulting Group so many years ago. Experience curve analysis initially gained popularity by showing that achieving lower costs could be achieved in far more businesses than originally thought. Now in the 1990s, firms have discovered that cutting costs can be accomplished in a much broader way than simply learning to do the task better.

In sum, like the popularity of the technique they sought to discredit, critics' attacks on the BCG were an overreaction. Today, more than ever, prices and costs are important. For that reason, the BCG's contribution is an important, if heavily criticized, one. It set in place a trend that continues to this day.

NOTES

[1]Frank Andress, "The Learning Curve as a Production Tool," *Harvard Business Review,* January–February 1954, pp. 87–97.

[2]Winfred Hirschmann, "Profit from the Learning Curve," *Harvard Business Review,* January–February 1964, pp. 125–39.

[3]A detailed review of the history of the learning curve and experience effects is provided by Louis E. Yelle, "The Learning Curve: Historical Review and Comprehensive Survey," *Decision Sciences,* April 1979, pp. 302–28.

[4]Walter Kiechel, "Oh Where, Oh Where Has My Little Dog Gone? Or My Cash Cow? Or My Star," *Fortune,* November 2, 1981, p. 149.

[5]R. G. Hammermesh, M. J. Anderson, Jr., and J. E. Harris, "Strategies for Low Market Share Businesses," *Harvard Business Review,* May–June 1978, pp. 95–102.

[6]Carolyn Woo, and Arnold Cooper, "The Surprising Case for Low Market Share," *Harvard Business Review,* November–December 1982, pp. 106–13.

[7]William Fruhan, "Pyrrhic Victories in Fights for Market Share," *Harvard Business Review,* September–October 1972, pp. 100–07.

[8]Jaclyn Fierman, "How to Make Money in Mature Markets," *Fortune,* November 25, 1985, pp. 47–53.

[9]David Aaker, and George Day, "The Perils of High-Growth Markets," *Strategic Management Journal,* September–October 1986, pp. 409–21.

[10]Donald Hambrick, and Ian MacMillan, "The Product Portfolio and Man's Best Friend," *California Management Review,* Fall 1982, pp. 84–95.

[11]H. Kurt Christensen, Arnold Cooper, and Cornelis A. DeKluyver, "The Dog Business: A Re-examination," *Business Horizons,* October–December 1982, pp. 12–18.

[12]"AM International: When Technology Was Not Enough," *Business Week,* January 25, 1982, pp. 62–68.

[13]William Abernathy, and Kenneth Wayne, "Limits of the Learning Curve," *Harvard Business Review,* September–October 1974, pp. 109–19.

[14]William Alberts, "The Experience Curve Doctrine Reconsidered," *Journal of Marketing,* July 1989, pp. 36–49.

[15]*Perspectives on Experience,* The Boston Consulting Group, 1968.

[16]Zachary Schiller, "Ed Artzt's Elbow Grease Has P&G Shining," *Business Week,* October 10, 1994, pp. 84–86.

CHAPTER 5

GENERIC STRATEGIES

If the 1970s was the decade of the experience effects and the growth-share matrix then the 1980s was the decade of generic strategies. The Boston Consulting Group favored the low-cost option of creating imperfect competition. But that is only a single strategic choice. In his landmark 1980 Free Press book, *Competitive Strategy,* Michael Porter added *differentiation* and *focus* as alternative paths to business success.[1] More than a decade later, Michael Treacy and Fred Wiersema proposed *customer intimacy, product leadership,* and *operational excellence* as strategic options.[2] What makes both efforts unique is that they recognize that there is more than one way to create imperfect competition.

PORTER'S THREE GENERIC STRATEGIES

An old adage holds that the way to succeed in business is to "buy low *and* sell high." Porter disagrees. He argues that firms should *either* differentiate their goods and sell at a higher price, or do as the Boston Consulting Group advises, and lower costs and sell at lower prices. But, they *should not do both.*

Porter also proposes a third generic strategy whereby firms succeed by limiting the *scope* of their operations. That is, some firms, without the resources (or desire) to compete across a broad mass market, should concentrate on a segment of the market. Segmenters can either differentiate or act as the low-cost producer in that segment. Exhibit 5.1 illustrates Porter's three generic strategies.

LOW-COST/LOW-PRICE SELLING

Firms that follow a strategy of "overall cost leadership" focus on lowering costs of production so they can lower prices to consumers. The competitive advantage of a low-cost, low-price seller lies in its ability to underprice the competition.

Exhibit 5.1
Porter's Three Generic Strategies

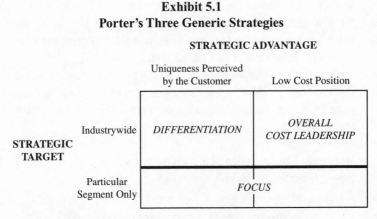

Low-cost, low-price sellers can be found in every sector of the economy. In retailing, for example, discounters such as Wal-Mart, Toys 'R' Us, the Price Club, and Sam's Club are efficient operators that sell at rock-bottom prices. They bargain hard with suppliers and pass along the savings to customers in the form of lower prices. In computers and consumer electronics, Packard-Bell, Emerson, and Korea's Samsung make standardized products that are designed for efficient production. They spend less on R&D and advertising than differentiators, and like many other low-cost, low-price sellers, are market followers, allowing others to innovate new product ideas, which they then imitate and produce in large volumes at very low costs. Large volume allows them to underprice the competition. In services, Southwest Airlines, and some of the more recent upstarts, follow a similar low-cost, low-price approach.

Low-cost, low-price sellers usually earn lower profit margins than sellers of differentiated goods, but they make up for it in high market share. Higher share gives them lower costs, which allows them to sell at low prices. It is the "supermarket" strategy of selling—make very little on each sale but sell enormous quantities. This type of low-cost producer is often the market leader. Staples and Packard Bell are examples of this kind of low-cost producer.

A second type of low-cost, low-price seller focuses slightly more on higher margins. This type of seller typically has a smaller market share than the market leader, but earns higher margins. Private label producers, for example, sell for less than national brands, but earn higher margins for retailers. They maintain a respectable share of the market but usually do not dominate their product category.

A low-cost producer creates imperfect competition by:

- *Reducing the bargaining power of suppliers.* High sales volume gives the low-cost producer bargaining power against suppliers. Suppliers value large accounts and are more likely to yield to demands they would not accept from smaller volume accounts.

- *Reducing the bargaining power of customers.* High sales volume gives the low-cost producer bargaining power with customers. Customers have little room to bargain against the firm that is already selling at the lowest prices.

- *Making substitutes less attractive.* Lower prices make substitutes less attractive. The low-price seller keeps the balance of price and performance tilted toward its products.

PRODUCT DIFFERENTIATION

Many products sell quality, status, service, and style rather than rock-bottom prices. A strategy of differentiation, as the term implies, tries to make products different, and usually better, than those sold by competitors. Differentiation can be based on either tangible or intangible product or service attributes. Consumers pay more for uniquely differentiated products while low-cost, low-price sellers focus solely on efficient production.

Almost every market has differentiated products. McDonald's, Nike, Grey Poupon mustard, Gucci, L'Oréal hair color, Merrill Lynch, Perdue Chicken, Crest Toothpaste, and L. L. Bean are but a few of the firms that successfully employ product differentiation.

Differentiators earn more on each item sold. They charge higher prices for superior quality products. Costs are never ignored by the differentiator. They are merely not the focus of all attention. Material prices may be higher, due to better quality. Expensive fine leathers may be used to make luxury handbags. Advertising expenses may be in keeping with the product's prestigious image. Tylenol, Bayer, Excedrin, and the other name-brand headache remedies charge much higher prices than the no-name generics that are often chemically identical, but the name brands are supported by campaigns that perpetually reinforce the superior quality image.

Market shares vary greatly for differentiated goods, typically in tandem with earned margins. Two patterns are common. Sellers of luxury brands, such as Mercedes, Hermès, or Cartier, earn huge profit margins on each item sold but hold only a tiny share of the market. In essence, their strategy marries differentiation to segmentation. By selling at such exclusive prices they inexorably target the high-income, upscale segment.

The second type of differentiator earns less exorbitant profit margins but possesses a huge share of the market. Most of the popular national brands, such as Coca-Cola, Campbell's soup, Quaker Oats oatmeal, Hellmann's mayonnaise, Gatorade, and Heinz ketchup, fall into this category. Often, they are the market leaders. They earn high margins *and* have high market share.

Differentiation creates imperfect competition in the following ways.

- *Reducing the bargaining power of customers.* The uniqueness of differentiated products lowers the bargaining power of buyers. Consumers either have to pay the price requested or settle for something else.
- *Making substitutes less attractive.* Unique products are not direct substitutes. They are purposely designed to be different. The greater that difference, the less likely consumers are to switch when prices are raised.
- *Reducing rivalry.* Differentiation lessens the likelihood of price cutting.

MARKET SEGMENTATION

Segmentation turns small size into an advantage. It seeks to avoid competition by focusing on a part of the market where the competition is not interested in reacting, or where larger competitors cannot react because of their large size.

The essence of segmentation is low market share. It is a specialization strategy that does not seek to satisfy all consumers. Instead, it offers something special to a small, defensible part of the market.

In virtually every market, sellers thrive by selling to segments. In the beer business, for example, microbreweries sell high-priced, high-quality, nearly homemade products to beer connoisseurs. Anheuser-Busch's premium brands, meanwhile, lose share. The brand name of the leading seller actually impedes its entry into small-scale brewing.

Market segmentation is not really a different generic strategy than differentiation and low-cost production but one that merely restricts the scope of competition using either one of those two strategies in order to lower the level of rivalry. According to Porter, there are two segmentation strategies: (1) a firm can offer unique products designed specifically for a segment, or (2) it can be a low-cost, low-price seller to that segment. What sets segmentation apart is its scope. Segmentation avoids competition across a broad market.

Many firms succeed by offering specialized products to a unique group of customers. Oshkosh Truck, for example, specializes in the manufacture of emergency crash and rescue vehicles used at airports. The firm also makes specially designed cement mixers. It does not compete against the big three auto sellers in the broader market for autos. It avoids competition.

Some firms target a segment and then produce and sell to that segment at very low prices. A specialty glass producer, for example, might efficiently focus on making glass doors for microwave ovens rather than engaging in the price competition found in commodity glass markets aimed at a broader market. Similarly, Guilford Mills, a textile firm, specializes in making the lacy material used in lingerie. Competitors have shown less interest in the efficient, but old fashioned, knitting process used by Guilford.

Market segmentation and product differentiation are different, but closely related, concepts. It is oftentimes difficult to tell which strategy is in action. Mercedes-Benz, for example, sells a clearly differentiated product for which consumers are willing to pay a premium price. But that high price means that Mercedes sells almost exclusively to a small group of very high-income consumers. Is Mercedes segmenting the market or differentiating its product? It is not an easy question to answer. Its focus on engineering excellence suggests differentiation while its customer base points to segmentation.

There is an inescapable definitional fuzziness to the terms differentiation and segmentation that arises out of their relatedness. They are slippery terms that escape precise definition and point up the artistic nature of many strategic marketing decisions.

A segmentation strategy creates imperfect competition in the following ways:

- *Reducing rivalry.* A firm that successfully attends to the needs of a segment avoids larger competitors. It relinquishes the larger market for a more secure share in a smaller segment. Segmentation is a strategy based on avoiding competition.
- *Reducing pressure from substitutes.* By focusing on the special needs of a segment a firm reduces the lure of substitutes. Substitutes appeal to either other segments or a broader market with a more diverse set of needs.

STUCK IN THE MIDDLE

Some firms have no strategy for combating competition. They are neither low-cost, low-price sellers, nor are they sellers of differentiated goods. Porter refers to such firms as stuck in the middle and notes: "The firm stuck in the middle is almost guaranteed low profitability."[3]

The U-shaped curve presented in Exhibit 5.2 illustrates Porter's concept of stuck in the middle. It shows that successful competitors either have a very high share of the market—they are the low-cost producers that sell on the basis of price—or specialize, focusing on only a segment of the market. Firms that are stuck in the middle do neither.

Exhibit 5.2
Porter's Concept of Stuck in the Middle

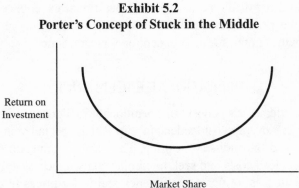

Reprinted with the permission of The Free Press, a division of Simon & Schuster, from *Competitive Strategy: Techniques for Analyzing Industries and Competitors* by Michael E. Porter, p. 43. Copyright © 1980 by The Free Press.

Firms get stuck in the middle for the following reasons:

- *Inexorable market changes.* Markets change perpetually. Those changes create opportunities for some firms but destroy the position of others. Consider the case of Woolworth, not the entire organization, which is a specialty retailer (it operates Footlocker, the athletic shoe store), but the variety store from which the organization arose. Little has changed at Woolworth's variety stores over the decades. As a result, its competitive advantage has been severely eroded. Does Woolworth sell something special? Are the prices especially low? Are its costs exceptionally low? The answer to each question is no. With its roots as a "general store," a form of retailing pioneered more than a century ago, Woolworth's variety stores have over time become the business equivalent of museum pieces. *Business Week* called them "an American Gothic, a part of retailing's past."[4] Is there really a need for a five-and-dime in the year 2000?
- *Competitor's actions.* Competitors can also force a firm to be stuck in the middle. In many markets low-cost entrants have garnered the low-price, high-share end of the market, while sellers of more expensive differentiated products have successfully served profitable market segments. That has left many mass market brands stuck in the middle.

TREACY AND WIERSEMA'S THREE VALUE DISCIPLINES

More than a dozen years after Porter offered his strategic insights, Treacy and Wiersema proposed a similar set of three "value disciplines." Like Porter's, their ideas started with an influential *Harvard Business Review* article and ended up as a best-selling business book.[5] According to these authors, the three different strategies—operational excellence, customer intimacy, and product leadership—emerged from a three-year study of forty companies noted for their exceptional performance.

OPERATIONAL EXCELLENCE

Treacy and Wiersema's concept of operational excellence is virtually identical to Porter's overall cost leadership. Firms that specialize in this strategic option lead the industry in price. They keep a constant eye toward lowering overhead costs and seek to eliminate any unnecessary production steps. Their goal is to increase efficiency and lower prices to consumers. As with Porter's and the Boston Consulting Group's concepts, firms following a strategy of operational excellence make money from lower costs rather than higher prices. Staples, Wal-Mart, and Dell computer are offered as examples of successful firms that follow this value discipline.

CUSTOMER INTIMACY

Customer intimacy combines aspects of Porter's differentiation and segmentation strategies. Firms following this strategy tailor their products to fit the specific needs of market segments. They compete on superior service and giving the consumer exactly what he or she wants rather than low prices. Customer intimacy is a recognition that some customers will pay extra for products made especially for them. Price sensitivity is reduced as a result.

Like Porter's differentiation strategy, customer intimacy implies that firms make money from higher prices rather than lower costs. Firms do more for customers in the hope of charging higher prices.

Firms following this strategy stress customer satisfaction and relationship marketing rather than efficient manufacture. Customer intimacy, as the name implies, emphasizes the long-term value of a customer to the firm, and the willingness to make products and services specifically for individual consumers. Nordstroms is an example of a firm that succeeds with customer intimacy.

PRODUCT LEADERSHIP

Treacy and Wiersema's concept of product leadership is unique. Firms following this value discipline stress speed and perpetual innovation. They eschew formal planning procedures and avoid bureaucratic systems, preferring, instead, to move quickly into new markets with innovative new products. Product leaders do not wait for competitors to make their products obsolete. They do it themselves, embracing Joseph Schumpeter's notion of creative destruction. These are the entrepreneurial innovators of the competitive arena. Product leaders introduce a rapid-fire array of new products that leave competitors perpetually playing catch-up.

They serve that group of customers who want new, different, and state-of-the-art products, even if they have to pay more for them. Nike is a prime example of a product leader.

THE RELATIONSHIP BETWEEN STRATEGIC CHOICE AND TARGET MARKET

Treacy and Wiersema specifically address the connections between the choice of a generic strategy and the market served. They note that choosing one of the value disciplines—operational excellence, customer intimacy, or product leadership—inevitably depends on the particular kind of consumer targeted. Operational excellence usually entails targeting consumers who care less about service or quality and more about price. Customer intimacy, in contrast, means targeting a segment with a product designed specifically for that segment. Finally, product leadership is a strategy that appeals to customers who want products that are new and different. Picking a segment to serve, in short, means picking a strategy. Conversely, picking a strategy inevitably means picking a group of customers to serve.

SHOULD FIRMS PURSUE ONLY ONE GENERIC STRATEGY?

Most of the criticism regarding generic strategies has centered on Porter's assertion that firms should pursue only a single choice. Porter is adamant on this point. He argues that success is "rarely possible" if a firm pursues more than one generic strategy. The skills required by each strategy are simply so different and so incompatible that pursuing more than one is likely to result in nothing being done well. The result is a firm stuck in the middle. As Porter notes, commitment and support "are diluted if there is more than one primary target."[6]

Critics argue otherwise. They contend that Porter's two generic strategies are neither mutually exclusive nor inconsistent.[7] In fact, in some situations differentiation and low-cost production can be observed simultaneously.

Their ammunition is drawn primarily from empirical studies that have shown that the most successful firms are *both* low-cost producers and differentiators.[8] One study, for example, examined sixty-four firms in eight industries and found that the most successful firms followed *both* strategies simultaneously. A subsequent study found the same result. Nineteen of sixty-nine businesses examined pursued *both* differentiation and low-cost production, and those businesses had higher returns on investment than businesses that followed only a single generic strategy. Another study examined 1,144 observations from 623 businesses contained in the PIMS database and found no support for the hypothesis that differentiation is incompatible with a strategy of low-cost production.

Interpreting those results, however, leads to two completely different conclusions. Critics see "dangers associated with the exclusive pursuit of a single generic strategy."[9] They point to firms such as IBM, Caterpillar, and Control Data that were so intent on producing highly differentiated products that they were hurt when low-cost producers entered their markets and stole share with lower prices. Likewise, firms that focus too obsessively on keeping costs low often avoid innovative new products that temporarily reduce efficiency. In other words, it is better to pursue a "mixed" strategy that combines aspects of differentiation and low-cost production rather than a "pure" strategy based on only one. Business today is simply too competitive, Porter's critics argue, to ignore any one aspect.

Critics further assert that differentiation and low-cost production are complementary rather than inconsistent. They observe that consumers are typically concerned with both price and quality, not with one to the exclusion of the other. It is the configuration of strategic attributes that matters, not merely choosing one generic strategy or the other. That is why the best firms have been found to follow both generic strategies.

Supporters of the one-strategy-is-best view interpret the results differently. They argue that the sequential use of Porter's two generic strategies works as follows. A firm establishes a dominant position by selling a highly successful differentiated product, such as Coca-Cola, Kellogg's cereals, or a host of other icons of American marketing. That success sometimes leads to high market share, which, in turn, leads to lower costs as a result of economies of scale and experience effects. In other words, a successful differentiator sometimes ends up as a market-leading low-cost producer.

Like Porter, Treacy and Wiersema argue that firms should narrow their business focus rather than broadening it. They contend that firms should strive to "become champions in one of these disciplines while meeting industry standards in the other two."[10] But, consistent with the findings of many empirical studies, Treacy and Wiersema also observed some examples of firms that are "masters of two"—that excel at more than a single value discipline. Still, these two authors, like Porter before them, argue that pursuing more than one value discipline is more likely to lead to confusion and dissipation of competitive advance rather than success. They, too, contend that it is better to focus on a single generic strategy.

Just because some extremely successful firms at the pinnacle of American business are fortunate enough to have achieved both enviable cost positions and highly differentiated goods does not mean that every firm should try to do the same. The empirical studies showing the success of "mixed" strategies are really observing the end result of a long evolutionary history that started with the use of a single generic strategy. In other words, pursuing a single generic strategy sometimes leads to success in the other. Porter's supporters advise that most firms should follow only one generic strategy. A firm that tries to do more is likely to end up doing nothing well.

NOTES

[1] Michael Porter, *Competitive Strategy,* New York: The Free Press, 1980.

[2] Michael Treacy and Fred Wiersema, "Customer Intimacy and Other Value Disciplines," *Harvard Business Review,* January–February 1993, pp. 84–93; and Michael Treacy and Fred Wiersema, *Discipline of Market Leaders,* Reading: MA: Addison-Wesley, 1995.

[3] Porter, *Competitive Strategy,* p. 41.

[4] "Woolworth Is Still Rummaging for a Retail Strategy," *Business Week,* June 6, 1983, p. 82.

[5] See note 2.

[6] Porter, *Competitive Strategy,* p. 35.

[7] Charles Hill, "Differentiation Versus Low Cost or Differentiation and Low Cost: A Contingency Framework," *Academy of Management Review,* July 1988, pp. 401–12; and Alan Murray, "A Contingency View of Porter's Generic Strategies," *Academy of Management Review,* July 1988, pp. 390–400.

[8] William K. Hall, "Survival Strategies in a Hostile Environment," *Harvard Business Review,* September–October 1980, pp. 75–85; Roderick E. White, "Generic Business Strategies, Organizational Context and Performance: An Empirical Investigation," *Strategic Management Journal,* 1986, pp. 217–31; and Lynn Phillips, Dae Chang, and Robert Buzzell, "Product Quality, Cost Position and Business Performance: A Test of Some Key Hypotheses," *Journal of Marketing,* Spring 1983, pp. 26–43.

[9] Danny Miller, "The Generic Strategy Trap," *Journal of Business Strategy,* January–February 1992, pp. 37–41.

[10] Treacy and Wiersema, "Customer Intimacy," p. 84.

CHAPTER 6

COMPETING ON PRICE

The dawn of the 1990s brought with it tremendous downward pressure on prices. The conspicuous consumption of the 1980s was clearly over. Consumers wanted lower prices and were willing to pass up products they deemed overpriced. Some experts believed the change was temporary and predicted it would reverse itself once the economy improved. Others saw a longer-lasting change. Low inflation, stagnant growth in real consumer incomes, global overcapacity, and brutally competitive international markets have conspired to force price to the forefront of consumer decision making.

The effect on companies has been dramatic. Whereas during the 1970s and 1980s they were able to pass along regular price increases to consumers with little resistance, by the 1990s firms that raised prices lost customers in droves. A 1993 *Business Week* cover story spoke of companies that were "stuck," unable to raise prices in the face of severe price resistance even though their costs were rising.[1] That pattern did not abate as the decade unfolded. Today, more than ever, there is a reluctance to pay extra for products and services that are deemed overpriced, as well as a continued decline in brand loyalty. Furthermore, there is a pervasive willingness to trade down to less prestigious, less expensive products. Those changes have created an opportunity for low-cost producers to gain share on sellers of differentiated goods.

CONDITIONS THAT FAVOR
SELLING ON PRICE

Exhibit 6.1 illustrates the strategy of low-cost, low-price sellers. They make money by lowering costs rather than raising prices. Consumer preferences for lower prices have created a boom market for low-cost, low-price sellers and tough times for differentiators.

Exhibit 6.1
Selling on Price by Lowering Costs

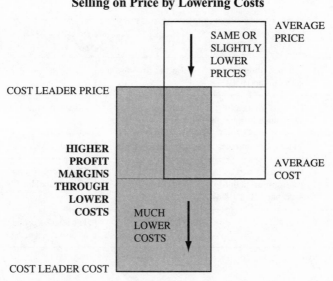

WHEN THE "GOUGE GAP" IS TOO WIDE

There is a limit to what consumers will pay for name-brand products. If the price difference between premium products and the low-price alternative is too great, then consumers can be convinced to opt for better value.

MINI-CASE: THE BATTLE BETWEEN NATIONAL BRANDS AND PRIVATE LABELS

According to a report issued in 1995 by two U.S. congressmen from the Northeast, between 1983 and the mid-1990s the price of breakfast cereals rose at twice the rate of other food products. Higher costs were not the cause. The politicians claimed that a lack of price competition and the absence of strong generics kept prices artificially high. Consumers simply had no alternative but to pay nearly five dollars for a box of cereal that cost mere pennies to produce.

That hasn't been the pattern in most other product categories. As manufacturers of national brands steadily raised prices throughout the 1980s in an attempt to capitalize on brand equity, many consumers concluded that lower-priced, private labels offered better value. As the 1980s ended, national brand sellers were unable to raise prices any higher. In fact, with few exceptions, private brands gained share at the expense of national brands in the cost-conscious 1990s.

Exhibit 6.2
Private Labels

RETAILER	PRIVATE LABEL MANUFACTURER	BRAND NAME	PRODUCT CATEGORY
Macy's	Started selling private labels in the 1940s	Loft & Brownstone	Clothing
Varied	Paragon (owned by Weyerhauser until 1993)	Store name	Disposable diapers
Loblaw	Varied, Cott in colas	President's Choice	Varied
Varied	Ralcorp (owned by Ralston-Purina until it was spun off in 1994)	Store name	The leading producer of private label breakfast cereals
Varied	Heinz	Store name	The leading producer of private label canned soups

Private brands come from many different sources and carry many different brand names. Examples of successful private brands are listed in Exhibit 6.2.

Retailers have welcomed the shift in power, finding that private labels offer:

- prices that are, on average, 15 to 40 percent below national brands
- lower costs to the retailer (since private labels are essentially "follower brands," where less advertising, promotion, and only minimal amounts of R&D are required)
- higher profit margins for the retailer, often 50 to 100 percent above national brands
- an exclusive franchise on the product (the retailer decides who can sell it)
- a gain in the bargaining power for the retailer and away from national brands

The recent rise in private brands is merely the latest surge in the ebb and flow of a long-running competitive battle. During the first half of the twentieth century, private brands were successful competitors. Retailers like A&P have a long history of selling branded products that they manufacture. The shift to national brands accelerated in the mid-1950s with the advent of television and television advertising. Heavily advertised brands drew a nationwide audience. The tremendous growth of General Foods, Procter & Gamble, and the other national brand giants occurred during that time. A short-lived threat to national brands occurred during the energy crisis in the recession-plagued second half of the 1970s when consumers embraced "generics," those no-frills, no-name products in austere packaging simply labeled "peas" or "beans." The Reagan economic expansion of 1983 ended the rise of generics and re-established the dominance of national brands. Tarnished with an image of "food for poor people," generics virtually disappeared from store shelves.

The most recent threat to national brands started in the early 1990s when consumers concluded that the price premium demanded by well-known national brands was simply not worth it. That started a shift back to private brands. What began as a classic battle between low-price sellers and sellers of differentiated goods, where the private brands stressed lower prices and national brands cultivated an image of premium quality, expanded into new areas. In more recent years, private brands have attempted to negate the long-term quality advantage of national brands in at least three ways.

1. *A stress on quality and brand recognition.* Gone is the poverty packaging of the late 1970s. In its place is a spiffy package designed to mimic national brands. A&P, which consolidated its many private labels under the patriotic-sounding "America's Choice," ran ads that claimed "Real Value, Real Savings, That's America's Choice" in the 1990s. The result is a private label that sounds remarkably like a national brand. Nowhere is that tactic more prominent than in the case of Loblaw's "President's Choice." The Canadian supermarket does not make its private-label merchandise. But it has so successfully cultivated the President's Choice label that it is now sold in New York at D'Agostino's, in Chicago at Jewel Foods, and at the Star chain in Boston. President's Choice is a national brand masquerading as a private label.

2. *Favorable shelf placements.* This allows private brands to sell on an equal footing with the national brands.

3. *Premium private brands.* Some retailers have even moved upscale, introducing premium private brands to complement their mainstream products. A&P, for example, sells both "America's Choice," its primary house brand, and "Master Choice," an upscale alternative that competes head-on with the national brands. Safeway's "Select" brand serves a similar role.

The strategy seems to be working. Whereas private brands were dogged with the image of lower quality in the past, a recent poll of two thousand consumers found that 67 percent of respondents "believe that private-label products are of the same quality or better than most national brands."[2] That is five percentage points higher than a poll taken five years earlier. A similar finding was reported in the September 1993 issue of *Consumer Reports.* A survey of the magazine's readers revealed that 64 percent "believe supermarket brands are about as good in quality as national brands."[3] It is no wonder that private brands racked up $30 billion in sales in 1993 and are approaching 20 percent of supermarket sales volume.

National brands have fought back in a number of ways.

1. Some sellers seek to *discredit private brands in ads,* hoping to scare consumers away.

2. Others rely on *relationship marketing.* Nestle's Friskies pet food tries to keep customers loyal by sending them issues of "Cat Club News," an informative special interest magazine that strengthens ties with the customer.

3. Some national brands have engaged in *promotional pricing.* Heavy couponing of breakfast cereals and other national food brands reduces prices to the price-sensitive segment of the market while maintaining high prices for consumers unwilling to bother with the clipping and sorting of coupons.

4. Some national brands have *lowered prices* to reduce the price differential. On April 2, 1993, Marlboro, the number-one-selling cigarette in the United States, cut prices by up to 20 percent to stem the loss of market share to generic brands. The cut reversed a long-running series of annual price rises and cost Philip Morris $500 million.

5. While private brands move upscale to meet the national brands, some national brands have *moved downscale* to challenge the private brands on their own turf. New or repositioned value brands scream "super value" in ads and on packaging.

6. Some national brands have challenged private brands with *innovation.* Gillette's Sensor razor, for example, switched consumers back to higher prices from low-price generics with a truly better product.

7. Finally, some national brand manufacturers have decided to *join the private branders* rather than fight. Many national brands, including Borden, Dole, Heinz, and Jergens, now make private brands for retailers. Both Philip Morris and RJ Reynolds make generic cigarettes in the United States. But, more typically, national brand manufacturers adopt strategies that avoid cannibalizing their premier brands.

Some firms restrict their actions geographically. Michelin, for example, is a leading maker of privately branded tires in the United States but sells only under its own name in France. Campbell's soup has a similar policy. It makes private branded soups outside the United States but, for the most part, does not compete with itself in the domestic market.

Other firms compete only in product categories where they are weak players to begin with. Ralcorp, for example, is the leading seller of private label breakfast cereals. Its national brands—Rice, Wheat, and Corn Chex—are not leading brands; thus it has less to lose from successful private labels than Kellogg and General Foods. On most supermarket shelves there is room for the number one, number two, and the store's private brand. As the *Wall Street Journal* noted in 1993, weak manufacturers "have two choices: Turn to private label or, sooner or later, go out of the business."[4]

The lesson to be learned from the battle between national brands and private labels is that when the "gouge gap" becomes too wide, the seller of differentiated goods is vulnerable to a share loss at the hands of a low-cost producer.

WHEN THERE IS A SHIFT IN THE POINT OF DIFFERENTIATION

Markets are constantly changing. Sometimes that creates an opportunity for a low-cost producer to gain share on a seller of higher-priced products.

MINI-CASE: HALLMARK CARDS—A SHIFT IN BUYING BEHAVIOR LEADS TO A DIMINUTION OF COMPETITIVE ADVANTAGE

Hallmark Cards was founded in 1910 by Joyce Hall in her room at the Kansas City YMCA. From those humble beginnings the firm has grown into a greeting card behemoth with 1994 sales of $3.8 billion. It is by far the world's largest purveyor of greeting cards. Hallmark is more than twice as large as Cleveland's American Greetings, the second largest seller. As a private company, Hallmark is two-thirds owned by the founder's descendants and one-third owned by its employees.

But this market leader is caught in a crushing environmental trend that is causing it to rapidly lose market share. According to *Business Week,* its share declined from 50 percent of the market in 1990 to 45 percent by 1995.[5] The reason is price competition caused by a change in shopper behavior.

Hallmark's strategy is clearly product differentiation. Its slogan, "when you care enough to send the very best," communicates its preference for prestige over low price. It also benefits from a market that disdains sending the very cheapest to a loved one or relative. Getting a good buy on a greeting card does not carry the same connotation as getting a good buy on a car or a winter coat.

Profit margins on greeting cards are huge but are also facing downward pressure. The price of paper, artwork, and pop poetry does not come close to matching the more than $2 price tag most cards carry.

But Hallmark's key competitive advantage is its lockhold on distribution. It distributes its cards through nearly ten thousand small, independently owned card shops that agree to feature Hallmark Cards and no one else's. Competitors cannot hope to match that advantage. Hallmark sells 75 percent of its cards through independent card stores. But that distribution advantage is fast becoming a disadvantage.

Women are the reason. They buy fully 90 percent of the $5.6 billion worth of greeting cards sold in the United States. The problem is they no longer shop at card stores in the numbers that they used to. According to *Forbes,* 50 percent of all greeting cards were bought at card shops in 1974.[6] By 1994 the figure had dropped to 30 percent. The trend toward joining the work force has left women less time to browse the independent card shops. Instead, they pick up cards at the large discounters, drugstores, and supermarkets where they shop for other items. Women pressed for time are willing to forego the larger selection offered at the card stores for the convenience of the discounters. Therein lies Hallmark's strategic dilemma.

Should Hallmark distribute its cards to large discounters such as Wal-Mart? Discounters would welcome the market leader's prestigious product but only if sold at a discount. Hallmark faces a difficult decision. If it cuts prices to discounters, and they discount Hallmark's cards to the consumer, then it undercuts the full-service card shops that constitute its primary competitive advantage. It also lowers its own profit margins for the product it worked so hard to differentiate. But if Hallmark does not sell to the discounters, it excludes itself from a growing share of the market.

The second-tier sellers gladly supply the large discounters. It was an easy move for them to make. Both American Greetings and Gibson Greeting (the number two and number three sellers respectively) were not tied tightly to the independent card stores and welcomed a way to avoid competition with Hallmark. It is no wonder that the business press estimates that sales and profits at American Greetings have soared while Hallmark has floundered.

Why not introduce a "discount" brand targeted to the discounters? Hallmark already has one—Ambassador cards—but Hallmark earns less on each low-end card and risks cannibalizing customers from its flagship brand. Furthermore, the major discounters want the flagship line and feel powerful enough to demand it on their terms.

In the end, Hallmark will have to deal with the discounters or find another way to maintain its commanding market share. The result will likely mean a diminished role for the card shops. But there is really no alternative. There has been an inexorable shift in buyer behavior that has negated the competitive advantage held by the market leader and allowed low-price sellers to gain share on the leading seller of differentiated goods.

WHEN PRODUCTS BECOME COMMODITIES

Price competition is heightened when consumers see no difference between products. In recent years, there has been a tendency for differentiated products to evolve into commodities as they progress from new to mature products.

The nature of competition changes once a new product becomes widely accepted. New products usually start out as unique creations that command premium prices. But once the market expands, there is a tendency for low-cost producers to enter the game and sell standardized products at very low prices. That brings in new customers who were not interested in buying when prices were high.

Low-price sellers typically have a simple strategy—they try to convince consumers that their product is just as good as more expensive entries. Such strategies promote the commoditization of markets. Once the market is flooded with efficiently produced, low-priced, standardized goods (often made with low-wage labor in third-world countries), it is difficult for differentiators to persuade consumers that their products are worth a higher price. When all entries are the same, price dictates choice.

There is sometimes an inevitable trend toward commoditization of markets about which differentiators can do little. Take, for example, personal computers. In the first half of the 1980s, IBM's differentiation strategy was universally deemed brilliant. Consumers willingly paid hefty price premiums for privilege of owning an IBM-PC. They knew that IBM would still be around when the shakeout came. Buyers knew they would not be left with an orphan computer a few years down the road. But by the 1990s, after IBM set the technical standard, personal computers became commodities. If they were all the same, consumers reasoned, why pay more for those three big-blue letters? Bad times followed for IBM.

Low-cost producers took advantage of that change in consumer thinking. Packard Bell, started by Beny Alagem and two partners in 1986, was one of the most successful. Its goal was to be the lowest-cost producer. It stressed low-rent operations, an absence of network advertising, and minuscule profit margins on each sale. Packard Bell sells primarily through mass market merchandisers and marketing consist almost solely of giving retailers money to advertise locally. The results have been spectacular. In 1995, Packard Bell sold 25 percent of all the personal computers sold in the United States. Sales surpassed $5 billion. The commoditization strategy has been so successful that other firms are starting to mimic and undercut Packard Bell.

Quality improvements throughout an industry can sometimes hurt existing market leaders who follow a differentiation strategy. Consider the case of Michelin, a premium brand that charges premium prices for its premium tires. Michelin was the first firm to introduce radial tires. As the technological leader, it routinely prices its tires at the top of the market. That has created problems for the differentiator. As one industry expert noted: "Today, consumers don't find a qualitative difference between tires. All tires are good."[7] As is the case with many other product categories, increased quality, vigorous price competition, and global overcapacity have conspired to focus attention almost solely on prices. As a result, Michelin has been forced to introduce a discount model, the "Michelin Classic." Its lower price directly affects profits by cannibalizing the premium brand.

WHEN MARKETS ARE DEREGULATED

Some products are protected from price competition by government regulations, which keep prices high and competition highly imperfect. Selling financial service products is a prime example. Before deregulation, prices were fixed so firms competed solely on the basis of higher service. Once deregulated, however, low-cost competitors such as Charles Schwab offered a less expensive alternative to Merrill Lynch and the other full-service brokerage firms.

The airline industry provides an even more stunning example. For four decades, fares and routes were regulated by the federal government. The airlines competed on service. It was a glamorous business where high costs were supported by uniformly high prices set by the regulators. After deregulation in 1978, however, all that changed. Low-cost operators like Southwest Airlines cut prices and stole market share from United, American, and Delta airlines. Price became the deciding factor as consumers viewed all airline seats as the same perishable commodity. Differentiation became exceedingly more difficult. Carriers fly the same planes from the same airports. When two airlines fly the same route, consumers logically choose the cheaper one. Deregulation changed a high-cost protected industry into a price-driven commodity business. The high-cost, brand-name airlines had to cut costs to remain competitive. Some were not successful. PanAm, Eastern, Braniff, and other major carriers went out of business.

Starting in April 1994, Delta embarked on a severe cost-cutting program aimed at making the airline competitive with low-cost producers such as Southwest and a bevy of other upstarts. Most other carriers did the same. The change is not popular with employees but the major carriers had no other choice. In a business with few ways to differentiate your product, price remains the deciding factor. And Southwest, with a cost of 7.1 cents to fly one passenger one mile is truly, as it states in its tagline, "the low-fare airline." The corresponding cost for the major carriers is 13 cents per passenger mile. As a result, it is no surprise that Southwest dominates the markets it flies. Only through re-regulation, industry concentration (which might lessen the intensity of competition and control price like an oligopoly), the creation of a new point of differentiation— such as safety—or by becoming low-cost producers themselves can the brand-name airlines thwart the share gains made by the low-cost producers in this commodity market.

WHEN THE LOW-PRICE FORMULA CAN BE APPLIED IN A NEW ARENA

The renewed importance of price in the 1990s created an opportunity for sellers to apply the low-cost, discounting superstore formula to product categories where it has not previously been applied. Following the model set by such successful retailers as Toys 'R' Us, Home Depot, and the Price Club, entrepreneurs have changed the dynamics of competition in an industry by generating huge economies of scale, and passing part of the cost savings along to customers in the form of rock-bottom prices. The growth of these operations has come at the expense of higher-cost sellers.

MINI-CASE: STAPLES—THE OFFICE-SUPPLY SUPERSTORE

One of the most stunning successes in low-cost, low-price retailing is Staples, the office supply discount chain. Staples sells huge volumes of merchandise at minuscule margins to small-business customers, such as lawyers and dentists.

Staples was started in 1986 by Thomas Stemberg. In the early 1980s, Stemberg was an executive at a northeastern supermarket chain. He was fired in 1985 after a dispute with the boss. Stemberg became a consultant who worked out of his West Hartford, Connecticut, home. At the time, personal computers were just coming to market, and computer supplies such as printer ribbons and disks were sold primarily through computer retailers like Computerland. Prices were high and hours of operation were limited. Like many other innovations, the idea for Staples came from personal experience. Later he recalled, "I was having trouble buying computer ribbons on Saturday," and "I was feeling ripped off on computer products."[8] Being from the supermarket business, Stemberg solved his personal problem, and what he surmised was a problem for many others, by applying the efficient practices with which he was familiar to an entirely new application. In essence, he created a stationery store that is always open, stresses high sales volume, and earns small profit margins on each sale.

The first Staples opened in Massachusetts in 1986. It offered customers two key benefits: (1) it was open seven days a week from early morning to late at night, and (2) it sold at very low prices. Spectacular growth followed. A decade later, in 1995, Staples had 375 stores, most in the Northeast and California. Sales in 1995 were estimated to be $2.9 billion, up 45 percent in a single year, and profits were estimated at $63 billion.[9]

Selling on price was a perfect strategy for office supplies. Since all sellers tend to carry the same merchandise, price is likely to be an important feature. Furthermore, before Staples, the industry was populated by small-scale, mom-and-pop retailers. These weak and unorganized sellers were an easy target for the economies of scale brought into the industry by Stemberg.

Competitors, with similar strategies, started in other parts of the country within a few years of Staples' entry. Office Depot, based in Boca Raton, Florida, has approximately four hundred stores with sales of nearly $3 billion per year. OfficeMax, started as a Kmart subsidiary, has fewer stores, and was located in the same mall as Sports Authority and Border Bookstores, which were also Kmart subsidiaries. The low-cost, low-price warehouse clubs, such as Price Club and Wal-Mart's Sam's Club, also allocate a sizable portion of floor space to office supply merchandise.

Staples and its primary competitors continue to expand. As they do, they increasingly compete with one another for the same customers in the same geographic areas. An OfficeMax executive told *Forbes* in 1993 that "his strategy is to choose store sites that intercept shoppers on their way to Staples."[10] Staples responded by cutting prices and becoming more efficient.

But, now, after making its name with low prices, Staples is trying to move forward on a second front. Influenced by Treacy and Wiersema's *Harvard Business Review* article, Stemberg now seeks to be a "master of two."[11] That is, in addition to low prices, Staples is setting out to become a higher-service operation. As Stemberg noted in 1995: "We clearly need to be more intimate with our customers."[12] In your opinion, is this a good idea, or will it dilute and possibly destroy the low-cost, low-price formula that made Staples such a success to start with?

HOW TO COMPETE ON PRICE

Firms compete on price using some combination of the following practices.

RUTHLESS COST CUTTING THROUGH REENGINEERING

The first requirement for competing on price is to lower costs. Coinciding with the demands of consumers for lower prices during the first half of the 1990s has been the trend among companies to cut costs through ruthless reengineering. This is a form of cost cutting that goes far beyond what experience curves call for. It entails brutal downsizing, massive layoffs, and outsourcing meant to reduce costs and reward shareholders rather than other stakeholders, such as employees. The demand for lower prices and the decline in brand loyalty has been mirrored by a decline in company loyalty to employees.

STRESSING EQUAL QUALITY AT LOWER PRICES

Successful low-price sellers stress greater value. Not only do they cultivate an image of having the lowest prices, but they work hard to convince customers that their products and services are of equal quality to the most expensive vendors. Only the price is different. That means that the packaging, advertising, and any other aspect of the product must avoid the implication that the low-price seller's goods are of lower quality.

SPECIALIZATION AND LOWER PRICES

Many low-price sellers specialize in a single product category and offer lower prices. Toys 'R' Us, Home Depot, Staples, and a host of other "category killers" offer low prices on a deep selection of related merchandise. Their huge volume in a single product category gives them economies of scale, bargaining power with suppliers, and a prominent place in the evoked set of consumers' minds for price and selection.

COPYING AND CUTTING PRICES

Many low-cost producers succeed by copying products and designs created by differentiators and selling them at lower prices. They avoid the expense and uncertainty of new product entry. Their skills lie elsewhere. Low-cost copycats wait until a market grows large enough to permit high-volume product efficiencies. They then produce a similar product inexpensively, typically in low-wage-rate countries, and pass along the lower costs in the form of lower prices, which often expands demand even further.

Aiwa, the Japanese personal electronics firm follows such a "copy-and-produce-it-cheaper" strategy. It moved production facilities from Japan to Malaysia and Singapore, where wage rates are much lower, and produced imitation personal stereos to compete with Sony's popular Walkman. The Aiwa stereos sell on price. While Sony, which created the market for personal stereos, sells a highly differentiated product that carries the prestigious Sony brand name, Aiwa sells stereos that are perceived to be of equal or near-equal quality at a price that can be 50 percent less. It is no wonder that Aiwa's president believes that "if you can make a copy of your competitor's product for half the price, you can take over the market."[13] Aiwa is currently the second largest seller of personal stereos, just behind Sony.

LETTING PRICES DICTATE COSTS

Price is of such strategic importance in some markets that some firms now set the price of a new product and *then* decide what costs to incur to produce it. That is the opposite of the typical practice of the past, when firms routinely focused on costs then added a markup to arrive at a selling price. That allowed costs to dictate prices. But the consumer does not see costs, she sees prices. In order to hit a target price, firms seeking to compete as low-cost producers must make costs follow prices.

THE EFFECTS OF LOW-COST COMPETITION

Competing on price is one of the oldest new strategies possible. But it has taken hold in the 1990s with a vengeance not seen in recent decades. A combination of low-cost imports and cost-conscious domestic operators have kept downward pressure on prices. That keeps inflation low and stockholders happy but keeps employee wage gains small and opportunities for long-term employment and advancement at large domestic producers slim to nonexistent. It is a trend that is both welcome and frightening. Shoppers and economists like the lower prices and low inflation. Workers suffer under the massive downsizing and worry about the possible disappearance of the American middle class.

NOTES

[1]Christopher Farrell, "Stuck!, How Companies Cope When They Can't Raise Prices," *Business Week,* November 15, 1993, pp. 146–55.
[2]"Private-Label Brands No Longer Retail's Stepchild," *National Petroleum News,* July 1995, p. 43.
[3]"Battle of the Brands," *Consumer Reports,* September 1993, pp. 565–67.

[4]Gabriella Stern, "Big Companies Add Private-Label Lines That Vie with Their Premium Brands," *Wall Street Journal,* May 21, 1993, pp. B1, B10.

[5]Susan Chandler, "Can Hallmark Get Well Soon," *Business Week,* June 19, 1995, pp. 62–63.

[6]William Stern, "Loyal to a Fault," *Forbes,* March 14, 1994, pp. 58–59.

[7]Roula Khalaf, "Le Tire, C'est Moi," *Forbes,* August 1, 1994, p. 46.

[8]Norm Alster, "Penny-Wise," *Forbes,* February 1, 1993, p. 48.

[9]Rahul Jacob, "How One Red Hot Retailer Wins Customer Loyalty," *Fortune,* July 10, 1995, p. 72.

[10]Alster, "Penny-Wise," p. 49.

[11]Michael Treacy and Fred Wiersema, "Customer Intimacy and Other Value Disciplines," *Harvard Business Review,* January–February 1993, p. 86.

[12]Jacob, "How One Red Hot Retailer Wins," p. 73.

[13]Neil Weinberg, "Good News, Bad News Man," *Forbes,* January 1, 1996, p. 58.

CHAPTER 7

DIFFERENTIATION
STRATEGIES

Differentiators sell quality rather than rock-bottom prices. They offer something special for which they charge a premium price. Just what that something special is can vary greatly from one seller to the next, even in the same market. It differs by product category, by market segment, and by individual seller. Some differentiators, for example, sell high-end luxury items that offer snob appeal at very high prices. Others stress superior reliability and durability at mid-level price points. Still other sellers offer consumers high performance. It is the difference that counts in differentiation.

As Exhibit 7.1 illustrates, a differentiation strategy succeeds by

Exhibit 7.1
Differentiation Strategy

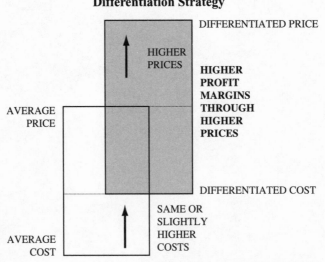

pushing up prices rather than cutting costs. It is not that costs are unimportant. They must not be allowed to run out of control. But costs are simply not the primary concern of a differentiation strategy. More expensive materials, greater advertising costs to reinforce a quality image, and higher overhead may even push up costs. Consumers are not fools. A company that claims to sell a special product or service must do something special to command the price premium, and that usually means high costs.

Like low-cost producers, differentiators also claim to offer better value, but whereas low-cost producers increase value by lowering prices and advertising that quality is the same as that sold by the differentiator, the differentiator stresses much higher quality at a price only slightly higher than the low-cost producer.

BASIS OF DIFFERENTIATION

There are nearly endless possibilities for differentiating products and services. The constraints seem dictated solely by the creativity of the differentiator. Typically, however, one or some combination of the following ten factors serves as the basis for differentiation.

1. SUPERIOR PERFORMANCE

One obvious way to differentiate a product is to make it "best-in-class." Mercedes, Sony, Tropicana, and Nike use a strategy based on performance excellence. Each sells the highest-performance products in its category, and charges a premium price for them.

Andersen windows is another case in point. It claims to sell more windows than the next three competitors combined. Andersen succeeds by selling the highest quality windows rather than the least expensive. The company's strategy is clearly stated in promotional literature: "Andersen products are different and better." They are promoted as the finest windows made.

The Minnesota-based company relentlessly pursues innovations that reinforce its claims of superior performance. Double-pane glass is filled with insulating argon gas, which the company claims is "different and revolutionary," and purportedly keeps the cold out better than competitive models. Frames and sashes are made only with high-quality wood, then sealed in vinyl making them virtually maintenance free. The result is a superior product that sells at premium prices to the largest share of the market. While other firms slash costs and prices, Anderson sells high quality to a huge share of the market.

2. SUPERIOR DESIGN AND STYLING

Styling and design excellence can be as important as performance. In fact, design has become such an effective point of differentiation that *Business Week* presents annual awards created to give recognition to the best product designs of the year.[1] It is also an area where American firms excel over foreign competitors.

Superior design and style can be used to differentiate products in categories where styling has historically played a minor role. Gillette's Braun uses European styling to differentiate its small appliances and personal care products. Consumers pay extra for the superior styling.

One of the most stunning examples of the strategic power of better design is Ford's Taurus. In the 1980s the uniquely styled Taurus, disparagingly called the "bubble car" by critics, helped push Ford's profits higher than General Motors' for the first time since the 1920s. Ironically, GM had surpassed Ford sixty years earlier with same superior styling strategy, when Ford was selling a car in one color (black) at very low prices.

MINI-CASE: OAKLEY SUNGLASSES

In some cases, styling is intertwined with performance. Consider the case of Oakley Sunglasses, which gained popularity in the early 1990s. Oakley charges premium prices for its fashionable sports sunglasses. Oakley "Blades" are wonders of modern technology. They have super-hard polycarbonate lenses that can withstand a shotgun blast at fifteen feet. Not that you will ever need that benefit or, if you do, that hard sunglasses will do much good for the rest of your body, but the emphasis on performance and sharp styling makes this product special, and more expensive.

Oakley sunglasses are the creation of James Jannard, who named the brand after his beloved Irish setter. He started by designing impact-resistant motorcycle goggles, which he gave away at off-road motorcycle races in 1979. The sleek styling caught the attention of sports legends, like Greg Lemond, who wore Oakleys when he became the first American ever to win the prestigious Tour de France bicycle race in 1985 and again in 1986. The fortunes of the tiny upstart turned rapidly upward with the burst of free publicity.

The Oakley "Blades" that followed had simple carbon fiber frames with interchangeable lenses. Oakley gave away many pairs to top athletes in many sports. Michael Jordan wore them when golfing. More free publicity. Andre Agassi did the same. Even Nike's Phil Knight sported Oakley Blades when seen in public.

The quality image was reinforced through a carefully planned distribution strategy. Oakleys are sold only at upscale retailers. Discounters such as Wal-Mart and Kmart are not allowed to carry the brand.

Prices are high for this clearly differentiated product. A low-end model is $40, and a top-of-the-line pair is priced over $200. Costs are low. An article in *Forbes* estimated "that a $100 pair of Blades costs Oakley about $15 to manufacture."[2] Such margins are *very* attractive to competitors, who have eagerly taken a piece of the action. Oakley's faddish sunglasses were widely copied in the mid-1990s.

3. A PRODUCT FOR EVERY PURPOSE

Alfred P. Sloan Jr., an early chairman of General Motors and a dedicated marketer, often summed up his firm's strategy as follows: "A car for every purse and purpose." Whereas Ford offered only a single model, GM offered consumers a wide variety of choices. In recent years, that trend has accelerated into a veritable explosion of product variety. Successful differentiators have splintered mass markets into ever-finer market segments by offering consumers products designed precisely for a specific purpose. In many product categories there are now many different products where there was once only a single offering. Consider, again, the case of athletic footwear. In the 1960s, canvas sneakers, either generic or under popular brand names such as Converse and Keds, were used by large numbers of people for a multitude of recreational activities. Kids played basketball in them, bicycled in them, and simply played in them. Then came Nike. Starting with the running shoe boom of the 1970s, this $4 billion a year company now sells a shoe for virtually every purpose. There are long-jump shoes, high-jump shoes, soccer shoes, basketball shoes, walking shoes, running shoes, golf shoes, and myriad other types of shoes, each with some design variation. Whereas the market was once populated by a few different models, by the 1990s Nike alone sold upwards of three hundred different models (nearly a thousand if different colors and styles are considered) for more than twenty sports.

The success of a product variety strategy in athletic footwear has inspired sellers of premium products in other markets to follow a similar differentiation strategy. Consider the case of Nikon Inc., which sells sunglasses designed specifically for skiing, rock climbing, hiking, driving, water sports, and skeet shooting. Nikon offers forty different frame styles, each with five different lens types. The consumer pays premium prices for such a finely differentiated goods. Nikon sunglasses range from $89 for a low-end model to $275 for the top of the line. Competitors Revco and Ray-Ban, both owned by Bausch & Lomb, offer even greater variety. Clearly, buying a pair of expensive sunglasses is less a function of price than personal choice.

⅓ 4. "ON-THE-EDGE" PRODUCT INNOVATIONS

Introducing a wide variety of products usually entails an emphasis on product leadership and "on-the-edge" product innovations. Some differentiators are "first-to-market," speeding new products to market before competitors have a chance to react. They move quickly to stay one step ahead of the competition.

In athletic footwear, for example, Nike constantly introduces new models and unique designs. That reinforces the firm's reputation as an innovator and keeps customers interested in the product category and excited about the firm's products. There is always something new in athletic footwear, and Nike is usually the first to introduce it.

Speeding a wide variety of new products to market usually means that some models live short lives. They are introduced and then, if not successful, are quickly withdrawn and replaced with yet newer models. The sheer number of new products offered to consumers usually results in some giant successes. Nike, for example, was the first to put "air insoles" in its shoes in the 1980s. That innovation was tremendously popular with consumers. It remains a mainstay of the Nike product line and has been widely copied by other sellers.

⅗ 5. LUXURY GOODS AND SERVICES

At an average price of $1,000 apiece, Tag Heuer's stainless steel sports watches are high-margin, high-status luxury goods. So are Louis Vuitton's $9,000 crocodile handbags. Germany's Mont Blanc pens sell for upward of $200, at least 250 times more than a low-end Bic. Even Jeep's $30,000 Grand Cherokees rough it in high-priced, high-profit luxury. Luxury goods are differentiated products that sell status and snob appeal at very high prices. That limits sales volume, but produces very high profit margins.

While most analysts have focused on the rise of price consciousness in the 1990s, some authors have recognized that the market for high-priced luxury goods remains strong, especially in Asian countries where there is a growing interest in acquiring prestigious goods with a strong European identity.[3]

The strategic dilemma for sellers of luxury goods is to balance "class versus mass." That is, the cachet of expensive consumer products is highly related to their scarcity. Not everyone can own a high-priced, high-margin luxury item. Brand dilution can be a problem. Sellers must resist the temptation to increase sales volume and risk debasing the exclusivity that created that demand in the first place.

During the 1980s, some sellers of luxury items devalued their prestigious brand names by licensing them to nearly anyone who showed up with a check. Gucci was one of the worst offenders. Its brand name was plastered on nearly twenty thousand items, some of which were made of plastic. All that changed in the 1990s, when the emphasis shifted back to the long-term preservation of brand identity.

Successfully selling luxury goods usually requires some combination of the following tactics:

- a statement of understated elegance, status, even snob appeal
- a long-term view of brand equity that avoids the gaudy, garish, and glitzy fads of the 1980s
- selling more than just a label—a luxury good must be the best possible product, made with the best material and workmanship, even if that drives *up* costs
- avoiding sales through discounters
- a clear focus on the highest end of the market—a conscious willingness to stress margins rather than volume
- global marketing of the brand

6. POPULAR MASS-MARKET BRAND NAMES

Brand names serve as a powerful basis of differentiation. Nearly every product category is populated by national brands that signify higher quality and, as a result, command higher prices. Coke and Pepsi, Quaker Oats old-fashioned oatmeal, Gatorade, Crest toothpaste, and countless other well-known brand names dominate their product categories even though they usually eschew outright price competition.

In an era of reduced free time, popular brand names offer consumers a convenient way to pick a product without conducting a thorough search of possible alternatives. Buying a well-known brand reduces a consumer's risk of getting stuck with a poor quality product.

While sales of some popular brands were hurt by competition from lower-priced private brands in the early 1990s, some national brands were able to withstand the onslaught and hold their share of their market. They did so by keeping the price premium or "gouge gap" reasonable, and continuing to build awareness with heavy advertising. Brands like Coca-Cola and Disney are still able to charge higher prices by offering a superior product supported by sufficient promotion.

With all of the fuss about the onslaught of private brands it is easy to forget the immense power of popular brand names. A recent issue of *Fortune,* for example, concluded that twelve out of the top fifteen companies on its list of most admired companies were popular household brand names.[4] How did they do it? According to *Fortune* they had learned the "most fundamental principle of brand building: that a brand has to be better than the rest of the competition. It has to deliver value." An earlier study published by *Advertising Age* found that most of the top-selling brands in twenty-five product categories in 1923 were still number one sixty years later.[5] Clearly, differentiation based on well-known, and well-managed, brand names provides a sustainable competitive advantage for those firms.

To appreciate the power of popular brand names, consider the case of Levi's jeans, an icon of American quality. Although a pair of the company's popular 501 model is made with less than two yards of denim, some thread, five buttons, and five copper rivets, it retails for far more than the cost of its component materials. In the United States, for example, the jeans sell for $30 to $50. But the price is even higher in foreign markets where the prestige of the brand name is even higher. In Britain, where American jeans are a fashion item, a pair of 501s retails for $85. That is why *Forbes* concluded that Levi's pricing strategy is "Whatever the traffic will bear—and it will bear plenty."[6] That is part of the reason why Levi's revenues reached $6.7 billion in 1995 and gross margins on sales were 40 percent.

7. EXCEPTIONAL SERVICE

Customer service standards have risen greatly in the past decade. Consumers now routinely expect liberal return policies, unconditional guarantees, courteous, knowledgeable, and instantly available sales help, as well as rock-bottom prices. Firms have to run faster just to keep up. Only exceptional service gets noticed.

Still, some firms differentiate themselves on the basis of exceptional service and, as a result, command higher prices. Nordstrom, the department store chain, is an often cited example. Its entire reputation is based on the premise that the customer comes first. Founded in 1901 as a Seattle shoe store, the $4 billion Nordstrom earns net profit margins that are 150 percent higher than Federated Department Stores, a key rival.[7] In addition, its sales per square foot are more than double. Nordstrom's rewards come from an attention to service rather than an obsession with costs. While costs are important in any business, Nordstrom is willing to carry a higher than average inventory in some product categories. In shoes, for example, the historical core of its business, some stores carry 28,000 pairs in inventory. That may be expensive, maybe even excessive, but Nordstrom fears disappointing a customer with the line "Sorry, we don't have your size in stock." With that strategy, Nordstrom can peacefully coexist side-by-side with much lower-priced, lower-frills rivals.

Nearly every sector of the economy has successful sellers mining the high-service option. It is the strategy selected by Merrill Lynch and the other full-service securities brokers. While the no-frill brokers, and lesser-frill brokers such as Charles Schwab, sell price, the full-service brokers sell service.

8. GREATER RELIABILITY AND DURABILITY

Some sellers charge premium prices for products that last forever and do not break down unexpectedly. For years, Maytag sold its large appliances on it's image of the lonely repairman. Its product carries a higher price but is perceived to be more reliable. Likewise, the Honda Accord, one of America's top selling cars, has an enviable reputation for both reliability and durability. Japanese cars, in general, continue to be viewed by American consumers as more reliable than cars sold by domestic producers, even though engineers argue that the quality gap has been narrowed or eliminated. That perception allows those sellers to charge higher prices for a valued consumer benefit.

9. CONVENIENCE

Time is especially valuable to today's consumers. Consumers are often willing to trade price for convenience. Even sellers of commodity produce, such as lettuce, have found ways to differentiate their goods by offering greater convenience. One notable example is the California-based Fresh International Corp., which perfected a way to keep lettuce fresh in the bag for weeks.[8] The result is "Fresh Express," a pre-packaged salad in a bag. Introduced in 1989, the fantastically successful new product fits nicely with the trend toward more healthful eating and growing numbers of working moms. The company garnered a 40 percent share of the $800 million business. The market for pre-packaged salads is now 50 percent the size of the market for raw lettuce. Most important, the pre-packaged salad carries a price tag of $2.99 versus 99 cents for the commodity product. Its huge success and higher margins have attracted hordes of competitors seeking to provide consumers with the benefit of convenience.

10. UNIQUE DISTRIBUTION CHANNELS

Finally, many products differentiate themselves by selling through different channels of distribution. Timex in watches, QVC in retailing, Avon in cosmetics, and many other companies, offer consumers similar goods through different channels.

PRICE AS A POINT OF DIFFERENTIATION

Lower prices can serve as a potent point of differentiation. Firms can just as effectively differentiate their wares with price as they can with the non-price variables described above. As a result, some observers argue that there is really no such thing as multiple generic strategies, there is really just one strategic choice—differentiation—where price is but one way to differentiate. Other experts reject that argument. Price competition is so qualitatively different from product differentiation, they argue, and so destructive to profit margins, that price is best treated as a distinct competitive strategy. Furthermore, price cuts are more easily matched than quality differences. Consequently, price is usually *not* considered a form of differentiation, but a distinct marketing strategy that requires unique special skills. Differentiation, by definition, dwells on nonprice variables.

THE HISTORY OF PRODUCT DIFFERENTIATION

The notion of product differentiation is deeply rooted in the economic concept of monopolistic competition and consumers' preference for product variety.

MONOPOLISTIC COMPETITION

Product differentiation is not a new idea. A definition almost identical to that used today was proposed by Edwards Hastings Chamberlin in his 1933 book *The Theory of Monopolistic Competition*. According to Chamberlin, a product is differentiated

> if any significant basis exists for distinguishing the goods (or
> services) of one seller from those of another. Such a basis may
> be real or fancied, so long as it is of any importance whatsoever
> to buyers, and leads to a preference for one variety of the prod-
> uct over another.[9]

Chamberlin's definition contains three key points. First, it recognizes that differentiation can be based on any criteria whatsoever. Second, it can be contrived by the seller, on the basis of artificial differences due to advertising and packaging, or the result of real, natural differences in consumer preferences. Third, the ultimate test is whether the difference is important to consumers.

Chamberlin recognized that sellers *deliberately* fragment markets into ever smaller segments in order to avoid competition and boost profits. That is not only true, it is the ultimate goal of monopolistic competition. It hints at the creation of mini-monopolies, where each seller has some control over the prices it is able to charge. Since highly differentiated products serve distinct segments, the power of substitutes is diminished. As a result, consumers are less likely to switch brands when prices are raised.

In recognition of his contributions to marketing, Edwards Hastings Chamberlin was awarded the Paul D. Converse award by the American Marketing Association in 1953.

CONSUMERS' PREFERENCE FOR VARIETY

Product differentiation is also rooted in the psychological observation that consumers prefer a greater variety of goods and services. That preference is partly driven by different tastes. The heterogeneity of demand ensures that a diversity of goods will be valued highly.

But differentiation also thrives because consumers value unique products and personalized service. They do not want products that are identical to those of their friends and neighbors, even though economies of scale might offer lower prices if everyone purchased the exact same model or style. It is almost anathema to American culture to prefer sameness. Alfred P. Sloan, Jr., the former chairman of General Motors, made a similar observation. He recognized that consumers would pay extra for cars that were different than those of their neighbors. While Henry Ford offered consumers a single, low-cost, low-priced model in only one color, General Motors embraced product differentiation through greater product diversity.

REAL VERSUS CONTRIVED DIFFERENCES

There is a long-running debate in economics over the extent to which differentiation is real or contrived. Critics of marketing argue that sellers create and manipulate perceptions of difference between otherwise similar products solely to avoid competition and boost profits. They argue that differentiation is contrived and wasteful. It keeps the volume of production small and prices high simply by advertising and superficial packaging differences. Laws and regulations should be enacted to stop such shenanigans, they argue.

Others see differentiation in a softer light. They recognize that consumers have different needs and wants. Families want minivans, young persons prefer sports cars, and the wealthy want luxury. Defenders of differentiation argue that life would be infinitely duller if all products were standardized on single model and style.

WHAT TO DIFFERENTIATE

Products can be differentiated in terms of tangible and intangible attributes. Furthermore, there are two types of tangible product attributes—core product features and cosmetic or incidental product features.

CORE PRODUCT FEATURES

The most obvious way to differentiate a product is to change its fundamental properties in order to stress a particular point of differentiation. Mercedes-Benz, for example, strives to make the best-engineered cars in the world. Sony does the same in consumer electronics. It innovates new technological advances in order to justify the premium prices it charges.

Technological breakthroughs create opportunities for differentiation. Many firms gain competitive advantage by quickly and creatively working new technologies into their products. Active matrix color screens, for example, were used to differentiate laptop computers.

The extent to which technological advances can be kept from competitors determines the sustainability of that point of differentiation. In some cases, technology is proprietary. That is, it is protected by law or the skill of only one seller. But in other instances, technologies are developed and then quickly put into the products of all sellers, where they becomes the standard for the entire product category.

INCIDENTAL PRODUCT FEATURES

Consumers are sometimes unable to evaluate fundamental product characteristics in many types of products. The circuitry of a stereo system, for example, is baffling to most consumers. Technical specifications are equally uninterpretable. Power ratings, distortion statistics, and other arcane electronic facts, make sense to engineers but can be used to mislead as easily as to inform consumers. Instead, consumers judge such products on the basis of cosmetic product features. A stereo with many flashing lights, dials galore, and an attention to detail might be judged superior to another seller's model. In such instances, it is not a clear understanding of the distortion range of the speakers that sells the product, but the implication that attractive incidental features signal good product quality. The incidental features become surrogates for judgments of actual product performance.

Incidentals can also be used to differentiate products that are otherwise same. IBM's butterfly keyboard attracted attention to its models even though most competitors sold similar models minus the unusual keyboard.

Cars are often judged using incidental criteria. To many consumers, the number of cup holders and lighted mirrors are more influential than displacement data and other engineering specifications. Frank Perdue differentiates chicken using cosmetic product cues. Contract chicken farmers feed Perdue chickens marigold petals to make the meat yellow. Yellow chicken meat is not more nutritious or delicious. It is, however, visibly different.

Examples of incidental differentiation abound. Loud vacuums, noisy lawnmowers, and ear-deafening leafblowers all imply superior product performance. Similarly, when freeze-dried coffee was first introduced it was made with bigger flakes because consumer testing found that bigger flakes signaled superior product quality, even though the size of the flakes had no real effect on product quality. It was merely a physical cue.

Incidental product features can also serve as a negative point of differentiation. In the early 1980s, Tandy's Radio Shack TRS-80 personal computer was nicknamed the "Trash 80" because it was housed in a cheap, gray, plastic case. It was fine machine with poor incidentals.

Packaging is a cosmetic product feature that often serves as a potent source of differentiation. Perfume is at least as much package as product. Perfume bottles convey status and earn high margins for the maker.

Cosmetic cues are especially influential when there is no physical product. Services rely heavily on incidentals. The fine wood paneling in a law office implies that quality lawyers are at work at that firm. Banks play a similar game to send signals to customers. Earlier in this century, banks sought to convey an image of permanence. Older bank buildings still have the feeling of a fortress, meant to stand a thousand years, protecting depositor's savings. Modern banks send a different signal. They attempt to reflect the warmth and friendship of a close personal friendship.

Services are sometimes forced to rely heavily on incidental cues of product quality since there is no tangible product for the consumer to examine. What the customer sees is used to draw inferences about the service offered. A shabbily dressed accountant or an ineloquent financial planner offers a different product to consumers than an accountant dressed in the conventional three-piece suit or a more silver-tongued planner.

PRODUCT INTANGIBLES

Products are rarely sold in isolation from the company's image and reputation, the salesperson with whom the customer interacts, and the services provided along with the physical product itself. Even when products are physically identical to one another, they are differentiated in terms of intangible attributes.

A product is often inseparable from its seller. Consider the purchase of one hundred shares of stock in General Motors—a commodity that can be bought from many sellers. The product can be purchased from Merrill Lynch, a full-service broker, or Charles Schwab, a discount broker. One sells service, the other trades on price. They are clearly differentiated services, even though they sell identical products.

Often, salespersons serve as the primary point of differentiation. Tom Watson, the former head of IBM, recognized the importance of intangibles. IBM employees, including sales staff, wore white shirts to convey a professional image of the firm.

Sometimes salespersons convey the wrong image. A sportswear firm trying to convey an image of youthful activity that is represented by an elderly salesperson is likely to present a confusing image to the retailers that buy the clothing line. Fortunately for such individuals, age discrimination laws protect against arbitrary forced retirements. Even in business, individual rights take precedence over strategic inconsistencies.

ACCOUNTING FOR INTANGIBLES

Intangibles may be important but they wreak havoc with accounting methods. Consider the case of *Wheel of Fortune,* one of the most successful programs in television history. The show successfully differentiated itself from game show competitors in the 1980s. What was its worth? Accountants valued it as the amortized cost of the rights to syndicate the program. By using that method the *Wheel* was worth nothing on paper, even though it had earned hundreds of millions. Traditional accounting methods emphasize bricks and mortar. As such they cannot adequately value intangible assets, service businesses, and idea industries.

Accounting for intangibles is in its infancy. Although intangibles contribute greatly to net worth, and add significantly to long-term profits, they are not considered assets on current balance sheets. Accounting rules do not permit it. Instead, intangibles are charged as expenses against current income.

But intangibles have long-term value. Advertising, contracts, patents, and R&D can all have long-term effects on shareholder equity. Coca-Cola, for example, possesses a world-class brand—an intangible asset—that is at least as important as its factories, plant, and equipment. Its physical assets can be easily replicated by competitors. Its intangible assets, however, offer a more sustainable advantage.

Intangible assets can also privide a more accurate picture of a firm's well-being than a traditional tabulation of its physical assets alone. Companies such as General Motors, IBM, and Digital Equipment all reported healthy financials long after their intangible assets had started to deteriorate. The data contained in their annual reports focused on only part of the picture and, as a result, gave a misleading report.

REQUIREMENTS FOR SUCCESSFUL DIFFERENTIATION

Differentiation requires a different set of skills than operating as a low-cost, low-price seller.

SUPPORT PREMIUM PRICES WITH SUFFICIENT MARKETING

Customers must be aware of a popular brand-name or high-performance product if they are expected to pay extra for it. That typically means the differentiator must spend more on advertising and other promotion tools to build brand and product awareness.

KEEP THE GOUGE GAP REASONABLE

Some markets accept huge price differences between sellers of premium-priced products and lower-cost generics. Other markets are less accepting. If the seller of differentiated goods raises prices too high then consumers may deem the difference "not worth it" and switch to the lower-priced alternative. Marketers must carefully test and monitor the limits of the "brand tax." The goal is to keep the price premium as high as possible without exceeding the limit that induces brand switching.

EMBRACE INNOVATION

Change can be used by differentiators to compete against low-cost producers. That is because once it is successful, a low-cost, low-price strategy driven by experience effects sows the seeds of its own destruction. As companies compete to drive down costs and prices, they sometimes become locked into their efficient production of a standardized product. Any radically new innovation disrupts the downward trend in costs. As a result, there is a tendency to ignore innovation and keep driving down costs and prices. That creates an opportunity for an innovator with a better, albeit more expensive, product.

The pursuit of experience effects often forces a focus on ever higher market share. It is needed to drive down costs and prices still farther. But as market share expands, it creates an opportunity for differentiators to segment a market and rip apart the leader's huge share with a new and innovative product.

KEEP COPYCATS AT BAY

Successful differentiation inevitably attracts copycats who try to mimic the differentiator's product and sell it at lower prices. Their goal will be to convince consumers that there is no difference between the two entries and that the smart shopper should choose the lower-priced brand. Differentiators must frustrate such efforts by whatever means possible, or face an erosion of profit margins. That can entail the vigorous enforcement of patents.

At the start of their popularity in 1995, Oakley sunglasses kept copycats away with vigorous litigation. It sued companies that mimicked its innovative designs. The firm's chief financial officer described Oakley's strategy as follows: "We work very hard to bust a few chops, make a few examples of people. It makes it easier [for competitors] to copy somebody besides Oakley."[10] It worked for a while, but once the style became too popular Oakley was unable to keep all competitors at bay.

PROTECT AGAINST THE "SQUEEZE PLAY"

Porter noted that some firms get stuck in the middle when they sell goods that are neither differentiated nor low priced. They get squeezed in the middle between low-cost producers and high-end differentiators. That sometimes happens to sellers of differentiated goods who establish a strong position in the high-volume mid-market price points. As the popularity of the product category grows, even more prestigious brands move down from the highest end of the market to challenge the mass-market differentiators. The luxury-good sellers expand sales beyond their small, very upscale segments. That can trap the differentiator in the middle, sandwiching it between low-cost producers and the upscale seller.

Consider the case of Levi, a differentiator that charges higher prices for its mass-market blue jeans. Wrangler and Lee, two competitive brands sold by the VF Corp., are priced lower than Levi's. So do the hordes of less prestigious brands that sell at a fraction of the Levi's price. Could Levi get stuck in the middle? Probably not, but the higher prices it charges customers in foreign markets leaves it vulnerable to a move downmarket from Ralph Lauren, Calvin Klein, and the other upscale designer labels. Levi, which positions its brand as reminiscent of the old American West, risks a challenge from the designer brands that sell outright fashion at similarly high prices. Can you envision a scenario where Levi would be stuck in the middle?

NOTES

[1]"Winners," *Business Week,* June 3, 1996, pp. 70–88.

[2]Josh McHugh, "Who's Hiding Behind Those Shades?," *Forbes,* October 23, 1995, p. 68.

[3]See, for example, William Echikson, "Luxury Steals Back," *Fortune,* January 16, 1995, pp. 112–19; John Bissell, "Mining Luxury Means Decoding Value," *Brandweek,* March 7, 1994, p. 16; Debra Sparks, "Stealth Wealth," *Financial World,* March 28, 1995, pp. 26–27.

[4]Betsy Morris, "The Brand's the Thing," *Fortune,* March 4, 1996, p. 74; and Anne Fisher, "Corporate Reputations," *Fortune,* March 4, 1996, pp. 90–98.

[5]"Old Standbys Hold Their Own," *Advertising Age,* September 19, 1983, p. 33.

[6]Robert Lenzer and Stephen Johnson, "A Few Yards of Denim and Five Copper Rivets," *Forbes,* February 26, 1996, p. 82.

[7]Seth Lubove, "Don't Listen to the Boss, Listen to the Customer," *Forbes,* December 4, 1995, pp. 45–46.

[8]Seth Lubove, "Salad in a Bag," *Forbes,* October 23, 1995, pp. 201–3.

[9]Edwards Hastings Chamberlin, *The Theory of Monopolistic Competition,* Cambridge, MA: Harvard University Press, 1933, p. 56.

[10]Ibid., p. 70

CHAPTER 8

SEGMENTATION STRATEGIES

Market share is what makes segmenters different. They are special-ists who focus on only a part of the market with the intent of more closely serving the needs of customers and avoid competitors focused on larger markets.

Consider the case of Sub-Zero refrigerators. The fifty-year-old pri-vate firm based in Madison, Wisconsin, holds only 1 to 2 percent of the 8.5-million-unit refrigerator market, which is dominated by industry giants with huge economies of scale. But according to *Forbes,* Sub-Zero holds 70 percent of the superpremium segment.[1] It specializes in very expensive, super-luxurious built-in refrigerators that start at $3,500 each. The product is popular with architects and designers working for the very affluent. To own a Sub-Zero refrigerator is to have something special.

The basic premise of market segmentation is rooted in the funda-mental principle of military strategy—the concentration of forces. In marketing, as in war, the smaller army is best advised to concentrate its forces at a point where the larger opponent's forces are weakest rather than to compete (or fight) across a broad front. Only in that way have marketers and military commanders alike won battles when greatly out-numbered.

THE DIFFERENCE BETWEEN DIFFERENTIATION AND SEGMENTATION

The terms "product differentiation" and "market segmentation" are widely used and just as widely defined. A review of the literature by James Dickson and Peter Ginter concludes that the terms mean different things to different authors and are often used interchangeably.[2] It is sim-ply not clear whether they mean the same thing, must be used together, or chosen between.

THE ARGUMENT FOR ALTERNATIVE STRATEGIES

Some marketers argue that product differentiation and market segmentation are alternative strategies. A firm picks one or the other, but does not use both simultaneously. A landmark article by Wendell Smith published in 1956 epitomizes that view.[3] He makes the following distinction: "differentiation is concerned with the bending of demand to the will of supply." In other words, product differentiation focuses on the supply of goods. Demand is changed to favor goods produced by a particular firm. According to that argument, differentiation is a "promotional strategy." It seeks to bring consumers to the firm's products.

Segmentation, in contrast, focuses on the demand side of the equation. It is a "merchandising strategy" by which products are adjusted to serve a particular group of users. Supply is made to fit demand.

The difference between differentiation and segmentation is best drawn by an analogy with cutting a cake. Differentiation seeks a broad share of the total market. It seeks a horizontal layer of the cake. Segmentation seeks depth of market. It takes a deep slice of the cake.

CLAIMS FOR COMPLEMENTARY STRATEGIES

Economists argue that product differentiation and market segmentation are really two sides of the same coin. A firm differentiates its products to appeal to specific market segments. Selsun Blue, a dandruff shampoo, is a clearly differentiated product targeted directly at that segment of consumers who have that unfortunate malady. The product is differentiated. A segment is served.

RECONCILING THE RELATIONSHIP BETWEEN DIFFERENTIATION AND SEGMENTATION

Which argument is right and which wrong? Both are right. Each looks at a particular aspect of differentiation and segmentation. The relationship between product differentiation and market segmentation can be summarized as follows:

1. *Segmentation requires differentiation.* A firm must change something real or imagined about the product if it wants to appeal exclusively to a segment. It is impossible to appeal exclusively to a target segment without goods that are different than those sold to other groups of consumers. That difference can be real or imagined but it must be a difference.
2. *Differentiation does not require segmentation.* Products can be made

Exhibit 8.1
Segmentation Strategies

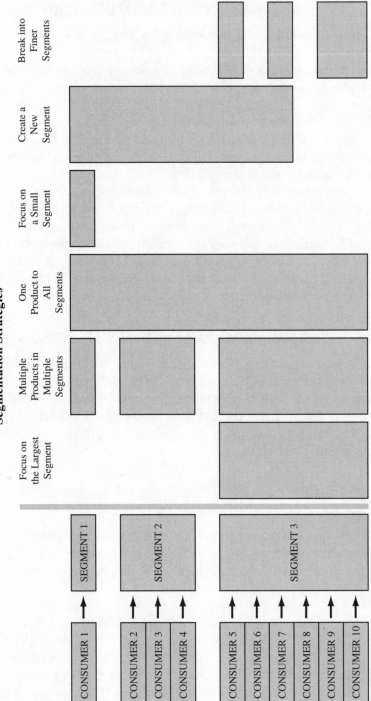

different without appealing to a segment of the market. Many, if not the majority of, differentiated products—such as Kellogg's corn flakes and Coca-Cola—serve broad markets rather than specific segments.

SEGMENTATION STRATEGIES

Most markets exhibit a clustered demand preference pattern. That is, not all consumers want the exact same product. Ideally, consumers might demand unique products tailored precisely to their individual needs. But usually that is neither practical nor cost effective. Most markets lie somewhere in between. Consumer preferences are neither entirely homogeneous nor entirely diffused.

The presence of clustered preference patterns creates an opportunity for segmentation. Even the simplest market structures allow for numerous possible segmentation strategies. What follows is an adaptation of an example first presented by Nelson Foote in 1969.[4]

Consider a hypothetical market consisting of only ten persons, one redhead, three blondes, and six with brown or black hair. In this simple example, we are interested in the preference pattern for ice cream. Assume that market research discovers that redheads like strawberry ice cream, blondes like vanilla, and the brunettes prefer chocolate. As Exhibit 8.1 illustrates, the ten persons then break out into three unequal-size segments. As the exhibit also shows, there are at least six possible segmentation strategies in a market described by those simplifying assumptions.

1. GO FOR THE LARGEST SEGMENT

The first possible segmentation strategy a firm might pursue is to target the largest segment. That is, a firm might specialize in selling chocolate ice cream to brown- and black-haired consumers. The intent is to build a strong position in the most attractive segment and to concede smaller segments to smaller firms.

2. SELL MULTIPLE PRODUCTS IN MULTIPLE SEGMENTS

A grander segmentation strategy might be for the firm to sell all three flavors. That would allow the firm to cover the entire market with three different product offerings.

Many large firms follow a multiple coverage segmentation strategy. For decades, Coca-Cola sold a single soda—sugared cola in a bottle. Then it started selling diet colas to the weight-conscious and caffeine-free soda to the health-conscious. Products are packaged in twelve-ounce cans for individual servings and giant plastic bottles for families and "heavy-user" households. In addition, it offers consumers Minute Maid orange juice, orange-flavored soda, and Powerade, a performance-based sports drink. Coca-Cola, along with a host of other admired markets, covers every conceivable segment with a bevy of liquid refreshments.

3. SELL A SINGLE PRODUCT TO ALL (OR MOST) SEGMENTS

Some sellers forego segmentation entirely. In the ice cream example, the firm might decide to sell an efficiently produced block of ice cream containing all three flavors. The firm hopes that consumers in many segments will be lured by very low prices. The product many not be exactly what they want but it is acceptable given the price. This is the strategy most often followed by low-cost, low-priced sellers.

4. FOCUS ON A SMALL SEGMENT

A smaller firm without the resources to battle across the entire market, or even to fight it out in the largest segment, might choose to build a solid reputation for selling the best strawberry ice cream. Strawberry is only a small segment of the overall market but it is the segment least likely to attract large competitors. Focusing on that segment is a strategy that trades sales volume for a defensible market position.

Many smaller firms have succeeded by focusing on smaller segments of the market where they can exploit their competitive advantages. Consider the success of A&W root beer. From 1919 to 1971, A&W root beer was sold only at A&W root beer stands. In 1971, United Brands bought the rights to sell the brand and operated it like a classic cash cow. They invested little, and withdrew much cash. In 1986, A&W management precipitated a leveraged buyout and adopted a segmentation strategy that was based on three distinct actions. First, they convinced independent bottlers to add A&W root beer to their trucks, which were delivering Coke or Pepsi anyway. A&W root beer would supplement bottlers' product lines, not replace Coke and Pepsi.

Second, A&W introduced a cream soda—a product where the A&W label could easily be transferred. At the time, there was no national cream soda. Hence, there was no direct competition.

Third, A&W acquired two other niche players—Squirt, a grapefruit soda, and "The Original Vernors," a strange-tasting ginger drink with strong regional appeal. They also won the rights to distribute General Food's Country Time Lemonade. Competition was minimal in these markets.

The results of avoiding larger competitors were impressive. While total soft drink sales rose less than 5 percent per year in the late 1980s, sales of A&W products rose a whopping 25 percent. Sales reached $100 million in 1988 while profits soared to $7 million. As one industry analyst recognized: "The key to this business is knowing how to market, and these people are very good marketers."[5] They successfully served segmented markets by avoiding more powerful competitors.

5. CREATE A NEW SEGMENT

Some firms use innovation to create entirely new segments. In the ice cream example, a firm might decide to sell frozen yogurt to a newly defined segment cutting across redheads, blondes, and brunettes all in search of fewer calories. The new product might reconfigure the market before industry incumbents realize that the new product is neither a fad nor a farce. The history of business is full of examples of entrenched industry leaders that failed to react to new products that forever changed their markets.

6. BREAK SEGMENTS INTO EVEN FINER SUBSEGMENTS

Within the chocolate segment there might be an opportunity to introduce chocolate with almonds, double chocolate, and a host of other flavors more precisely tailored to the desires of consumers in that segment. In effect, the firm is breaking the segment into ever finer subsegments. The result is that where there was once a single segment for chocolate ice cream there are now a half-dozen distinct segments based on ever-finer gradations in demand.

Many firms have succeeded by segmenting big segments into many smaller segments. Consider the case of Thor-Lo sport socks.[6] Founded in 1953, the North Carolina company started by selling socks to the military and under private label. Then it stumbled into the sport sock business, which was dominated by large efficient producers such as Wigwam Mills, Burlington, and Fox River. The industry giants sold a generic product, usually called "crew" socks, that, at best, was only mildly differentiated in the minds of consumers. Such socks were worn for whatever sport the consumer happened to be playing. Thor-Lo's owner and president, James Thornburg, changed all that. Following the strategy used so successfully by Nike, he designed socks specifically for eighteen different sports. He started with golf when a professional player on the women's tour asked him to design a sock that would not slide into her shoe. He made one that had a soft cylindrical band at the ankle. Then in the mid-1980s he introduced the very popular Thor-Lo Padds sport socks, which have heavy padding on the bottom to cushion the foot. Design variations for tennis, running, walking, basketball, aerobics, and virtually every other sport followed. Where there had once been a single sport sock segment, there were now many. His product gained near-cult status. Martina Navratilova called Thor-Lo-Padds "the best sock I ever put on" and agreed to serve as a spokeswoman. Consumers had to pay extra for the more precisely defined product—Thor-Lo Padds are priced at $7.50 per pair—but they willingly did so, allowing the tiny segmenter to gain share in a market dominated by giants and characterized by ruinous price competition from imports.

THE BASIS OF SEGMENTATION

The number of possible segmentation strategies grows quickly as a market becomes more complicated. In the simple ice cream example presented earlier, for example, segmentation was based on hair color only. In the real world there are many choices. A landmark review article by Yoram Wind described some of the more popular criteria for segmenting a market.[7] These include: (1) demographics, psychographics, and lifestyles, (2) benefits sought, (3) product usage, (4) product preference, price sensitivity, and (5) brand loyalty. The possibilities are nearly endless.

A REGIONAL FOCUS

Many firms have succeeded against national competitors by focusing their efforts on a single geographic region. Hardee's, the fast-food chain, seeks market dominance in the southeastern and middle-western United States. It does not attempt to compete with McDonald's on a nationwide basis. To do so would be to spread itself too thin. It is a much smaller firm. As a result of its focus, Hardee's is the number two or three chain in 75 percent of the markets it serves. It competes on an equal footing with larger competitors, but only within its scope of operations. Hardee's tight focus allows it to move quickly against rivals in its own markets.

In another example of a regional focus, very small microbreweries have succeeded by serving small localized markets with a high-quality, distinctive product. Microbrews sell minuscule volumes in comparison with the large national brands but usually target an upscale market with a more expensive brew. They thwart competition from national brands by focusing on very small geographic segments.

DEMOGRAPHICS

Demographics are used to segment many markets. In the 1970s, for example, sellers of cigarettes targeted women with new products such as

Virginia Slims and Benson and Hedges to replace male smokers who gave up the habit. As a result, cigarettes successfully expanded into a demographic segment where they had previously been weak.

PRODUCT USAGE

Product usage varies greatly among consumers. It is often possible to classify consumers into three groups: heavy users, light users, and nonusers. Heavy users consume most of the product. They are the embodiment of the age-old "80/20" principle, wherein 20 percent of the market typically consumes 80 percent of sales. In the beer industry, for example, popular domestic brands serve a large market, including heavy users. Light users can also be an attractive segment. Higher priced imports, like Beck's, and microbrews are popular with light users. Lower volume is offset by higher prices.

More recently, brewers have targeted nonusers. The introduction of nonalcoholic beers such as Sharp's, O'Doul's, and Coors Cutter is an attempt to offer a product more in tune with a society increasingly intolerant of drunk drivers, and clamoring for further restrictions on the consumption of alcoholic beverages.

QUALITY NICHES

David Garvin has noted that many sellers follow a strategy of "quality niches." He argues that firms should "single out a few dimensions of quality as their focus instead of striving to be number one in all categories."[8] With quality niches, different sellers excel at one dimension of quality and meet minimum expectations at other dimensions. As Exhibit 8.2 illustrates, the Toyota has a strong record on reliability, while Volvo stresses safety and BMW focuses on performance.

THE INDIVIDUAL CONSUMER

One of the latest trends in marketing is to target individual consumers through database marketing techniques. This is the ultimate in market segmentation—a system where each consumer is treated as an individual segment. It starts with the development of a list of consumers. It might be a list of "good" customers gleaned from company records, data collected from supermarket scanners, or the result of a joint marketing program such as GM's Mastercard. Once that database has been built, marketers zero in on specific customers with special offers tailored specifically to their needs. GM, for example, sends cardholders informa-

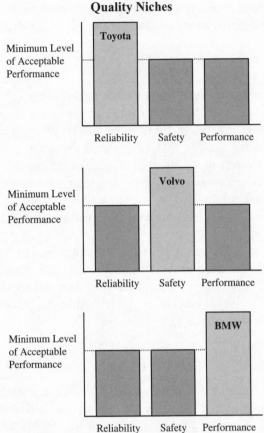

Exhibit 8.2
Quality Niches

tion on new vehicles in which they have expressed interest when it seems likely the customer is ready to buy. Casinos build relationships with their best customers by sending personalized birthday cards and offering special programs to keep those people coming back to the tables. In each case, personalized attention is paid to each customer as though he or she were a separate segment of the market.

MARKET RESEARCH AND SEGMENTATION

Most of the work in market segmentation research has gone into the creation of techniques aimed at identifying segments. Two basic approaches have been developed. In the first, management selects the basis for segmentation beforehand—be it age, region of the country, or benefits—then uses a statistical technique to describe the characteristics of those segments. That is called the "a priori" approach to segmentation.

An alternative approach allows mathematical techniques to decide the basis of segmentation. Generally, these techniques cluster consumers with similar characteristics into the same segment. They "build" market segments from individual consumer profiles. While the technique decides who falls into which segment, judgment is still important. Someone must decide how many segments are selected, and what their labels should be. Often, segments with titles such as "upscale singles," "happy homemakers," and "young newlyweds" are the result of clustering techniques.

Exhibit 8.3 illustrates the basic philosophy of segmentation approaches. The aggregation approach moves from left to right, starting with individual consumers who are grouped into segments on the basis of profile similarities. The disaggregation approach moves from right to left. It starts with the entire market, then breaks that market into distinct segments. One approach is not necessarily better than the other. They are merely choices available to marketers.

Exhibit 8.3
Aggregation Versus Disaggregation

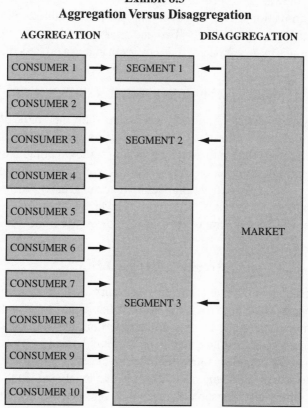

QUESTIONS ABOUT SEGMENTATION

The following questions are often asked about segmentation research.

ARE SEGMENTS CREATED OR DISCOVERED?

Some segments exist naturally in a market, waiting to be discovered by astute marketers as times change. Others are created by marketers who see an opportunity to change the status quo. The need for underarm deodorants and mouthwash, for example, were created largely by marketers seeking to build demand for new consumer products.

Which is more common—created segments or discovered segments? It is not clear. In the 1970s, William Moran argued: "More often than not, product market segments are made, not born."[9] He cites the examples of Land's Polaroid camera, which created the segment for instant photo processing, and Clarence Birdseye's frozen foods, which created the segment for convenience foods, to support his claim. Others disagree. They argue that those segments always existed, technological innovation merely made it possible to satisfy them better than had previously been possible. Segments can be created, they argue, especially for line extensions and other variations on existing innovations. But discovery is more common. Most segments already exist, waiting to be identified and exploited. According to that view, segmentation is more a process of discovery than it is a process of creation.

TO WHAT EXTENT DO SEGMENTS OVERLAP?

Many segments are not mutually exclusive. The members of one segment can easily be classified into another as well. In toothpaste, for example, families that value decay prevention may include children who favor flavorful toothpaste, as well as singles who value white teeth. Likewise, targeting autos to women can overlap greatly with segments defined as "upscale" or "suburban." These examples show that the boundaries of segments are often roughly drawn, not ironclad.

ARE SEGMENTS STABLE?

It is often said that change is the only certainty. That observation suggests that segments, once identified, do not last for long. The few studies that have examined this issue contradict the assertion that segments are unstable. One study looked at how segments for retail banking services changed over a two-year period. It found that (1) the benefits sought remained stable, (2) the size of the segments did not change much, *but* (3) the segments into which individual consumer households were placed did change.[10]

IS COUNTERSEGMENTATION A VIABLE OPTION?

Some markets have been broken into such small niches that opportunities exist for marketers to combine market segments and move back in the direction of mass marketing. That reverse process has been termed countersegmentation.[11] But claims that markets will move en masse away from segmentation and back toward efficiently produced mass-market products have been made for almost twenty years with few indications that it has happened or will happen.

IS SEGMENTATION FOR SMALL FIRMS ONLY?

Segmentation is often the only strategy available to smaller firms but it is not limited to them alone. Large firms can also pursue a strategy of segmentation, particularly if they cover multiple segments with differentiated goods. Large firms simply have more options open to them than smaller firms. It is an issue of resources. Small firms are constrained by the need to concentrate their scant resources on a part of the market that can be defended. Smaller firms simply have fewer options.

NOTES

[1]Joshua Levine, "Cool!," *Forbes,* April 1996, p. 98.

[2]Peter Dickson and James Ginter, "Market Segmentation, Product Differentiation, and Marketing Strategy," *Journal of Marketing,* April 1987, pp. 1–10.

[3]Wendell Smith, "Product Differentiation and Market Segmentation as Alternative Marketing Strategies," *Journal of Marketing,* July 1956, pp. 3–8.

[4]Nelson Foote, "Market Segmentation as a Competitive Strategy," in *Current Controversies in Marketing Research,* Leo Bogart (ed.), Chicago: Markham Publishing Company, 1969, pp. 129–39.

[5]Claudia H. Deutsch, "A&W: Prospering by Avoiding the Big Boys," *New York Times,* January 15, 1989, Section 3, p. 10.

[6]This mini-case is based on an article by Gretchen Morgenson, "The Foot's Friend," *Forbes,* April 12, 1992, pp. 60–62.

[7]Yoram Wind, "Issues and Advances in Segmentation Research," *Journal of Marketing Research,* August 1978, pp. 317–37.

[8]David Garvin, *Managing Quality,* New York: The Free Press, 1988, p. 62.

[9]William Moran, "Segments Are Made Not Born," in *Marketing Strategies: A Symposium,* Earl L. Bailey (ed.), New York: The Conference Board, 1974, p. 16.

[10]Roger Calatone and Alan Sawyer, "The Stability of Benefit Segments," *Journal of Marketing Research,* August 1978, pp. 395–404.

[11]Alan Resnick, Peter Turney, and Barry Mason, "Marketers Turn to Counter-Segmentation," *Harvard Business Review,* September–October 1979, pp. 100–6.

CHAPTER 9

COMPETITIVE DYNAMICS

Competition is dynamic, not static. Consumer changes, technological innovation, and moves by competitors seeking to gain advantage all conspire to change stable markets into free-for-alls. As in war, competitive attacks can come from above, below, or across the battlefield. Sometimes such attacks come from obvious enemies. But other times they come suddenly from unexpected sources, wreaking havoc on industry incumbents.

Competition is also multifaceted. It is sometimes not clear just where the boundaries of competitive battles lie. Cola soft drinks, for example, compete with one another but they also compete with other types of carbonated soft drinks as well as newer entries such as Gatorade and canned ice teas. They even compete with fruit juices for what some industry experts call "share of stomach."

Rarely is the outcome of a competitive battle predetermined. Instead, attackers and defenders try their best to catch the other off guard. What follows is a discussion of some of the more commonly encountered competitive situations.

COMPETITION BETWEEN PRICE POINTS

One kind of competition pits higher-priced, higher-quality merchandise against lower-priced, lower-quality products. As noted in previous chapters, this is the classic case of low-cost producers competing against sellers of differentiated goods. Consumers have a choice in such markets. They can pay more for higher-quality products or opt for lower prices and lower quality, where quality is defined broadly as more than products that are merely reliable and durable. In this type of competition consumers must trade price for quality.

VERTICAL DIFFERENTIATION

Economists have a name for such competitive situations—they call it "vertical differentiation." Exhibit 9.1 illustrates the competitive situation

Exhibit 9.1
Competitive Dynamics

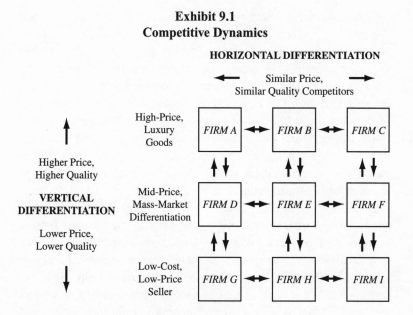

where low-cost, low-price sellers compete directly against higher-priced differentiators. The figure shows a hypothetical three-tier market where high-priced luxury goods compete with middle-price-point, mass-market goods and low-cost, low-priced products. That is, firms A, B, and C compete against firms D, E, and F, and both groups compete against firms G, H, and I.

1. DRAWING CUSTOMERS UP-MARKET WITH HIGHER QUALITY

Competition among vertically differentiated sellers typically involves tradeoffs between price and quality. Sellers of highly differentiated products and services stress quality and/or prestige in an attempt to win share from low-cost producers. Basically, such sellers try to convince consumers that their wares are worth the higher price. They entice customers up the price-quality ladder using any one or some combination of the differentiation strategies discussed in the previous chapter.

MINI-CASE: GILLETTE'S SENSOR RAZOR VERSUS THE LOW-PRICED DISPOSABLES

In a decade dominated by lower costs and lower prices, some sellers have succeeded in stealing share back with higher-priced, higher-quality differentiated goods. Gillette's stunningly successful Sensor razor is a case in point.

Disposable razors, which were first introduced in the 1970s, changed the nature of competition in the shaving business. Bic, the low-cost leader in disposable pens, was ready to introduce a disposable razor in the U.S. market in 1976. Gillette was forced to preempt Bic's move by introducing its own "Good News" disposable. But the Good News proved bad news for Gillette. What had been a high-margin, high-quality business based on sales of replacement blades (mostly for Gillette shavers) quickly became a low-cost, low-price commodity business where consumers simply bought whichever bag of razors happened to be on sale in a particular week. Cheap disposables cannibalized Gillette's high-margin products.

By the early 1990s, disposables made up nearly 50 percent of all blade sales. Furthermore, they were particularly popular among younger men, the future of the business. Something had to be done. Gillette decided to introduce a new and innovative razor, a strategy that had worked well in the past in creating renewed interest in the firm's products. For decades, Gillette had introduced new blade systems such as the Trac II and Atra, which caused a buzz in the business and generated excitement and sales growth.

But this time the company faced many daunting obstacles. First, price was now a potent factor. Gillette's new razor would cost twice as much as the low-cost disposables. Marketers had to convince men that it was worth the extra price to accomplish an unpleasant chore. Second, men already thought they were spending twice as much on shaving as they actually did. Not only was the new product more expensive, but consumers perceived it to be even more expensive than it was. Finally, even if the product gave a better shave than the disposables, Gillette could not count on extensive word-of-mouth advertising. Virtually no one talks about shaving and razors with friends and family. Clearly, Gillette faced an uphill battle.

Nonetheless, the Boston-based firm spent $200 million developing the new Sensor razor. Introduced in January 1990, Sensor was supported by a $110 million first-year ad budget. It sold for $3.75 and came with three replacement blades. Newspapers were flooded with price-off coupons that ran as high as $2 off around Father's Day 1991. By combining retailer discounts and price-off coupons, some smart shoppers could get the Gillette Sensor for almost nothing.

Gillette's Sensor was an instant success. It garnered more than 3 percent of all U.S. blade sales after only three months on the market. By September 1992 it held 17 percent of the market. Annual retail sales reached $400 million by 1992. Men who were used to bad shaves from cheap razors proved willing to pay more for product quality.

After such stunning success, Gillette set out in search of expansion opportunities.

1. *Sensor for Women.* The market for women's shavers is only one-third the size of the men's market. In the past, it was a neglected niche. Disposables were simply colored pink and sold as womens' models. Many women used their man's disposable. Gillette set out to design a version of the Sensor specifically for women. The first thing it did was put a woman in charge of the design team. She knew that existing disposables were ergonomic nightmares. Whereas men shave their faces in front of a mirror, women shave in hard to reach places and they tend to shave in the shower. Most of the design money was spent on the development of a large, cool-green handle that was easy to hold in the shower. Since the blades had already been designed, the women's Sensor needed only a token $10 million in R&D (versus $200 million for the men).

Sensor for Women was introduced in the summer of 1992. It was priced at $3.99 and supported with a meager $14 million ad budget. It, too, was an astonishing success, selling 7.6 million units in the first six months and garnering 60 percent of the entire women's shaving market.

2. *SensorExcel.* When sales slowed in 1993 Gillette had to look elsewhere for fast growth. It decided to go further upscale with the equally successful SensorExcel. Introduced in late 1994, SensorExcel was advertised as "the next revolution in shaving closeness." The revolution was caused by five flexible microfins, which "gently stretch your skin, causing your beard to spring upward so the blades can shave you closer." Consumers had to pay extra to participate in the revolution. SensorExcel carries a 15 percent price premium over the pre-revolutionary Sensor. SensorExcel was supported by a $40 million advertising budget.

3. *Toiletries.* Gillette also reemphasized men's and women's shave cream and aftershave lotion. Here the record was mixed. In the past, its Right Guard and Foamy lines were criticized for fuzzy marketing. And there was heavy competition from the likes of Procter & Gamble's Old Spice and Noxzema and Colgate's Mennen.

4. *Going global.* Gillette's success in U.S. markets, and its dominant position in many developed countries, is being followed by a push into developing countries where growth is high and the demand for high-quality Western goods is growing.

5. *Upstream pulls in other markets.* Finally, Gillette's success in stealing share back from disposables prompted a move into other markets dominated by low-cost, low-price sellers. In pens, for example, Gillette now owns Parker Pen, Waterman, and PaperMate, once-leading companies decimated by low-priced disposables such as Bic. Watch for another

attempt to pull consumers up-market with higher-quality, highly differentiated goods.

   Sensor is now the number one shaver in the United States. Cumulative worldwide sales were more than $2.2 billion by 1994. Schick is a
distant second with only a small share of the market. Most important,
Sensor is a high-margin product (32 percent margin on blades) that
stole share back from low-cost, low-price sellers. With those facts in
mind, is Gillette's success at charging higher prices temporary or will it
be long-lived? What do you think of its other expansive moves? Will
they succeed? What else could they do to continue to grow?

2. LURING CUSTOMERS DOWN-MARKET WITH LOWER PRICES

The second kind of competitive move among sellers of vertically differentiated goods occurs when low-cost producers lure customers downward with lower prices. Their strategic message is often the same. They
argue that customers can obtain equal quality at lower prices. Chapter 6,
on low-cost, low-price sellers, details the mechanisms of this competitive
dynamic.

3. PUSHING PRODUCTS UP-MARKET

Another way in which firms can increase market share is by "stretching"
their product lines from one end of the market toward the other. Whereas
the previous two strategies tried to convince *customers* to move upstream
or downstream to the firm's product, this type of competitive maneuver
move the firm's *products,* or at least the appeal of those products,
upstream or downstream to meet the demands of new groups of consumers. Vertical movements can be in either direction. "Up-market"
moves occur when a low-cost producer with an established beachhead at
the lower end of the market moves toward the more profitable, higher
end of the market. Many low-cost, low-price sellers, especially foreign
competitors with lower costs, get their start in the United States by estab-
lishing a solid position at the bottom of a market. They build a reputation
for producing inexpensive goods that provide good value to consumers.
Once that position is firmly established, however, those firms look for
growth by moving up-market.
   Consider the case of Japanese automobiles. Throughout the 1960s,
the Japanese built a solid reputation for producing low-priced econo-
boxes that served utilitarian needs. Once that position was firmly established, however, they started to march up-market by introducing more

expensive models that carried higher margins. Toyota introduced the Camry, then the Cressida. By the late 1980s, entire new divisions of the major Japanese automakers were created to compete at the highest end of the market. Lexus by Toyota, Infiniti by Nissan, and Acura by Honda are premium-priced, luxury automobiles that compete head-on with the prestigious German entries. From a beginning at the bottom of the market, the Japanese automakers moved vertically until they competed over the entire spectrum of the auto market.

The primary barrier to moving up-market is that consumers will not always pay premium prices for goods that are perceived to have a pedestrian image. That is why many upstream movers pick a different brand name.

Take the case of Gallo wines, the California giant with a strong position at the lower end of the market. Gallo operates the world's largest winery. It sells an astonishing one out of every four bottles of wine sold in the United States. Its operations are a testament to low-cost efficiency. But it is less well known for premium quality. With a tremendous marketing effort, Gallo has succeeded in moving upstream from its position of strength in the $3 to $5 per bottle category to the $5 to $7 varietals. Now it wants to move further upstream into the $8 to $10 bottles, where its product line has been virtually nonexistent. Gallo's history is more closely aligned with screwtops than corkscrews. The question is whether the firm should use its own name on the label, or pick another label, as did the Japanese carmakers when they moved into the premium products segment. In reality, it is not a question. Ernest Gallo is adamant about keeping his name on the high-end product. He argues that he will be able to convince both consumers and wine critics that Gallo can make and sell a fine wine that sells at a premium price. Do you agree?

4. PUSHING PRODUCTS DOWN-MARKET

While Gallo moves up-market, Mondavi, another California seller, moves in the opposite direction. Mondavi's strength lies at the high end of the retail wine market, where bottles typically sell for more than $14. Margins are high at that end of the market but sales are small, only about 3 percent of total wine sales. To increase sales, Mondavi has moved down-market. In the $7 to $14 mid-market segment it sells its Costal line of wines, while its Woodbridge line competes in the below $7 a bottle segment. Like Gallo, Mondavi also prominently displays its name on its low-end wines. But, unlike Gallo, Mondavi faces a different risk by moving down-market. By serving the mass market, it risks diluting the cachet of the brand and destroying the illusion of exclusivity that first created that brand. Many critics claim that is what happened to the American Express card.

MINI-CASE: THE AMERICAN EXPRESS CARD

For many years the prestigious American Express charge card had an air of exclusivity not found in Visa and Mastercard. Amex charged extra— to both merchants and cardholders—for that intangible tinge of luxury. Throughout the 1980s, Amex claimed that its card was not for every- one. But as it moved down-market in search of larger numbers of card- holders and more merchants who would accept the card, it diluted its point of differentiation from the mass-market credit cards. Consumers and merchants alike started to wonder whether it was worth paying more for something so similar to the lower-priced alternative. Exclusivi- ty started to seem pretty ordinary once the number of its platinum, gold, and green cardholders neared 30 million.

Then came the issue of who should be allowed to accept the Amex card. As the use of charge and credit cards spread to new locations, Amex had to decide whether or not to go along. Should Amex be allowed at Kmart and McDonald's? What about at self-service gas sta- tions and movie theaters? To say "yes" may violate the principle of exclusivity but to say "no" may forego an opportunity for growth and cede an important part of the market to downscale competitors. Even wealthy cardholders sometimes eat at fast-food restaurants and go to movies. They might not want to carry a card that was not accepted at many everyday locations. What strategy would you set for the Ameri- can Express card?

COLLISIONS IN VERTICALLY DIFFERENTIATED MARKETS

It is important to note that as some competitors move down-market, they inevitably run headlong into other sellers moving up-market. That is what happened with credit and charge cards. As Amex moved down-mar- ket it collided with Visa and Mastercard, which were moving up-market with the introduction of "gold" cards and features such as buyer protec- tion programs and car rental collision insurance that mimic the prestige of key Amex products. The result is a blurring of the points of differenti- ation. Whereas there used to be clear differences between charge cards and credit cards, those distinctions are now less prominent.

INTENSITY OF RIVALRY IN
VERTICALLY DIFFERENTIATED MARKETS

In some product categories there is vigorous competition between low- cost producers and higher-priced differentiated goods. National brands, for example, battle fiercely with private labels. So do full-price brokerage houses, which compete head-on with discounters. But, in other markets, competition between price points is virtually nonexistent. Each price point is a distinct segment. In the watch industry, for example, price-based rivalry between distant price points is less intense than it is within price points. A 10 percent discount on a $20 Timex is unlikely to have any effect whatsoever on demand for a $1,000 Tag Heuer. The products are so different, and serve such different purposes, as to be completely noncompetitive.

INCREASING PRODUCT VALUE

Vertical differentiation implies different combinations of price and quality but equal levels of product "value." Product value is an important term used to describe the balance between price and quality. All of the tiers in a vertically differentiated market offer the same level of product value. The balance between lower prices and lower quality of the low-cost producer may be the same as the balance between higher prices and higher quality of the seller of differentiated goods.

An alternative strategy to "tradeoffs" between price and quality occurs when a firm seeks to tilt the price-quality balance in its favor by increasing product value to the customer. Such firms can argue that their product offers:

- higher quality at the same low price
- the same quality at a lower price
- much higher quality at a somewhat higher price
- somewhat lower quality for a much lower price
- best of all, higher quality at lower prices

COMPETITION BETWEEN DIFFERENTIATORS

Not only do low-cost producers compete with differentiators, but each group of competitors competes with similarly priced rivals within its own price point.

HORIZONTAL DIFFERENTIATION

When competition occurs within a single price point, economists call it horizontal differentiation. Many similarly priced goods are highly (horizontally) differentiated. The price may be the same, but each product excels at a different dimension of product quality. Within these "quality niches" different sellers stress different combinations of benefits or product features. A $1,200 stainless steel Tag Heuer sports watch, for example, is highly differentiated from a $1,200 hi-tech ceramic Rado fashion watch, which is also different from a $1,200 classically designed Raymond Weil dress watch. All carry the same price, but they are not direct substitutes. They stress different features and styles and tend to serve very different segments. Rivalry can be greatly reduced for such horizontally differentiated goods.

SHIFTING POINTS OF DIFFERENTIATION

Change can create opportunities for some firms and destroy opportunities for others. The well-being of a firm following a differentiation strategy is particularly susceptible to such changes. Its reputation may be wrapped up in a vulnerable part of the business. Changes in consumer tastes, economics, and technological innovation can diminish the hard-earned point of differentiation for a firm's products and services.

MINI-CASE: NIKE VERSUS REEBOK

That is what happened to Nike between 1986 and 1988 when Reebok surpassed Nike in the athletic footwear market. Each of the firms had a specific point of differentiation. Nike stressed technological leadership and superior product performance. Founder Phil Knight's background as an elite track runner in the 1960s ensured that the firm's strategy would be "if we build the best shoe, the consumer would buy it."[1] Reebok, and others such as L.A. Gear, focused, instead, on trendy fashion. They made colorful aerobic shoes that sold mostly to women. Nike's fortunes faded with the running boom of the 1970s when it acted like a typical industry leader—Nike missed the trend toward women's aerobic shoes. As a result, Reebok surpassed Nike in 1986 to gain market leadership. Nike had a choice to make. It could doggedly stick to its performance-based differentiation strategy, or it, too, could focus on fashion and change with the times. Then the trend changed again. Like many fashion trends, the appeal of the flashy fashion athletic shoes was short-lived. Poor quality by Reebok, the introduction of Nike's wildly successful air insoles, and heavy advertising and endorsement efforts by Nike caused consumers, once again, to prefer performance over flashy fashion. Nike sprinted passed Reebok. After 1989 it was never even a contest. Nike's sales rocketed from $1.2 billion in 1988 to $2.2 billion in 1990, to $3.8 billion in 1993. According to data compiled by Sporting Goods Intelligence, Nike held 37 percent of the market in 1995 compared to Reebok's 21 percent share. Reebok's response?

Go for performance. With so-called innovations like "pump" shoes, which had to be pumped up with air, Reebok's CEO Paul Fireman set out to "attack Nike's jugular, the performance athletic shoe market."[2] Reebok's newest ad campaign (as of 1996) stressed preparing to win, a clear indicator of its performance-based strategy. Will it work? Can Reebok successfully change its point of differentiation? So far, Nike remains firmly in the lead, and over the past few years that lead has been widening. Other competitors, specifically Fila and Adidas, are gaining market share, although their combined share is still less than half that of number two Reebok. Reebok, meanwhile, has lost share. Can the trend be reversed? What would you do if you were Reebok's marketing manager?

COMPETITION BETWEEN LOW-COST PRODUCERS

Low-cost producers compete among themselves as well as with sellers of higher-priced, premium products.

A SUCCESSION OF LOW-COST PRODUCERS

Firms that sell strictly on the basis of price run the risk that other sellers, with even lower cost structures, will enter the market and gain share by offering even lower prices. Often, a succession of lower-cost entrants enter sequentially as the market expands and sales volume grows.

MINI-CASE: MICROWAVE OVENS—A SUCCESSION OF LOW-COST PRODUCERS

The microwave oven is one of the most influential innovations of the postwar period. It was first conceived in 1942 when Percy Spencer, an engineer at the Raytheon Corp., discovered a chocolate bar in his pocket had melted while he worked on a radar system to detect Nazi planes. Spencer instantly glimpsed the commercial possibilities of his discovery. He cut a hole in a kitchen kettle and inserted a radar-producing magnetron, thus creating Raytheon's first, crude "Radarange."

The earliest microwave ovens were cumbersome devices that stood six feet tall, weighed 750 pounds, and sold for up to $3,000 in the late 1940s. In 1955, the Tappan Stove Co. released a prototype of a "miniature" 170-pound air-cooled, $1,195 microwave oven. That was before experience effects kicked in. Prices were so high and reliability was so incredibly poor that few consumers were interested in the new cooking wonder.

By 1965, a total of only ten thousand microwave ovens were in use in the United States. Heating food from vending machines was a popular use. College students would purchase frozen food from a dormitory vending machine and heat it up in a nearby microwave. At about the same time, Raytheon acquired the Amana Refrigeration Company of Iowa.

Demand for microwave ovens started to grow in 1970. Sales reached 55,000 units a year and experience effects began to accumulate. Retail prices fell to about $600 a unit. Raytheon's Amana and Litton were the two leading sellers.

But the April 1973 issue of *Consumer Reports* argued that microwave ovens might leak "radiation" into consumer's homes. It concluded: "we are not convinced that they are completely safe to use. We've therefore designated them all Not Recommended."[3]

Even with negative publicity, sales of microwaves grew to 314,000 units in 1972. To counteract fears of radiation, both Amana and Litton adopted a strategy of selling high-quality, premium-priced products. Neither firm wanted to compete on price. Instead, they offered additional features such as Amana's "Touchmatic" controls and temperature probes.

The Japanese electronics giants entered in the mid-1970s with a low-cost, low-price strategy. They had accumulated considerable experience producing small, no-frills, inexpensive microwave ovens for the Japanese market where small living spaces valued those products. Sharp quickly became the leading import, selling ovens under its own name and as a private label for Sears. The Japanese sellers were willing to accept lower profit margins. They focused on gaining market share.

For a while it looked like the market would support both strategies. But, by 1980, price emerged as the most important feature. As the market expanded, the entire product category transformed itself from one of differentiated goods to low-priced commodities. That favored the Japanese sellers, who offered consumers the low-priced, no-frills ovens they wanted. The American sellers were doomed. They found themselves selling a premium product that few consumers would pay extra for. Sharp's share of the market rose rapidly in the early 1980s, pushed by relentless price cutting.

Sales of microwave ovens skyrocketed to 10.9 million units in 1985. Experience effects pushed prices down to $150 for the smallest units. By then microwave ovens were little more than a low-priced commodity. Consumers judged all ovens to be of acceptable quality and picked the least expensive. Margins turned razor thin.

The Koreans entered the market in the early 1980s with even lower prices than the Japanese. Just as the Japanese had gained share from the American sellers with lower prices so, too, did the Koreans now gain share from the Japanese. Korea's Samsung relied on reverse engineering. It examined ovens from the world's top producers, selected the best features of each, then applied a talent for low-cost manufacturing to win private label business from price-conscious sellers in the United States. Samsung started with a small order from J.C. Penney, then produced low-end models for GE. Korea's Goldstar made low-end models for Kmart, J.C. Penney, and Magic Chef.

In 1987 sales reached a record 12.6 million units. But imports held a 75 percent share of that market. By 1990, Litton was down to a 3.9 percent share while Amana held a sad 4.5 percent of microwave sales. Sharp, in contrast, had 13.5 percent while GE held 11.2 percent of the market selling Korean-made ovens.

The case of microwave ovens illustrates that there are sometimes waves of low-cost producers that enter once the market starts to grow and volume increases. What is surprising is that the Koreans ended up dominating the market even though they started from scratch with no experience.

In your opinion, is there anything the U.S. sellers could have done to maintain their market share in the face of such brutal competition?

PRICE SHIFTING

Competition among low-cost producers can be so brutal that prices sometimes fall below costs. Consider the case of record, tape, and compact disc retailers. The market for their products is growing. Sales rose steadily during the first half of the 1990s. But retail profit margins fell as competitors sought to build sales volume with ever-lower prices. As a result, many record retailers are either losing money or making only a tiny profit. The economics of the industry tell why. It costs record producers roughly one dollar to make a CD, which wholesales for about $10.[4] The retailer then sells that CD for as low as $8, even though the list price can be $18. Why does that happen? The record producers—Sony, Warner, MCA, Polygram, EMI—make a tidy profit. But retailers battle with price. Many large retailers sell CDs as a "loss leader," in the hopes that consumers will pick up something else when they come in to buy a record. The loss on records is made up for by the profits on other products. Record-only retailers are at a price disadvantage. They carry only records and have no opportunity for cross-subsidization. The price war forces them to keep costs as low as possible so they can compete in a low-margin business.

A similar situation has evolved in computer software. CompUSA and the other big computer retailers sell software at below or near cost in order to build traffic for hardware in their superstores. That squeezes the profits out of software-only retailers who cannot cross-subsidize.

Price shifting can be driven by other motives as well. Some manufacturers entice customers with low prices on the initial purchase then make extraordinary profits on replacement parts or complementary products. For years, Polaroid sold its instant cameras at near cost and made profits on film sales. Price competition was nonexistent since its film was protected by strong patents. A similar situation exists in the ink-jet printer business. Market leader Hewlett-Packard prices its printers low then makes margins as high as 60 percent on sales of its ink-jet cartridges, which sell for about $30 apiece. Competitors charge "that H-P specifically designs into its ink-jet refills some sort of mechanism that rejects other products."[5] That creates imperfect competition that keep prices high and competitors at bay.

Competitors are kept out by the threat of protracted legal suits. Companies such as Dallas-based Nu-kote recycle H-P cartridges, refill them, and then sell them at lower prices. H-P has reacted to the newfound price competition with charges of patent infringement.

EVERYDAY LOW PRICES VERSUS HIGH-LOW
PROMOTIONAL PRICING

Competing on price usually entails using one of two competing pricing strategies. The first, "high-low" promotional pricing, sets very low prices—either near or below cost—on a few featured specials and earns profits on the rest of the items in the line (or in the store), which are priced much higher. The other choice, everyday low prices (EDLP), avoids loss leaders. It charges the lowest possible prices for every item in the store (or in the line) all the time. Advocates of EDLP include Wal-Mart, Price Club, Toys 'R' Us, and Home Depot.

Each strategy has its own unique set of advantages and disadvantages. High-low promotional pricing gives the sheen of very low prices, even though only a fraction of the merchandise is really on sale at any one time. It also allows consumers to engage in a form of self-selected price discrimination. Consumers willing to clip coupons and stock up during specials end up paying much lower prices. Those that do not pay much higher prices. Most estimates hold that, on average, prices paid under a high-low promotional pricing system are about 10 percent higher than under an EDLP system.

The downside of high-low pricing is that the system has gotten out of hand. Wholesalers and retailers have become addicted to case-off deals, slotting fees, store performance incentives, and popular practices such as forward buying.

EDLP saves money by eliminating many of those wasteful practices. It sends a quieter, more stable message to customers. It implies that the firm offers consistently better value. Consumers no longer have to worry whether the price they paid will be lower or higher tomorrow. The disadvantage of EDLP is that it does not allow firms to focus on that one featured loss leader.

Low-price sellers using both strategic approaches to pricing can be found in most markets.

COMPETITION BETWEEN SEGMENTERS AND MASS MARKETERS

Some markets are characterized by increasing industry concentration. Large firms merge with even larger firms in order to increase their bargaining power with suppliers and customers and dominate the markets they serve. That puts small sellers at a disadvantage. Unable to achieve the economies of scale held by the largest sellers, they are easy prey to price cutters. Home Depot in hardware, Toys 'R' Us, and Wal-Mart versus the small town independent retailers are a few examples of large firms that use size to consolidate markets.

WHEN A SEGMENT GROWS LARGER AND MORE ATTRACTIVE

Often a small firm starts out in a segment that is too small to attract large competitors. The small firm is left alone to serve some tiny corner of the market. But sometimes, the segment grows larger and attracts the interest of powerful market leaders with great resources and a desire to have a piece of the action. That creates a dilemma for the segmenter. The firm faces not only the good times created by a growing market but also the bad times brought on by more formidable competitors. The outcome can go either way.

MINI-CASE: BRIAN MAXWELL'S POWERBARS

In the late 1970s, Brian Maxwell was a top-rated marathoner. There was only one problem. If he ate something substantial before a big race he got severe cramps and diarrhea, which, needless to say, hindered his performance. If he had nothing to eat, he ran out of energy before the race ended. Either way, he could not perform to his maximum. That personal dilemma led him to develop a high-energy, low-fat, easy-to-digest "sports bar." Between 1983 and 1986 he mixed a variety of grains, proteins, and other wholesome ingredients into more than eight hundred experimental "powerbars," as the product was later branded, and spent his weekends handing out the bars at races near his San Francisco–area home. Slowly but surely he honed in on the right formulation. His market research consisted solely of asking others what they liked best. Then, in February 1986, he and his wife-to-be Jennifer put their life savings into a single production run of 40,000 PowerBars. Through word of mouth and direct mail selling the Maxwells found themselves with a thriving business based on an innovative new product. They ran a bare-bones operation throughout most of the late 1980s as they poured money back into the business to fund further growth. Retailers picked up the product nationwide. By 1994 sales had reached $30 million per year and their firm was growing by 40 percent per year. The two-and-a-quarter-ounce product packed with vitamins, minerals, and carbohydrates contained just 230 calories with only 2 grams of fat. At a retail price of $1.69 couch potatoes joined elite athletes in chowing down on the taffy-like substance. What Gatorade did for drinks, PowerBar was doing for sustenance. What had been a small niche product was now becoming a high-growth market. Brian and Jennifer Maxwell had inadvertently created an entirely new food product category. That attracted the attention of large sellers in allied fields. Quaker Oats, in particular, threatened to step into the market with its Gatorade brand. With $30 million in annual sales, the Maxwells could not hope to match the resources of the food industry giant. Hoping to capitalize on its brand equity Quaker Oats named its entry "GatorBar." It then replaced PowerBar as the official sponsor of the prestigious Hawaii Ironman Triathlon. As of 1996, PowerBar still holds the commanding market share position. The Maxwells can now produce more than 100,000 PowerBars a day in their own factories. They claim that offers to sell out to a larger company are pouring in.

In your opinion, what will the competitive outcome be? Will the Maxwells sell out? Should they try to compete? Is their brand name powerful enough for the small firm to be able to maintain its leadership position or will a larger firm win out?

WHEN SEGMENTERS STEAL SHARE FROM MARKET LEADERS

Sometimes markets expand beyond the mass-market offerings of the largest sellers. That creates an opportunity for a small segmenter to move way upscale and offer a cachet and exclusivity not available to the large seller. In fact, the brand name of the market leader may actually be an impediment to a competitive response. The large seller may have become so successful that its name cannot be transferred to small, premium-priced products at the highest end of the market. In such instances, some consumers are willing to pay extra for a much higher quality product.

MINI-CASE: SPECIALTY COFFEES VERSUS
FOLGERS AND MAXWELL HOUSE

Per capita consumption of coffee in the United States has been stagnant for decades. Procter & Gamble's Folgers and Philip Morris's Maxwell House dominate the $4 billion retail market with efficiently produced brands that often compete on the basis of price. First one seller cuts prices to gain share, then the other follows. This push for lower prices has resulted in lower cost and lower quality coffee beans. Bitter taste has followed lower prices.

That has created an opportunity for sellers of premium coffees that sell at much higher prices. By 1995 almost 20 percent of all coffee sales were in the form of whole beans, which are ground by the consumer. The fresh coffee segment represents one of the few bright spots in an otherwise stagnant market. The segment, which is growing by 10 percent per year, is dominated by small specialty sellers, not the two major brands. The segmenters excel on quality while the two large sellers compete strictly on price.

Maxwell House tried to react by introducing an upscale version of its standard brand, called Maxwell House "Private Collection," but the brand name did not transfer well. Consumers would not pay a premium price for a mass-market brand. What else could they have done to gain a position in this growing segment of the market? What are the advantages and disadvantages of the large and small sellers in this specialty market?

MINI-CASE:MICROBREWERIES VERSUS
ANHEUSER-BUSCH AND MILLER

Segmenters have also gained share at the expense of large industry leaders in the beer industry. Microbrews come in some odd flavors at much higher prices but offer higher quality, deeper taste, and the mystique of homemade charm missing in the mass-market brands. It is truly a competition between giants and Lilliputians. Whereas Anheuser-Busch sells more than 40 million barrels of Bud every year, a typical microbrewer is lucky to sell fifteen thousand barrels. But the prices are higher at the microbreweries, and the product category represents one of the few growing areas in the otherwise mature, and in some cases even declining, market. In this case, though, the large brewers have reacted in kind. To insure against further inroads by the small microbreweries, both Bud and Miller have introduced their own bevy of specialty brews. Anheuser-Busch sells Red Wolf, Elk Mountain, Crossroads, and Redhook Ale. Miller sells Red Dog and Ice House. Coors comes in with Sandlot and George Killian. Unlike the case of specialty coffees, the large sellers do not use their own brand names. The goal is to appear to be a micro-brewer. They understand that consumers in search of home brew do not want one from a huge company. The huge brewing giants are using their distribution muscle to entice bars to stock only their brands. Their many brews now fill up the taps at local watering holes. Patrons often have no choice but to select the small-volume beers of the large sellers. As a result, microbrews are forced to find other channels of distribution, often selling in their own small-scale brew pubs, which further enhances their reputation for uniqueness. Will the microbrew segment continue to grow? Or is it merely a fad? Will it stay in the hands of the small sell-ers? Is there anything else the large sellers can do to enhance their posi-tion in this most attractive segment of the market?

WITHIN-SEGMENT COMPETITION

Competition within narrowly defined segments can be especially brutal. By definition, customers are the same and prices tend to be the same, as are features and styling. Even distribution tends to be the same. These similar-priced products are so tightly defined that it is more difficult to engineer in truly important differences. Consider, again, the case of watches. Timex sports watches compete head on with Casio and Lorus (Seiko) sports watches. Most have similar features and prices. Substi-tutability is high.

NOTES

[1]Barbara Buell, "Nike Catches Up with the Trendy Frontrunner," *Business Week,* October 24, 1988, p. 88.
[2]Geoffrey Smith, "Can Reebok Regain Its Balance," *Business Week,* December 20, 1993, p. 108.
[3]"Microwave Ovens: Not Recommended," *Consumer Reports,* April 1973, p. 221.
[4]Amy Feldman, "Somebody's Eating My Lunch," *Forbes,* December 4, 1995, pp. 166–67.
[5]Michael Unger, "Seeing Red Over Color Ink-Jets," *Newsday,* Money & Careers Section, December 3, 1995, p. 4.

CHAPTER 10

MARKET-SHARE STRATEGIES

Over the years, more attention has been paid to market share than any other marketing variable. That interest results from a long history of research that shows that higher share leads to higher profits. This chapter examines four possibilities: (1) gaining share, (2) holding or maintaining share, (3) harvesting, and (4) divestment or abandonment. Exhibit 10.1 illustrates each of those strategies arrayed as to their level of commitment to the product or service.

GAINING MARKET SHARE

Gaining or building market share is an offensive or attack strategy aimed at trying to increase market position at the expense of competitors. A

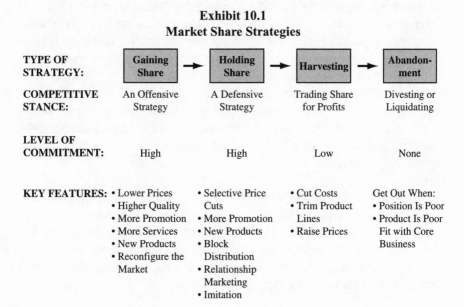

Exhibit 10.1
Market Share Strategies

TYPE OF STRATEGY:	Gaining Share	Holding Share	Harvesting	Abandonment
COMPETITIVE STANCE:	An Offensive Strategy	A Defensive Strategy	Trading Share for Profits	Divesting or Liquidating
LEVEL OF COMMITMENT:	High	High	Low	None
KEY FEATURES:	• Lower Prices • Higher Quality • More Promotion • More Services • New Products • Reconfigure the Market	• Selective Price Cuts • More Promotion • New Products • Block Distribution • Relationship Marketing • Imitation	• Cut Costs • Trim Product Lines • Raise Prices	Get Out When: • Position Is Poor • Product Is Poor Fit with Core Business

firm builds market share by stealing it from others. There is a conspicuous sense of a battle. Discussions of share gaining are rife with allusions
to military combat.

WHEN TO GAIN SHARE

Gaining share is expensive and risky and takes more than desire on the part
of the firm wishing to gain share. The overwhelming conclusion of research
on the topic is that it is not always possible nor advisable to gain share.
Firms should seek share gains only when the situation is right and when
they have the appropriate resources. Share gains are most appropriate when
one or some combination of the following five conditions is present.

1. In High-Growth Markets. Competition is often thought to be less severe
in high-growth markets. That is a central premise of the product life cycle.
The argument is that building share is easiest when a market is new and
competitors have not had a chance to establish an impenetrable position.
Competitors are less likely to fight hard when their own sales are growing.
There are fewer reasons to start a price war when the pie is expanding.

2. When the Firm Has Developed a Breakthrough Innovation. The
introduction of a major new product creates an opportunity to gain share
from an existing product. That new product may offer consumers better
performance or lower costs.

3. When an Acquisition Can Be Expanded. A small startup with a hot
product may be starved for cash for expansion. When a large firm with
deep pockets acquires the small firm, it may be able to transform it into
a larger market opportunity. That is what happened with Gatorade when
it moved from the University of Florida in the 1960s to Stokely–Van
Camp in 1967 and was then acquired by Quaker Oats in 1983. At each
step more money was pumped into the growing acquisition, transform-
ing it from a small beverage aimed at serious athletes to a strong contender in soft drinks. Gatorade is now the number one sports drink in the
world and the number one product within Quaker Oats.

4. When a Competitor Is Unwilling to Fight Back. There are five reasons why a market leader may be unwilling to defend its share.
    First the leader may be unwilling to sacrifice profit margins. Consider
the case of Sorrell Ridge, a small jam seller that gained share on Smucker's, the market leader. Sorrell Ridge sweetens its jams with 100 percent
fruit, a more expensive but higher-quality approach. Smucker's uses cane

sugar and corn sweeteners, which costs less than half as much as pure fruit. Jams and jellies sweetened with fruit are the fastest-growing segment because of their natural appeal. Smucker's dilemma is as follows: Do they match Sorrell Ridge, and raise their costs and lower profits greatly? Or, do they ignore the attack and hope it goes away? In 1989 Smucker's introduced an all-fruit knock-off but they would prefer consumers simply to continue to buy the traditional Smucker's product. To paraphrase Smucker's ad byline, with a strategy like that it has to be good.[1]

Second, the share leader may be preoccupied with opportunities in other industries. It may be focusing its attention elsewhere and not on the point of the challenge.

Third, the share leader may be unwilling to spend the funds necessary to defend its dominant share of the market. It may be willing to cede market position rather than spend to defend.

Fourth, in some industries there may be no history of vigorous competition. In fact, competition may be viewed as a "gentlemen's game," where retaliations are considered undignified.[2] Twenty years ago, in the wine industry, for example, there was little advertising, few promotions, and meager competition in comparison to soft drinks, beer, and other beverage markets. That all changed when Coca-Cola entered the market, trying to gain share in that gentlemen's market. A similar situation exists in the professions, where lawyers, doctors, dentists, and accountants still argue over whether advertising is beneath their dignity.

Fifth, and finally, some market leaders are "asleep at the wheel." They seemingly invite new entrants to attack their markets. But sometimes those lackadaisical sleeping giants are awakened by the shock of a new entrant in their midst. Consider, once again, the wine industry in the early 1980s. When Coca-Cola entered the industry with the intent of gaining share for its newly acquired Taylor brand it conducted taste tests and other marketing practices unheard of in the refined business of selling wine. Industry incumbents were shocked when Taylor gained share. But they also awakened a sleepy giant. Gallo, the industry leader, possessed overwhelming economies of scale. As a result, Coca-Cola divested Taylor a few years later. Competition at the low end of the wine market turned out to be higher than expected.

5. When a Competitor Is Unable to Fight Back. Defending share is expensive. In some situations a competitor may have the desire to defend its share but lack the strength to do so. There are two basic reasons why a competitor would be unable to respond to the competitive threats of an attacker.

First, the defender may be a large firm in financial trouble. The rash of takeovers and leveraged buyouts that occurred in the 1980s left many firms starved for cash. They could not respond to increases in advertising and promotion that less leveraged competitors used in an attempt to gain share by raising the marketing stakes. Those market leaders had to concentrate on paying the banks. They could not afford to pay attention to their competitor's actions. Many lost share.

In the Northeast, Home Depot, the home improvement powerhouse, entered just as Rickel's, a regional chain, was struggling to survive the effects of heavy debt brought on by a leveraged buyout. Not only is Home Depot a potent competitor in its own right, but it faced a weakened competitor with no money to compete. Rickel's simply closed up shop in locations where Home Depot entered.

The same thing happened to Ticketron, the leading computerized ticketing service. Until the mid-1980s, if you wanted to buy a ticket to a concert or a sporting event you almost certainly would have done business with Ticketron. But Ticketron was owned by Control Data, which in 1985 defaulted on nearly $400 million of debt due to its ailing mainframe computer business. There was no money to battle Ticketmaster, a spunky upstart. Little by little, Ticketmaster stole accounts and market share from Ticketron, which could not fight back.

It is important to note that share battles are expensive for both the attacking firm and the defender, and come at the expense of short-term profits. A firm must have the resources and the willingness to fight the battle or lose share.

The second reason why a defender would be unable to fight back is because of a resource mismatch. Small firms simply cannot match the marketing muscle of large, well-financed giants. That is why large chains of drugstores, hardware stores, bookstores, toy stores, and real estate offices have stolen share from independent mom-and-pop operators with far fewer resources. They pit strength against weakness.

Consider the case of bookstores. Ten years ago, the market was populated by many independent sellers. Then the chains moved in. Barnes and Noble, Borders, Dalton, and a host of others built big box bookstores that dwarfed mom-and-pop operators. The chains had the buying power of large volume, heavy discounts, and new sit-and-browse formats. The independents had higher costs, lower volume, and higher prices. One by one they went out of business. They could not compete.

HOW TO GAIN SHARE

Gaining share can be accomplished in a number of ways, the more important of which are described in the following discussion.

1. Lowering Prices. One of the most common ways to gain share is to lower prices. Firms strive to build a lower cost position than competitors and pass those savings along to customers in the form of lower prices.

2. Increasing Promotion. Alternative approaches to building market share favor non-price actions. One is to increase advertising and promotional expenditures vis-à-vis competitors. There are two variations on that theme. The first is a strategy of sheer financial power, which entails huge promotional expenditures to overcome the advantage of the incumbent. Bud Light, for example, has used a no-holds-barred advertising blitz, spanning decades, to buy the leading share of the light beer market. A second option looks for markets where promotion has been underspent in the past. A large firm then steps in, raises the level of advertising, and gains share against weaker or less committed opponents. Coke's foray into wines, for example, increased promotional spending in an underspent market and led to share gains.

3. New Products. New products create excitement in an industry and can be used to build share. A firm that increases its rate of innovation and speeds new products to market can easily gain share on a more stodgy competitor.

4. Improving Product Quality. Extensive research has shown that a strategy of selling better products (where better is defined broadly) can gain share just as easily as a strategy based on lower prices. One landmark study found that increasing quality led to higher market share and higher profits.[3] An earlier study using the PIMS database found that share gains were related not only to quality improvements but to new product activity and an increase in marketing expenditures as well.[4] Most often, a combination of those factors was responsible for the gain in market share. Interestingly, the study found no relationship between price cutting and share gains. Price cuts, they surmised, were too easily matched.

5. Increasing Service. As C. Davis Fogg argued more than twenty years ago, improving the level of service, a part of the total product offering, can be used to gain share.[5]

6. Breaking the Rules. Changing a product or market in some way that negates the market leader's advantage or doing something different that shakes up the industry can create an opportunity to gain share. It can entail pioneering a new channel of distribution, as Timex did in low-end watches, or eliminating middlemen, as YKK, a leading seller of zippers, did. Or, it can consist of making instead of licensing a prestigious fashion item as some apparel companies do. The possibilities for gaining share by breaking the rules are nearly endless. They require creativity and risk taking, and a willingness to rethink the entire appeal of a product or market needs. When Perrier was introduced in the United States, for example, it was positioned as a healthful alternative to soda pop. Before that time, most sellers sold bottled waters as a way to avoid pollution that might be present in tap water.

In sum, whatever the means, gaining market share is an expensive proposition with high risks and heavy short-term costs. Building share requires a strong commitment from the attacker, and, it is hoped, a lesser commitment from the defender.

HOLDING SHARE

Holding or maintaining market share is a defensive strategy that seeks to protect what has already been gained. It is a reaction to an attacker's challenge.

The advantage in holding share belongs to the defender. As in war, it is almost always easier to hang on to the share you have than to steal some from someone else. Theory backs that commonsensical observation up. Market leaders purportedly have stronger experience effects than lower-share firms. They also have more money to wage marketing battles.

Commitment is a key component of a successful defense. The attacker is sure to ask whether the market leader has strongly defended its share in the past. Procter & Gamble, a superb marketer, entered the well-defended market for orange juice with its Citrus Hill brand in the 1980s and had little success gaining share. Tropicana, which is owned by Seagram's, and Minute Maid, owned by Coca-Cola, vigorously defended their shares. In the absence of any special product feature, P&G could only cut prices. That drove up costs and never led to any appreciable share gains. As a result, P&G liquidated its Citrus Hill product without ever having gained a significant share of the market.

HOW TO HOLD SHARE

The tactics for defending share are basically the same as those used to gain share.

1. Selective Price Cuts. In theory, market leaders can cut costs more effectively than smaller attackers. But market leaders also have more to lose if the price cut is made over the entire volume of sales. Since market leaders have the dominant share they have greater experience effects but they also take a bigger hit to margins. As a result, market leaders are often reluctant to make outright price cuts. Selective price reductions that target the attacking product are an option. By targeting the price cuts to only part of the market, or to only a few products in the line, the defending firm exposes only part of its sales to lower prices. That strategy works especially well against smaller competitors with no other source of income. They cannot retaliate across a broad front.

Hershey Food Corp., for example, tried to enter the cake frosting business with the intent to gain share. Their luscious chocolate entry should have been a strong contender. Instead, it failed badly. Market leaders cut prices on their cake frostings and raised prices on their cake mixes. Hershey could not retaliate. It had no cake mix. The defense was successful. Hershey gained no share.

2. Price Cutting in the Attacker's Home Market. A variation of selective price cutting is to cut prices in the attacker's home market, sapping the attacker's source of funds. Consider the case of a small airline expanding into the profitable route of a larger carrier. The small airline is funding its entry from profitable routes it already runs. A cross-parry by the larger airline would entail expanding into the profitable routes of the smaller airlines and cutting prices. The goal of that strategy is to sap the financial strength of the weaker opponent.

3. Heavy Promotional Spending. Heavy spending on advertising and promotion also favors the share leader. The defender has a larger volume over which to spread promotional expenditures. In an all-out war the advantage in promotional spending lies with the market leader.

4. A Focus on Cutting Edge Innovation. Innovation can also be used defensively. As detailed in the chapter on differentiation, market leaders can thwart the moves of aggressive competitors by flooding the market with new products, leaving no room for the attacker to leapfrog current products.

5. Blocking Access to Distribution. The rapid introduction of new products offers another benefit to market leaders. It leaves no shelf space for competitors' new products. The introduction of "make-believe" microbrews by major beer sellers is largely an attempt to thwart distribution for smaller sellers. Exclusive agreements, backward integration, and other defensive measures can be used to keep others from gaining share.

6. Signaling Commitment. Firms looking to gain share will look for opportunities where competitors will not fight back. That makes it easier for them. Competitors will be reluctant to attack committed competitors.

Attacking new products in test markets is one way to signal commitment. It shows the ferocity of competitive retaliation if the attacker enters the larger market. Often, defending firms offer two-for-one coupons or blanket a test market area with free samples of their own product while a competitor's test market is in progress. More insidious, defending firms sometimes buy up large quantities of the test-marketed product to analyze and reverse engineer. As a result, the firm running the test market might mistakenly conclude that it has a sure winner on its hands when it really has a dog.

Fighting brands are also used defensively. Fighting brands are peripheral brands used to fend off attacks on the mother brand. Pick a fight with the mother brand and the defending firm will counter with the fighting brand.

Commitment is the key to market share retention. If competitors think that the defender is not interested, and that they can enter unopposed, they will do so.

7. Relationship Marketing. The recent interest on forming tying relationships with customers has the effect of precluding competitors from gaining share. A customer who has promised loyalty to a single seller (in return for some valued reward) is unable to satisfy a competitor's lust for additional share.

8. Vigorous Later Entry. Often, a market leader misses a major new product opportunity in its home market. It allows an attacker to win share with a strategy of innovation. But all is not lost. Sometimes the defender can regain the lost share through vigorous later entry. Entering a market after the attacker, with a competitive advantage, can often serve as the best defense against an attacker's offensive use of innovation. As Exhibit 10.2 illustrates, many of the most prominent innovations of the past few decades were pioneered by attackers but ultimately dominated by market leaders that were later entrants. They did so by using some combination of the following three strategies:

Later entrants often regain the share lost through imitation and improvement. They introduce a superior product that is *second but better.* To do so, the defender must have an advantage in brand name, reputation for quality, or distribution.

Another response is *imitation coupled with heavy promotional expenditures.* Large market leaders, like Coke and Pepsi, for example, possess an unmatchable competitive advantage in terms of promotional expenditures over smaller rivals such as Royal Crown Cola. Once the market proves itself, the large firms step in with advertising and distribution advantages and dominate the market.

Finally, some leaders *cut prices* for a simpler version of the new product, which is targeted more toward the more price-sensitive mass market.

Exhibit 10.2
Seventeen Cases Where Imitators Surpassed Pioneers

Product	Pioneer(s)	Imitator/Later Entrant(s)	Comments
1. Automated Teller Machines (ATMs)	Britain's DeLaRue (1967) Docutel (1969)	Diebold (1971) IBM (1973) NCR (1974)	The pioneer was a small, entrepreneurial upstart that faced two types of competitors: (1) larger firms with experience selling to banks and (2) the computer giants. The pioneer did not survive.
2. Ballpoint Pens	Reynolds (1945) Eversharp (1946)	Parker "Jotter" (1954) Bic (1960)	The pioneers disappeared when the fad first ended in the late 1940s. Parker entered eight years later. Bic entered last and sold pens as cheap disposables.
3. Caffeine-Free Soft Drinks	Canada Dry's "Sport" 1967 Royal Crown's RC100 (1980)	Pepsi Free (1982) Caffeine-free Coke, Diet Coke, Tab (1983)	The pioneer had a three-year head start on Coke but could not hope to match the distribution and promotional advantages of the giants.
4. CAT Scanners (Computed Axial Tomography)	EMI (1972)	Pfizer (1974) Technicare (1975) GE (1976) Johnson & Johnson (1978)	The pioneer had no experience in the medical equipment industry. Copycats ignored its patents and drove the pioneer out of business with marketing, distribution, and financial advantages, as well as extensive industry experience.
5. Commercial Jet Aircraft	deHavilland Comet 1 (1952)	Boeing 707 (1958) Douglas DC-8	The British pioneer rushed to market with a jet that crashed frequently. Boeing followed with safer, larger, and more powerful jets with an unsullied safety record.

(continued)

Exhibit 10.2 *(continued)*

Product	Pioneer(s)	Imitator/Later Entrant(s)	Comments
6. Diet Soft Drinks	Kirsch's No-Cal (1952) Royal Crown's Diet Rite Cola (1962)	Pepsi's Patio Cola (1963) Coke's Tab (1963) Diet Pepsi (1964) Diet Coke (1982)	The pioneer could not match the distribution advantages of Coke and Pepsi. Nor did it have the money needed for massive promotional campaigns.
7. Dry Beer	Asahi (1987)	Kirin, Sapporo, and Suntory in Japan (1988) Michelob Dry (1988) Bud Dry (1989)	The Japanese pioneer could not match Anheuser-Busch's financial, marketing, and distribution advantages in the U.S. market.
8. Food Processors	Cuisinart (1973)	Lower-priced Copies by Black and Decker (late-1970s) Sunbeam "Oskar" (1984)	The pioneer failed to sell lower-priced models. A leveraged buyout drove it into bankruptcy when the market became price sensitive.
9. Light Beer	Rheingold's "Gablinger's" (1966) Meister-Bräu "Lite" (1967)	Miller Lite (1975) Natural Light (1977) Coors Light (1978) Bud Light (1982)	The pioneers entered nine years before Miller and 16 years before Bud Light but financial problems drove both out of business. Marketing and distribution determined the outcome. Costly legal battles were commonplace.
10. Mainframe Computers	Atanasoff's ABC computer (1939) Eckert-Mauchly's ENIAC/UNIVAC (1946)	IBM (1953)	The marketing muscle of IBM, in particular its powerful sales force, proved no match for the tiny upstart. When the giant entered, it moved quickly to the forefront.
11. Money-Market Mutual Funds	Reserve Fund of New York (1973)	Dreyfus Liquid Assets (1974) Fidelity Daily Income Trust (1974) Merrill Lynch Ready Assets (1975)	The tiny pioneer could not match the marketing, distribution, and financial advantages, as well as the reputation benefits, held by the imitators. Size mattered more than first entry. The later entrants swamped the pioneer with product variety.

Exhibit 10.2 *(continued)*

Product	Pioneer(s)	Imitator/Later Entrant(s)	Comments
12. MRI (Magnetic Resonance Imaging)	Fonar (1978)	Johnson & Johnson's Technicare (1981) General Electric (1982)	The tiny pioneer faced the huge medical equipment suppliers, which easily expanded into MRIs. The pioneer could not hope to match their tremendous market power.
13. Non-Alcoholic Beer	G. Heileman's "Kingsbuy" (early 1980s) Switzerland's "Moussy" (1983)	Miller's "Sharp's" (1989) Anheuser-Busch's "O'Doul's" (1989) Coors "Cutter" (1991)	The innovators had a six-year head start but first-mover advantages were no match for the marketing and distribution advantages of the later entrants. Heileman was in bankruptcy by the time the imitators entered.
14. Personal Computers	MITS Altair 8800 (1975) Apple II (1977) Radio Shack (1977)	IBM-PC (1981) Compaq (1982) Dell (1984) Gateway (1985)	The pioneers created computers for hobbyists, but when the market turned to business uses, IBM entered and quickly dominated using its reputation, marketing, and distribution skills. The cloners then copied IBM's standard and sold at lower prices.
15. Pocket Calculators	Bowmar (1971)	Texas Instruments (1972)	The pioneer assembled calculators using TI's integrated circuits. TI controlled Bowmar's costs, which rose as calculator prices fell. Vertical integration was the key.
16. Projection Television	Advent (1973) Sony (1973 with an industrial model) Kloss Video (1977)	Panasonic (1978) Mitsubishi (1980)	Everything seemed to be arrayed against the pioneer. It had no money and was beset by internal strife. It also faced Japanese giants who lowered prices and introduced a new design that rendered the pioneer's product obsolete. The pioneer went bankrupt.
17. Telephone Answering Machines	Code-A-Phone (1958)	Panasonic (mid-1970s) AT&T (1983)	The pioneer was late to move production overseas. It could not match the low-cost production of the later entrants with shared experience in related products.
18. Word-Processing Software	Wordstar (1979)	WordPerfect (1982) Microsoft Word (1983)	The pioneer was stuck with an obsolete standard when it failed to update. When it did update, Wordstar abandoned loyal users, offered no technical support and fought internally. The followers took advantage.

HARVESTING STRATEGIES

Harvesting is a compromise between defending and divesting. Harvesting extracts cash from products that face imminent decline or prolonged stagnation of demand. It is a recognition that the business or product can still generate income, but that future prospects do not justify heavy reinvestment. Harvesting is, in essence, a tax of products that face a bleak future. The receipts of that tax are better spent on more promising opportunities. A euphemism for harvesting is "managing for cash flow."

The decision to harvest is a delicate one that depends on the answers to two key questions:

1. *What are the future prospects for the product or service?* Generally, harvesting is an option when a product or service competes in a declining market or has a poor market position. If there is no potential for future growth, profits are poor, and there is a better use for the money elsewhere, then harvesting should be considered.
2. *What will happen if investment in the business is reduced?* Will sales plummet or petrify? Amazingly, sales of many products do not decline rapidly when promotion is withdrawn or slashed drastically. Instead, market share and sales fall but level off at some lower level. In the parlance of harvesting, sales "petrify."

   Petrified demand occurs when promotional support is reduced or withdrawn from a brand, but the brand still attracts customers and is widely recalled by consumers. Many well-known brands continue to sell even though they receive little promotional support.

SUSTAINED HARVESTING

There are two very different types of harvesting. The first, sustained harvesting, extracts a moderate amount of cash over a long period of time with the intention of staying in the business for years to come. The guiding principle of sustained harvesting is to extract cash without destroying the product that provides that cash in the first place. Moderation is the key. The intention is to reduce costs drastically while reducing sales and market share only slightly. In many markets, petrified sales is a very attainable goal.

SEVERE HARVESTING

The second type of harvesting extracts a large amount of cash over a much shorter period of time. The goal is to get as much cash as possible out of the business before the bottom falls out of the market. There are many situations where severe harvesting is an option. Short-term harvesting is the best choice when a technological innovation has made an existing product obsolete. Compact discs, for example, have greatly affected the future prospects, and company support, for cassette tapes, once the most popular medium for music sales. Similarly, a model change may be in the works. Or, the market might simply be disappearing. In each instance, severe harvesting is the best choice.

HOW TO HARVEST

All harvesting is accomplished using the same basic set of marketing tools. They differ only in the degree to which they are applied. Severe harvesting uses them vigorously. Sustained harvesting applies them in moderation.

The essence of harvesting is to cut costs to the bone. These cost savings can come from many aspects of the business.[6]

- *Cutting marketing expenditures.* Firms routinely spend 3 percent to 6 percent of sales (depending on the product category) on advertising. Cut these expenditures and the money falls directly to the bottom line. Phil Kotler advises that firms should provide "splash advertising" to give the appearance of being interested. Offering deals to suppliers also helps gain continued distribution. It is important not to signal competitors or the trade that you are not interested in the business.
- *Cutting research and development expenditures.* At some firms, R&D costs can run between 3 percent and 6 percent of sales. Cuts in those costs also go directly to the bottom line.
- *Cutting plant and equipment expenditures.* In sustained harvesting it is often unnecessary to spend anywhere near as much as the product generates. In severe harvesting few investments are made at all. Broken windows are fixed but not much else.

Advertising, R&D, and plant and equipment expenditures build for future profits. Cutting them on viable products and services is a shortsighted tactic. But when their future is bleak, cutting them offers the only opportunity to obtain profits that would otherwise be lost. There is nothing to build for. The firm willingly trades a nonexistent long-term potential for quick profits.

- Service is expensive. *Service cuts* can be made in the amount and selection of inventory carried, delivery schedules, and the size and quality of the sales force.
- Small customers often take a disproportionate amount of the service effort. *Dropping small customers* can lower the costs of service with only a small loss in volume.

- Carrying many products in each line increases costs unnecessarily in a declining market. *Trim the number and depth of product lines* and the few remaining customers will be forced to choose from a more limited menu.
- A harvesting strategy may warrant the *substitution of cheaper materials.*
- Finally, in a declining market it is sometimes possible to *raise prices.* Remaining customers with ties to the declining product may be forced to pay more to gain supplies.

In essence, harvesting is a strategy that lives off the past good will of consumers. Abusing that good will can quickly boomerang unless the following steps are taken.

- *Feigning commitment.* A firm that sends clear signals that it is not interested in a product category and is harvesting profits will find wholesalers and retailers are reluctant to carry the product. It is important to show some commitment to the trade, the market, and customers if harvesting is to continue. Even stagnant markets are competitive.
- *Maintaining employee morale.* Employees must also be considered. Good employees will leave and bad employees will sabotage a business targeted for severe harvesting. Likewise, management careers are rarely built by presiding over decline. It is often desirable to bring in management that is experienced in harvesting.

In sum, harvesting is a fascinating but dangerous strategy that sometimes deserves consideration but must be carefully applied and monitored if it is to be successful.

ABANDONMENT

Abandonment is the ultimate lack of commitment to a product or service. A firm that divests seeks to sell or abandon the business. There are two primary reasons why a firm would want to divest: (1) when the product or service has a poor market position, or (2) when it does not fit into the company's strategic base of businesses.

POOR MARKET POSITION

Low-share products or services are sometimes uncompetitive. Without a "critical mass" of market share, it might not be worthwhile to continue competing. In many markets there is only enough room for two, three, or four major players. All others must segment, or face a bleak future of slim profits. Many firms decide that it is better to withdraw than fight under such circumstances. They may have tried to gain share but been unsuccessful, or their share may have been eroded by a more determined competitor. In either case, divestment may be the only viable option. A firm with limited funds for market share battles, or too many opportunities to pursue simultaneously, may opt for divestment of their weakest market links.

Consider the case of Eagle Snacks, an Anheuser-Busch subsidiary that was abandoned in February 1996. It started in 1979 when Anheuser decided to expand its marketing and distribution expertise into snack foods. The synergies would be significant. Beer truck drivers would merely add high-margin snack foods to their beer runs. But Anheuser faced Pepsico's Frito-Lay, the entrenched market leader. Frito-Lay blitzed new products to market, cut costs, dominated distribution, and cross-subsidized various parts of its product line. Eagle Snacks never gained more than a minuscule share of the market. Its poor position placed it at a competitive disadvantage from which it could not recover.

A POOR FIT WITH THE FIRM'S OTHER PRODUCTS

Divestment is also a good strategic choice when the product or service is a poor match for the company. Today, firms want to be able to say what business they are in. Divesting far-flung, unrelated businesses compiled during a bygone era that valued conglomeration makes sense in our time. It allows the firm to concentrate, and build a competitive advantage, in one area of business. Usually, that is an area in which the firm has a dominant position.

Sometimes one firm will pay handsomely for what seems like a mangy mutt to another; that is, a poor fit for one firm may fit nicely into the portfolio of another. The divesting firm may have a poor position in the market but the acquirer may be seeking to build a critical mass of market share, or be seeking to consolidate the industry. In either case, the acquirer is enhancing its own market position. It is able to achieve what the divesting firm could not.

NOTES

[1] Joshua Levine, "Sorrell Ridge Makes Smucker's Pucker," *Forbes,* June 12, 1989, pp. 166–68.

[2] Michael Porter, *Competitive Advantage,* New York: The Free Press, 1985.

[3] Lynn Phillips, Dae Chang, and Robert Buzzell, "Product Quality, Cost Position and Business Performance: A Test of Some Key Hypotheses," *Journal of Marketing,* Spring 1983, pp. 26–43.

[4] Robert Buzzell and Frederick Wiersema, "Successful Share-Building Strategies," *Harvard Business Review,* January–February 1981, pp. 135–44.

[5] C. Davis Fogg, "Planning Gains in Market Share," *Journal of Marketing,* July 1974, pp. 30–36.

[6] Philip Kotler, "Harvesting for Weak Products," *Business Horizons,* August 1978, pp. 15–22.

CHAPTER 11

THE EVOLUTION OF PRODUCTS, MARKETS, AND NEW TECHNOLOGIES

Innovation has proved to be one of the most potent competitive weapons of the twentieth century. It has probably caused more industry changes and competitive shifts than any other individual strategic factor. History is replete with firms that gained market leadership by introducing radically new products that forever reconfigured their industries. This chapter is about technological change. It details the process whereby innovations make their way from an inventor's mind to widespread market acceptance.

TYPES OF INNOVATIONS

Not all innovations are created equal. Some are more important than others and have more consequential effects. The continuum of innovations ranges from minor incremental innovations that are little more than slight adaptations of existing products to radically new technological products that have a profound effect on future markets.

INCREMENTAL INNOVATIONS

Incremental innovations are product adaptations that take a small step forward. They are often minor product adaptations that serve to refine an existing product to make it better. Examples abound of firms adapting an existing product with a new flavor filling or coming out with a "new-and-improved" model.

Incremental innovations also occur on more important kinds of new products. Take the emergence of steam-powered ships, for example. Sailing ships evolved slowly, but steadily, into steamships over the course of decades. There was no one point at which steamships were "invented" making sailing ships obsolete. The change occurred gradually, cumulatively, and incrementally. The first steam engine placed on a ship was a crude, unreliable device used to supplement sail power for short periods. But, as time went on, the engines grew larger and more reliable, and the sails grew smaller, and then disappeared altogether.

Most innovations are incremental. Also known as "continuous" or "micro" innovations, they point up the gradual nature of evolutionary change found in many product categories. Economists call this phenomenon "technological drift." Companies in search of profits intentionally search for ways to improve existing products. It is through the process of product perfection that many technological changes occur. They occur slowly, gradually, and with a cumulative effect. The future builds steadily upon the past.

NEW-TO-THE-WORLD INNOVATIONS

The second type of innovation is the great leap forward. New-to-the-world innovations are discontinuous. They mark a clear break with the past. As in the case of computers, the telephone, the electric light, nuclear energy, the transistor, and even the entire industrial revolution, new-to-the-world innovations forever change what went before.

New-to-the-world innovations do not occur as often as incremental innovations but their effect is more important. They create new industries and destroy others.

New-to-the-world innovations also have fewer connections to the past. It is difficult to establish predecessors to "macro," "breakthrough," or "discontinuous" innovations.

THEORIES OF PRODUCT EVOLUTION

Theories of economic evolution have been derived from theories of biological evolution. At least three unique perspectives have been held during the twentieth century.

THE "GREAT MEN" THEORY

During the first two decades of the twentieth century it was widely believed that technological progress pushed forward as a result of the heroic actions of a few "great men." (Women were not included in those early years.) The basic idea was that the inventive genius of great men caused change to happen. The implication is that without the likes of

Thomas Edison the world would have remained in darkness—both figuratively and literally—for years to come. It was only through their overwhelming brilliance that such men were able to change the world. They were more than mortal.

Like many popular beliefs, the great men theory of invention was based on available examples of the day. Alexander Graham Bell's telephone, Thomas Edison's light bulb and phonograph, and Henry Ford's mass-produced automobile were among the many innovations commercialized during those decades.

GRADUALISM

An alternative view of product evolution started to take hold in the 1930s when S. C. Gilfillan published his landmark book, *The Sociology of Invention,* in 1935. He, and others at the time, disputed the view that breakthrough innovations appeared fully formed from the genius of individual inventors. Gilfillan viewed innovation as a series of small, gradual, and cumulative changes in product design. These gradualists proposed that products, like species, evolve slowly over time in response to pressures from environmental changes. Products, like species, adapt to unfolding events. Successful adaptations thrive while unsuccessful adaptations decline, or face extinction.

Economic gradualism has its roots in Charles Darwin's 1859 book *On the Origin of Species,* which argued that gradual changes in species occur in response to gradual changes in the environment. Species adapt slowly over millions of years to changes in their environment. Those that adapt successfully thrive, those that remain the same decline. Darwin's theory is called gradualism because it proposes slow, adaptive changes.

Economic gradualism is based on the cumulative effect of a series of small incremental innovations. That is, each new product builds on existing products. No new product is radically new—and it is certainly not a breakthrough—it is merely a small step forward. Over time, these small innovations result in the appearance of large changes. According to this view, innovation is largely a process of "accretion," the slow, gradual buildup of technical knowledge over time. In more recent years, George Basalla has emerged as a key economic gradualist.[1]

Other similarities exist between biological and economic evolution. As in biology, products also exhibit trends toward greater diversity, greater efficiency, and increasing complexity.[2] As product categories evolve the variety (diversity) of products usually increases. Similarly, products typically start off as crude early models—such as the first VCRs, which recorded for only an hour—but progress to more efficient models as refinements are made. Finally, products often become more complex. They rely on new and more elaborate technologies and incorporate more advanced features.

Although there are many similarities between technological and biological change, there are also many differences.[3] First, technological change is much more rapid than biological change. Second, it is reversible. If the new product proves to be a fad, it is possible to step back to the product that preceded. Biological evolution is irreversible. Third, interbreeding is possible in technology, but not in biology. Many major technological innovations occur from the creative combination of existing ideas that had never before been combined. In biology it is impossible for a horse to breed with a mouse. Even given those differences, however, it is clear that Darwin's view of gradual evolution has many applications to marketing.

PUNCTUATED EQUILIBRIA

The third view of product evolution is the most recent and relies most heavily on new-to-the-world innovations. It holds that many markets experience long periods of stability, only to be thrown into brief periods of catastrophic change when a "breakthrough" innovation is introduced. Slide rules and electromechanical adding machines, for example, were viable and stable product lines characterized by incremental improvements in product design until the sudden appearance of the electronic pocket calculator.

This view of product evolution is called punctuated equilibria and, unlike gradualism, it proposes two very different kinds of time periods:

- *Stasis*—those long periods of stability when products change very little
- *Sudden Appearance*—short periods of very rapid change caused by the rapid diffusion of new-to-the-world innovations

One expert compared punctuated equilibria to the life of a soldier during wartime, which "consists of long periods of boredom and short periods of terror."[4]

Like gradualism, punctuated equilibria also has its roots in biology. As a student, Charles Darwin was greatly influenced by the work of Charles Lyell, a noted nineteenth-century geologist. At the time, there was a great debate in geology between proponents of gradual versus catastrophic change. Lyell argued that geologic change was gradual. Darwin followed the same line of reasoning in biology.

In recent years, punctuated equilibria has caused a great debate in both biology and economics. In biology, it started in the late 1970s when Stephen J. Gould, the noted Harvard paleontologist, and Niles Eldredge, then curator of the American Museum of Natural History, argued that Darwin was mistaken. The fossil records they studied showed little evidence of slow, continuous change. Instead, there are long periods where species hardly change at all. Those periods are interspersed with short periods where the mix of life changes very rapidly in response to catastrophic changes in the environment. Gradualists claim the fossil record is incomplete. Proponents of punctuated equilibria argue that it is the theory of gradualism that is incomplete, not the data. The interested reader is referred to a short and highly readable article by Gould or a weighty treatise on the subject of punctuated equilibria by both Gould and Eldredge.[5] Joel Mokyr presents an excellent discussion of the importance of macro innovations in product evolution.[6]

PATTERNS OF PRODUCT EVOLUTION

Exhibit 11.1 shows an idealized plot of how "new-to-the- world" (macro) and "incremental" (micro) innovations interact.

MACRO THEN MICRO

Macro innovations create large leaps that often break with the past. These are new-to-the-world innovations. Once they occur, a process of steady improvement in product design proceeds. That is, macro innovation is usually followed by a series of micro innovations. According to this view, macro innovation precedes micro innovation and creates the opportunity for micro innovation to occur.

Exhibit 11.1
The Relationship Between Macro- and Micro-Innovation

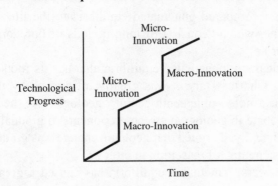

Consider the case of mainframe computers. Univac was a crude machine when first introduced in the late 1940s. But, it was a new-to-the-world innovation that presented a giant leap forward over the card-based, mechanical tabulating machines of the day. But Univac was followed by a near-half-century-long period of incremental innovation that continues to this day. Similar patterns were followed in telephones and automobiles.

ACCUMULATION OF MICRO LEADS TO MACRO

But micro innovation can also result in macro innovation. Long, sustained periods of gradual, incremental innovation can result in a product so radically different than the original invention that it appears to be a macro change. Cars, for example, have changed incrementally since the start of the twentieth century. As a result, today's cars bear little resemblance to early models. Similar patterns have been observed in many other product categories.

MICRO RUNS OUT IF NO MACRO

The opportunity for incremental innovation often diminishes in the absence of macro innovation. That is, unless there are periodic breakthroughs in technology there are fewer chances to create incremental improvements. As time passes, there are fewer and fewer opportunities to improve upon what already exists.

THE PRODUCT LIFE CYCLE

Marketing's contribution to product evolution has focused almost exclusively on the product life cycle (PLC). In essence, it is a view of product evolution that in its purest form is portrayed as an S-shaped pattern showing how new products are introduced, enter a period of rapid growth, stabilize at "maturity," then decline when replaced by subsequent innovations. This idealized pattern is chronicled in textbooks as though it were descriptive of the evolutionary path followed by many different products.

But even a cursory examination of actual sales histories shows widespread variability in the patterns actually observed. These include: (1) "scalloped demand," wherein new uses are found for a product entering maturity, which causes renewed growth, (2) "cycle-recycle," wherein decline is transformed into renewed growth by the actions of creative marketers, and (3) "extended maturity," where a product remains stuck in maturity for decades. There are also fads, where decline sets in soon after growth.

In the 1960s numerous empirical studies searched for families of life cycle patterns. One study fit six life cycle patterns to sales of 258 prescription drugs. Nearly half of the series (48.2%) exhibited a cycle-recycle pattern inconsistent with the type of most commonly espoused product life cycle pattern.[7] A subsequent study of 140 nondurable goods tested two assumptions of the PLC: (1) whether PLC stages followed each other as expected (i.e., maturity follows growth), and (2) whether the timing of stages was equal.[8] The results were inconclusive. The PLC did significantly better than chance in only 34 percent of the cases tested, but fully 92 percent of the sales series showed greater consistency than a matched, simulated series of random numbers.

A review of the literature found twelve different life cycle patterns that had been identified in the years since the concept was first proposed.[9] This review concluded that there is strong support for the basic, bell-shaped, product life cycle pattern. Others disagree vehemently.

CRITICISMS OF THE PRODUCT LIFE CYCLE

Criticisms of the PLC started to appear in the 1970s. Typically, they cluster around six issues.

1. *Curve-pattern variability.* Curve fitting as an approach to verify the PLC was abandoned by the early 1970s. It seemed to prove little. Researchers would fit many curves to many sales series and report which curves fit which series. The more curves that were applied to actual data series, the more patterns that fit at least some of those series. Curve fitting violates many rules of good research design. But more important, it shows that there is great variability in how products evolve. Anyone who has examined simple plots of yearly sales series quickly becomes appreciative of the wide variability there is in the evolutionary process. The differences sometimes seem to outnumber the similarities.

2. *No predictive validity.* It is not possible to know *beforehand* which pattern a particular product will follow. Curves are fit only to events that have already occurred. Consequently, the PLC is limited to "post-hoc" explanations of evolutionary behavior. It tells what has happened but offers no power to predict.

3. *Difficulty in estimating current status.* It is often not even possible to identify which stage of the PLC a particular product is currently in. Neat and orderly patterns are rare outside textbooks. Does a sales

downturn, for example, signal the onset of maturity, or is it merely a temporary slowdown? The choice is often difficult to make.

4. *Skipped stages.* At its heart, the PLC is rooted in the aging process of individual organisms. It holds that products, like people, are born, grow old, and die. But unlike biological aging, which is immutable and irreversible, the evolution of products is replete with rejuvenations, reversals, and skipped stages. Some products go straight from rapid growth to rapid decline. Other products spend decades in maturity, and never decline.

5. *Erratic timing.* The amount of time a product spends in each stage also varies. Some products grow for short periods, while others grow for years at a time. There seems to be no rhyme or reason to the timing of life cycle stages. Again, variability seems to be the rule rather than the exception.

6. *The product life cycle as a tautology.* The most damning criticism is that the PLC is a tautology. That is, the pattern proves itself. How do you tell a product is in the growth stage of the cycle? Because it is growing. In the decline stage? Because it is declining. Such explanations are not explanatory. They are tautological. The stage of the life cycle is identified by the trend in sales, which, in turn, identifies the stage of the life cycle. The concept proves itself and nothing else. Shelby Hunt, the noted marketing theorist, puts it best: "If the level of sales determines the stage of the life cycle, then the stage in the life cycle cannot be used to explain the level of sales."[10]

Breaking the life cycle down into two component parts illustrates the tautological criticism further.

Introduction to Maturity. The first half of the PLC postulates that sales follow an S-shaped curve. That is, after experiencing a slow start, sales grow rapidly as the product gains widespread consumer acceptance. Then, growth slows as the market saturates. Two problems arise. First, many S-shaped patterns have been observed. Low-tar cigarettes, for example, were on the market for many years before sales soared. Another product in the same category, 100mm cigarettes, grew immediately upon introduction. Like children learning to print the alphabet, the shape of an "S" varies greatly from child to child and from product to product.

Products also saturate markets at different levels. Telephones and refrigerators reach well over 90 percent of households while cornpoppers have penetrated less than 10 percent. None of this is known in advance.

Even more troubling is the observation that *products follow an S-shaped curve because the curve is applied only to products that have exhibited sustained growth.* It is never applied to product failures, such as the video telephone, CB radios, or artificial leathers. Consequently, by definition, sample products exhibit an upward trend in sales because the cycle is only applied to products that exhibit an upward trend in sales. The pattern is ensured by the nature of the sample used to test it, and the fact that all observations are made post-hoc. As a result, the PLC offers little explanatory or predictive power of product evolution.

Maturity to Decline. The second half of the PLC is subject to stronger criticism than the first. Myriad patterns are possible once growth abates. Sales might: (1) remain in maturity for decades (extended maturity), (2) resume growth (cycle-recycle), or (3) decline slowly or precipitously (the basic pattern). Numerous examples of each pattern have been observed. Exhibit 11.2 illustrates those possible patterns.

Critics claim that such observations offer little in the way of explanatory power. Instead, they reinforce the claim that the PLC is a tautology. It simply states: (1) sales may go up, (2) sales may go down, or (3) sales may remain the same. In violation of the basic principles of scientific theory building, the PLC concept cannot be refuted. No matter what the outcome, the concept holds. But, in the absence of any mechanism to select which pattern a product will follow beforehand, the concept offers little in the way of worthwhile explanations. It is indeed a tautology.

ARE LIFE CYCLES COMPLETELY CONTROLLABLE OR PREDETERMINED?

The idealized form of the product life cycle concept implies that sales histories are predetermined. Just as a living organism is born, grows,

Exhibit 11.2
Possible Life Cycle Paths After Maturity

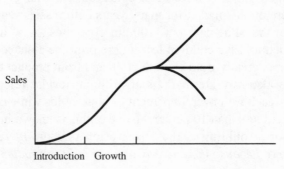

matures, and then dies, so too do products. That implies a complete lack of control over what happens to sales. Marketers are merely along for a roller-coaster ride. They cannot change the course the roller coaster takes: they can only hope to roll with the curves.

Critics take issue with that proposition. Dhalla and Yuspeh, for example, found no evidence at all that products follow life cycle patterns of any kind.[11] They argue that the future path of product sales histories is determined by marketing variables, such as advertising expenditures. Marketers, in other words, can influence the cycle not just observe it.

Critics contend that the PLC might mistakenly signal the inevitable end of a product's life. That might lead management to inadvertently milk bread-and-butter products on the assumption that they have no future rather than redoubling efforts to turn things around.

Some authors have taken a more extreme position. They argue that patterns can be completely controlled. In the parlance of regression analysis, they argue that the PLC is a "dependent variable," which is the result of marketing actions. Marketing controls the life cycle pattern, not the other way around.

Are life cycles really controllable? Or are they determined by outside forces? The answer, as with most issues, lies somewhere between the two extremes. Clearly, the life cycle is not predetermined. But neither is it totally controllable. The best sales and marketing efforts could not reclaim the 8mm movie camera and projector market. Their worlds were forever altered by forces beyond marketers' control. But marketers have considerable powers to influence. The important question is not what pattern will a product follow but what "drivers" will influence the evolutionary path.

DRIVERS OF PRODUCT EVOLUTION

In 1981, George Day succinctly summarized the status of PLC research: "Past attempts to validate the existence of the life cycle have uncovered many shapes, durations and sequences. These efforts have not been matched by systematic research into the reasons for the differences between shapes."[12] All that has changed. It is now widely accepted that products, like species, adapt to environmental changes. Those changes can be gradual or rapid, controllable or uncontrollable. The following are some of the more important drivers of product evolution.

THE SEQUENCE OF SUCCESSFUL INNOVATION

Exhibit 11.3 illustrates the three essential ingredients of successful innovation.

Exhibit 11.3
Sequence of Successful Innovation

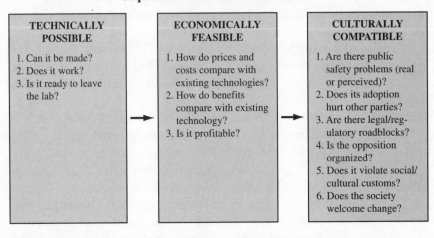

TECHNICALLY POSSIBLE	ECONOMICALLY FEASIBLE	CULTURALLY COMPATIBLE
1. Can it be made? 2. Does it work? 3. Is it ready to leave the lab?	1. How do prices and costs compare with existing technologies? 2. How do benefits compare with existing technology? 3. Is it profitable?	1. Are there public safety problems (real or perceived)? 2. Does its adoption hurt other parties? 3. Are there legal/regulatory roadblocks? 4. Is the opposition organized? 5. Does it violate social/cultural customs? 6. Does the society welcome change?

Technologically Possible. Before an innovation can be successful it must be possible to make it. There may be powerful consumer needs for inventions such as fusion energy and "*Star Trek*–like" human transporters but, to date, it is not possible to make them. Some inventions simply stay stuck in the lab until they are perfected.

Economically Feasible. Once it is possible to make a new product it must be cost and performance competitive with the existing way of accomplishing the task. The new device must be less expensive or perform the task better, or, in those rare cases such as computers, do both. It will not diffuse to the widespread public without favorable economics.

Culturally Compatible. Innovations must be introduced into a sympathetic social system. That system must welcome change. The product itself must fit with legal, regulatory, and safety norms. It must fit with the "spirit of the times." Cigarettes, for example, do not fit with today's times, and new cigarette products are likely to meet stiff resistance. Nike's move into running shoes, in contrast, was perfectly, if coincidentally, timed to match the fitness boom of the 1970s.

TEACHING CONSUMERS THE VALUE OF NOVELTY

Products do not diffuse in isolation. They diffuse in a context of existing consumer habits and industry trade practices. Sometimes those habits and practices are difficult to change. Innovators must teach consumers the value of novelty and overcome the inertia inherent in existing practices and beliefs.

Radically new products, with which consumers are unfamiliar, require a great deal of primary demand advertising. Marketers must teach, explain, and inform consumers of the product's benefits.

THE IMPORTANCE OF PRODUCT CONNECTIONS

Some new products "stand alone" while others depend heavily on complementary products. Thomas Edison, for example, had to invent not only the light bulb but the entire electrical generating system. The bulb by itself was useless. The same is true for CD players and VCRs. They needed discs and videocassettes, respectively.

The need for complementary products can hinder growth. Consumers are reluctant to purchase until complementary products are available. Suppliers of complementary products are reluctant to produce those items until a sufficiently large installed base of customers exists.

The need for complementary products also requires extensive coordination among buyers, suppliers, and firms in allied industries. All must do their part. Products that stand alone have no such hindrances.

THE EFFECTS OF PRODUCT STANDARDS ON PRODUCT GROWTH

Standardization facilitates early product growth. It prevents consumer confusion over which type of product will dominate and allows manufacturers to concentrate on promoting growth rather than competing as to which standard will emerge as the dominant one.

But setting standards too early can hinder future innovation. Once a standard is set it is very difficult to change. Of the world's three standards for television, the United States has the oldest and, as a result, the crudest. But changing it requires that broadcasters and consumers abandon existing equipment and buy into the new standard. So far, all parties have been reluctant to do so.

Not setting standards usually results in the market, or the most powerful player, picking the standard. It works as follows: Various versions of a new product are introduced. Eventually, a "dominant design" emerges, which then becomes the de facto standard for the rest of the industry.

PERCEIVED ATTRIBUTES OF INNOVATION

The success of an innovation is driven by the extent to which it is perceived to have advantages over the existing way of doing things. Lyman Ostlund studied the perceived attributes of innovations and found a number of growth drivers:[13]

- *Relative advantage over existing products:* products that perform the task better or are less expensive are more likely to grow quickly.
- *Compatibility:* products that are consistent with existing practices, and do not require major changes in consumers' lives to use the new product promote growth. (Products that are incompatible require greater buyer learning.)
- *Design simplicity:* products that do not require consumers to obtain a graduate degree in order to to operate or understand them are likely to grow quickly.
- *Use on a trial basis:* products that do not require a large and nonrefundable payment to test the product before using promote growth
- *Clearly observable benefits:* products grow more quickly when consumers can see the advantage of using them.

CHARACTERISTICS OF EMERGING MARKETS

Innovations may exhibit a number of common patterns as they make their way from lab to market, some of which are described below.

LONG, LONG USELESS STAGE

In 1935 S. C. Gilfillan concluded that innovations get stuck in a long, long useless stage.[14] That is, once conceived, it typically takes years—and sometimes decades—for an idea to transform itself into a commercially successful product. After more than half a century, Gilfillan's findings still ring true. Many innovations still spend years incubating in laboratories and in the marketplace before consumers show interest.

There are two parts of the long, long useless stage. First, there is the lag between the time a product is first conceived of and when it first reaches the market. Second, there is the lag between when it is first placed on the market and when it achieves commercial success.

Consider some specific cases of products that spent time in the long useless stage.

- In light beer, for example, there was a nine-year gap between the time of Rheingold's Gablinger's entry and the stunning commercial success of Miller's Lite beer.
- There was, at least, a ten-year gap between the entry of the first diet soft drink and the first sustained commercial success.
- First invented in 1946, it took ten years for the microwave oven to get to market. But it took another twenty years for the product to gain commercial acceptance.

In many cases, either the product is not ready for the market or the market is not ready for the product.

EARLY MODELS AS CRUDE FIRST ATTEMPTS

Many new product are not fully formed when they are first brought to market. Often technically crude and based on first-generation technologies, they are little more than first attempts to move the product out of the lab and into the marketplace. As such, they wear their weaknesses on their sleeve.

Consider the following cases:

- The first ballpoint pens introduced in the mid-1940s were crude devices that leaked, skipped, smudged, and generally failed to write the way they were supposed to.
- Magnavox Odyssey, the first home videogame, had incredibly crude graphics and required users to hang an acetate sheet on the television as a background playing field.
- The first diet soft drinks were targeted to diabetics and teenagers with acne.

THE IMPORTANCE OF MARKET TIMING

Most successful new products enter just as demand is about to explode. Like the stars of ancient astrologers, the technological, economic, and social factors are aligned in the best possible configuration. Often, and usually by sheer chance, the seller just happens to be *in the right place, at the right time, with the right product.*

- Consider the case of nonalcoholic beers, which have been on the market for decades. Sales were minuscule for years, but in the late 1980s, when inebriation became socially unacceptable and the trend against drunk driving accelerated, sales of nonalcoholic beers spurted upward.
- A similar pattern was observed in charge cards. Throughout the early 1950s, social mores held that buying on credit was somehow immoral. By 1958, however, times had changed. Consumers become more comfortable with credit. That change corresponded almost perfectly with American Express's entry.
- Nike's timing was most fortunate. Formed on a shoestring in 1964 to sell running shoes to the minuscule market of dedicated track athletes, by 1974, ten years later, sales had climbed only to a paltry $4.8 million. Then the market exploded. Weekend athletes and nonathletes entered

the market in droves as the trend toward "health and fitness," which had started in the 1960s, accelerated in the 1970s. Nike found itself in an enviable position—it had the right product in the right place at the right time. By 1976 sales had still reached only $14 million. By the early 1990s sales soared to an astounding $3 billion.

INCUMBENT INERTIA

One of the most stunning observations about innovation is the overwhelming tendency for large market leaders to misread the true potential of innovations that threaten their current product lines. Typically, they let upstarts enter their markets with impunity and are then forced to play catch-up once the magnitude of the opportunity becomes clear. Incumbents, in other words, exhibit inertia when it comes to pursuing products that are natural extensions of their business. Consider the following list of seventeen cases where industry incumbents missed major market opportunities.

1. *Ballpoint pens.* The three major fountain pen sellers—Parker, Sheaffer, and Waterman—showed no interest in the new technology.
2. *Caffeine-free soft drinks.* Coke and Pepsi entered after Canada Dry and Royal Crown.
3. *Commercial jet aircraft.* Neither Douglas, the market leader in propplanes, nor Lockheed, another incumbent, seemed interested in cannibalizing existing products.
4. *Diet soft drinks.* Coke and Pepsi entered after Kirsch and Royal Crown.
5. *Digital watches.* Digital watches were based on electronics technology. The leading Swiss watch makers did not have expertise in that area and did not respond.
6. *Food processors.* Food processors did not come from the major appliance sellers but from a small, entrepreneurial upstart.
7. *Frozen yogurt.* Frozen yogurt was not pioneered by the major ice cream sellers, even though it should have been viewed as a natural extension of their current business.
8. *Herbal teas.* Herbal teas did not come from Lipton. That honor went to Celestial Seasonings, an entrepreneur from the mountains of Colorado.
9. *Inline skates.* Rollerblades, founded by two hockey enthusiasts, created the product. The major ice skating or sporting goods companies did not see much chance for success.
10. *Light beer.* Light beer first came from small, regional brewers. Only later was it copied by the industry leaders.
11. *Mainframe computers* Mainframe computers were not pioneered by IBM, or the other office machine suppliers. Sperry Univac was the pioneer.

12. *Money market funds.* This innovation was not pioneered by the major financial houses such as Merrill Lynch, nor was it introduced by the major mutual funds—Dreyfus and Fidelity.

13. *Mountain bikes.* Individual biking enthusiasts pioneered the product. Schwinn, Huffy, and the other industry giants reacted to the trend long after it began.

14. *Paperback books.* Paperbacks were not introduced by the major publishing houses.

15. *Personal computers.* Personal computers were not pioneered by the major mainframe sellers, such as IBM. Nor were they pioneered by mini-computer sellers, which had entered unchallenged in minis. They came from Apple and Osborne.

16. *Pocket calculators.* Calculators did not come from the major sellers of "portable" electro-mechanicals. Monroe, Sweda, or Friden never made the switch to the new technology.

17. *Projection TV.* Projection TV did not come from the major television set manufacturers. It came from tiny Advent.

There are four reasons for incumbent inertia.

1. *Incumbents do not perceive the threat as real.* It is often viewed as a short-lived fad that will soon fade away. That view is often well-founded. Many times, there is a long history of failure preceding the latest innovation. Incumbents expect that pattern to be repeated. But the opposite happens. The backwater product emerges as a major market opportunity.

2. *Incumbents may feel few pressures to react because they do not have to.* Advantages in marketing, distribution, and financial resources may allow them to succeed should the product take off and show itself to be a real rather than an imaginary opportunity.

3. *Incumbents are shortsighted, defining their markets in terms of current product lines rather than broad market needs.* They may exhibit "product provincialism."

4. *Industry incumbents may be reluctant to cannibalize current product lines.* Why replace sure-shot winners with risky, unproven new products? Incumbents are often unwilling to engage in "creative destruction," a term popularized by the economist Schumpeter and adapted by others in subsequent decades.

CREATIVE DESTRUCTION

The concept of creative destruction is that technological innovations make existing products obsolete, or at least relegate them to a minor economic role. Creative destruction is the cost of technological progress. It produces long-term economic gains at the expense of short-term costs to individual firms. Workers in old industries are displaced while opportunities in new industries are created.

Incumbents are advised to engage in creative destruction because if they do not someone else will destroy their current product lines for them. By focusing too intently on current products, incumbents typically miss opportunities pursued by more entrepreneurial pioneers with less to lose in the way of current product lines.

MARKET ENTRY STRATEGIES

Pioneers benefit from "first-mover" advantages, which result from their being first to market. But pioneers do not possess all of the competitive advantages. "First-mover" advantages are counterbalanced by "free-rider" effects, which accrue to imitators and later entrants. Which effect is stronger? Rhetorically, the outcome of that argument depends on the metaphors used to describe each set of advantages.

Proponents of pioneering view "first-mover" advantages as a five-kilometer footrace, except in this race the pioneer leaves the starting line before the other contestants. The greater the length of the pioneer's lead, the less likely it is that later entrants will ever catch up. Only when the later entrant possesses outstanding physical talents, or reacts quickly to the pioneer's entry, can the overwhelming odds of leaving the starting line after the first entrant be overcome to win the footrace.

Proponents of "free-rider" effects rely on a metaphor drawn from geographic exploration. According to this view, pioneers took enormous personal risks to explore the uncharted Western United States. They opened up the wilderness for the settlers who followed. Some pioneers are immortalized in history textbooks, but most were not enriched financially for their trailblazing efforts. That benefit went to the settlers who created economic wealth. The pioneers got the glory, but the followers reaped the largest economic rewards.

FIRST-MOVER ADVANTAGES

Pioneers are the beneficiaries of numerous first-mover advantages, which are summarized below.

IMAGE AND REPUTATION

Pioneers enjoy important reputation benefits that derive from their innovative products and early entry. Pioneers bask in the glow of a positive image infused with innovativeness and progressiveness while later entrants are stuck with a copycat image, which tarnishes the appeal of their products.

BRAND LOYALTY

Pioneers have an opportunity to create loyal customers for their innovative products. Consumers become familiar with—and even form habits around—the first product that they try. There is no reason for satisfied consumers to experiment with similar products sold by imitators and later entrants.

AN OPPORTUNITY TO PICK THE BEST MARKET POSITION

If pioneers can pick product attributes that are most important to consumers and preempt the most favorable market position before later entrants even have a product on the market later entrants will be forced to pick between two unappealing choices: (1) they can adopt an inferior product position, or (2) they can copy the pioneer's product position and be saddled with the perception that their product is a "me-too," second-rate entry. Both strategic choices place the later entrant at a competitive disadvantage.

TECHNOLOGICAL LEADERSHIP

The pioneer is likely to have a head start in technology as well as market position. While competitors play catch-up, the innovator can pursue the next technological generation, staying one step ahead of lagging entrants.

AN OPPORTUNITY TO SET PRODUCT STANDARDS

Pioneers have an opportunity to define an emerging product category in terms of their own products. They can set industry standards, which later entrants are forced to follow. The first group of customers becomes familiar with the pioneers' product. As that installed base of users grows, it becomes harder and harder for later entrants to switch the market to its own proprietary standard. The later entrant is forced to imitate the pioneer's product and adopt a subservient position.

ACCESS TO DISTRIBUTION

In many cases, there is room for only a limited number of brands in distribution channels. By virtue of being first, pioneers ensure that their products have access to preferential distribution. Later entrants are less fortunate. They may find themselves shut out of the distribution network simply because of their later entry.

EXPERIENCE EFFECTS

The first entrant slides down the experience curve faster than later entrants. The cost advantages thus gained place later entrants with less experience at a competitive disadvantage. That gives the pioneer a price advantage that cannot be matched by later entrants.

PATENTS AS A BARRIER TO ENTRY

Patents granted on innovative products can be used to lock out later entrants. Innovative pioneers are able to gain control over the essence of innovative products, which allows them to reap the economic benefits.

SWITCHING COSTS AS A BARRIER TO ENTRY

Pioneers can also raise barriers to entry by building mutually beneficial relationships with their customers. Those relationships keep customers loyal to the pioneer's product and keep competitors at bay. Long-term contracts, familiarity with the first supplier's product, a lack of incentive to switch, and other intentional and unintentional inhibitors serve to bind the buyer to the first seller.

FREE-RIDER EFFECTS

Critics contend that the benefits of pioneering have been grossly oversold. While first-mover advantages appear to be strong and immutable in theory, they prove to be weak and vulnerable to the actions of crafty later entrants in practice.

AVOIDING PRODUCTS THAT HAVE NO POTENTIAL

Later entrants avoid spending time and money on products for which there turns out to be no demand. Their strategy is to sit back and watch. Only when the market potential becomes clearly favorable do they move in and gain a viable and oftentimes commanding lead.

There is considerable risk inherent in pioneering new and unproven markets. By focusing solely on the successes, many studies have inadvertently ignored the fact that many pioneers simply are not around to study. A study by Golder and Tellis examined patterns of pioneering and later entry in fifty product categories and found that 47 percent of pioneers failed.[15] The authors conclude that previous studies did not adequately consider survival bias.

LOWER COSTS

It is clearly cheaper to imitate than innovate. One study examined forty-eight product innovations in the chemical, ethical drug, electronics, and machinery industries and found that, on average, imitation costs were only 65 percent of innovation costs.[16] Later entrants avoid many of the costs that must be borne solely by the first entrant. The question is not whether imitation is less expensive than innovation—it clearly is—but whether sustainable benefits accrue to the pioneer who takes on those enormous expenses. That point is debatable.

Lower Research and Development Expenditures. Innovators are forced to spend heavily on research and development. That expense is justified by the assumption that innovators gain a long lead on imitators, who are simply unable to catch up. But imitation often occurs quickly. Companies learn about each other's new product development projects: (1) by monitoring each other's patent applications, which require going public with the firm's innovative ideas, (2) through papers and presentations at professional and academic conferences attended by scientists and engineers, and (3) when technical and marketing personnel switch jobs, taking with them inside information and then either unintentionally or maliciously spreading knowledge.

Lower Costs of Educating Consumers. By being first pioneers must spend heavily to inform and persuade consumers as to the merits of a new product. That is especially true for radical innovations with which consumers are unfamiliar. In such instances, the innovator must incubate a new technology over long periods before it attracts large numbers of paying customers. During that incubation period, costs are high and revenues are low as the product prepares for life outside the pioneer's womb.

AN OPPORTUNITY TO GAIN SHARE WITH HEAVY PROMOTION

Later entrants may also be able to make up for their slow start by spending heavily on marketing. That is, they may be able to trade up-front R&D expenditures for later promotional spending. They might be able to nurture what they are unable to conceive. A study of the new product practices of two hundred firms by Robert Cooper found that "marketing resources appear to be the most critical in deciding a successful new product program."[17] Some firms rely more heavily on marketing than on R&D to push their products and gain a dominant position.

TECHNOLOGICAL LEAPFROG

Sometimes pioneers find it difficult to switch technologies once they have invested so much in the first generation. The switch from 8-bit to 16-bit personal computers, Wordstar to WordPerfect then Word in word processing software, and CP/M to MS-DOS in operating systems was anything but smooth for the pioneers involved. In each case, as well as many others, the change in technology favored later entrants over pioneers.

STICKING THE PIONEER WITH AN OBSOLETE STANDARD

Standards are often set by larger, more powerful, later entrants, who, though not first, have a superior product. In the case of VCRs and personal computer operating systems, as well as many other product categories, later entrants were unencumbered by investments and reputation in first-generation designs.

AN OPPORTUNITY TO BENEFIT FROM MARKET CHANGES

Not only are products not fully formed when they are first brought to market, but the market for those products is often poorly formed as well. The kinds of consumers who purchase at the beginning are often different than those who enter later in larger numbers. The earliest customers for personal computers and computer software, for example, were technology-oriented hobbyists who needed little customer service and support. That changed when the market turned mainstream, attracting business users lacking technical skills. Distribution and customer service became key. It changed again when the product turned into a virtual generic. At that time, mail order sales boomed, price became the most important criteria, and the power of prestigious brand names to command higher margins declined.

AN OPPORTUNITY TO USE SHARED EXPERIENCE

Shared experience occurs when a firm has or does something closely related to what the pioneer claims as new. The later entrant may, for example, sell products that are similar, have experience with similar production methods, or distribute its products through similar channels. In addition, the later entrant may possess the marketing skills to sell similar products, which can be used to develop the market created by the pioneer. In short, the pioneer may be moving into a market where a dominant market leader holds all the cards.

ARE INVENTIONS INEVITABLE?

The "great men" theory of invention has been discredited, replaced by theories of the micro innovations of gradualism and the mix of micro- and macro-innovations of punctuated equilibria. But implicit in the technological drift of those two newer theories is the idea that individuals are not important to the invention process. It is a belief that technology rolls forward without regard to unique individual effort. That is a fascinating but chilling hypothesis.

THE PHENOMENON OF SIMULTANEOUS INVENTIONS

A review of the history of innovation reveals a stunning observation— for most inventions, during most time periods, discoveries were made at about the same time by more than one person. That is the phenomenon of simultaneous invention. It is not a new observation. As long ago as 1922, Ogburn and Thomas tallied 148 important inventions and new ideas of previous decades that had been created simultaneously, including the sewing machine, the typewriter, the phonograph, and the telephone.[18] The same is true today. The discovery of DNA, the development of the jet airplane, and just about every other important invention of recent decades were all accomplished by two or more independent teams working at about the same time.

That observation suggests that there is a certain inevitability to technological progress. Individual genius becomes less important than the accumulation of knowledge, to the point where multiple inventors deduce the same conclusions from the same set of data and take the next technological step forward. Had Thomas Edison, Alexander Graham Bell, or for that matter, Robert Noyce (co-inventor of the integrated circuit) or Stephen Jobs (Apple) picked careers in professional sports, we would still have their inventions in pretty much the same form. That is the most profound lesson of the evolution of products, markets, and new technologies.

NOTES

[1]George Basalla, *The Evolution of Technology,* New York: Cambridge University Press, 1988.
[2]Gerard Tellis and Merle Crawford, "An Evolutionary Approach to Product Growth Theory," *Journal of Marketing,* Fall 1981, pp. 123–32.

[3]Chris DeBresson, "The Evolutionary Paradigm and the Economics of Technological Change," *Journal of Economic Issues*, June 1987, pp. 731–72

[4]Stephen J. Gould quoting the British geologist Derek Ager in *The Panda's Thumb, New York:* W.W. Norton, 1980, p. 185.

[5]Gould, "The Episodic Nature of Evolutionary Change," *The Panda's Thumb,* pp. 179–85; and Stephen Gould and Niles Eldredge, "Punctuated Equilibria: The Tempo and Mode of Evolution Reconsidered," *Paleobiology,* Vol. 3, 1977, pp. 115–51.

[6]Joel Mokyr, *The Lever of Riches,* New York: Oxford University Press, 1990.

[7]William Cox, "Product Life Cycles as Marketing Models," *Journal of Business,* October 1967, pp. 375–84.

[8]Rolando Polli and Victor Cook, "Validity of the Product Life Cycle," *Journal of Business,* October 1969, pp. 385–400.

[9]David Rink and John Swan, "Product Life Cycle Research: A Literature Review," *Journal of Business Research,* 1979, pp. 219–42.

[10]Shelby Hunt, *Marketing Theory,* Columbus, OH: Grid Publications, 1976, p. 55.

[11]Narman Dhalla and Sonia Yuspeh, "Forget the Product Life Cycle Concept," *Harvard Business Review,* January–February 1976, pp. 102–12.

[12]George Day, "The Product Life Cycle: Analysis and Applications Issues," *Journal of Marketing,* Fall 1981, p. 61.

[13]Lyman Ostlund, "Perceived Innovation Attributes as Predictors of Innovativeness," *Journal of Consumer Research,* September 1974, pp. 23–29.

[14]S. C. Gilfillan, *The Sociology of Invention,* Chicago: Follett Publishing, 1935, p. 94.

[15]Peter Golder and Gerard Tellis, *Do Pioneers Really Have Long-Term Advantages? A Historical Analysis,* Report Number 92-124, September 1992, Cambridge MA.: The Marketing Science Institute.

[16]Edwin Mansfield, Mark Schwartz, and Samuel Wagner, "Imitation Costs and Patents: An Empirical Study," *The Economics Journal,* December 1981, p. 912.

[17]Robert Cooper, "New Product Success in Industrial Firms," *Industrial Marketing Management,* July 1982, pp. 215–23.

[18]William Ogburn and Dorothy Thomas, "Are Inventions Inevitable? A Note on Social Evolution," *Political Science Quarterly,* March 1922, pp. 83–98.

CHAPTER 12

SPEED AS STRATEGY

R emember the tale of the tortoise and the hare? Well, in today's intensely competitive marketplace, many firms (and a clutch of consultants) have concluded that the hare wins hands down. In other words, the strategy of speeding products to market is superior to moving cautiously after careful study.

The essence of speed as strategy is captured by the Nike slogan, "Just Do It." It is a strategy based on the proposition that since all firms sell similar-quality products at similar price points, then competitive advantage can be gained only by bringing new products to market more quickly than competitors, and distributing existing products faster than rivals.

Speed as strategy values action over analysis. It eschews market research and substitutes quick moves for lengthy deliberation. Firms that embrace this strategy move rather than mull, act rather than analyze, and try rather than try to predict. It is a strategy perfectly attuned to today's fast-moving times.

Speed as strategy started as an outgrowth of the "just-in-time" inventory methods of the early 1980s. It began in the auto industry, where U.S. sellers sought to catch up with the cost and quality advantages held by Japanese brands. By the mid-1980s it had expanded to include "quick-response systems" in the retailing and apparel industries, which tied together members of the channel of distribution in order to move goods more quickly from weaver to wearer.

At about the same time, interest emerged in speeding new products to market. Disillusionment with market research, and a tendency for the Japanese consumer electronics giants to flood the market with a never-ending series of new products, led many American sellers to increase the rate of new product introductions and let customers decide which products would be successful.

WHAT TO SPEED UP

There are two general marketing-related areas where speed can play a strategic role: innovation and distribution. The first, moving new products to market more quickly than competitors, entails streamlining the new product planning process in order to shorten the period between the initial conception of an idea and when it reaches retailers. The focus here is on *new* products and ideas.

The other general area where speed plays a strategic role is in the flow of *existing* goods and information through channels of distributions. Adopting standardized systems can speed the flow of information among channel members and accelerate production and delivery schedules. The result is it takes less time for existing products to go from maker to the ultimate consumer.

WHY SPEED IS IMPORTANT

Speed as a source of competitive advantage has grown more popular in recent years for at least nine reasons.

1. COMPETITIVE ADVANTAGE IS NOT SUSTAINABLE

A truly "sustainable" competitive advantage has proved to be an elusive goal for companies. Amar Bhide sums it up best when he notes: "Opportunities to gain lasting advantage through blockbuster strategic moves are rare in business. What mostly counts are vigor and nimbleness."[1] Speed as strategy sidesteps the problem of sustainable advantage by replacing it with quick response. If a firm cannot create a lasting competitive advantage, then it must move more quickly than rivals.

2. AVOIDING THE NEED TO PREDICT THE FUTURE

A longstanding criticism of long-range planning is that any plan for the years ahead either explicitly or implicitly assumes various things about market growth, competitor reactions, and economic growth, and frequent errors in those forecasts have ruined too many strategies. Firms end up prepared for a future that never comes. Speed sidesteps that shortcoming. Moving quickly with markets rather than trying to guess in which direction they will move substitutes flexibility for forecasting, and in so doing it jettisons an uncontrollable weakness of more traditional forms of planning.

3. THE LAW OF LARGE NUMBERS

It is never quite clear which new product introductions will turn out to be the next nylon and which will be the next Corfam (a failed leather substitute used to make shoes in the 1960s). Great outcomes sometimes come from humble beginnings, but so do inconsequential outcomes. A key benefit of speeding many new products to market without a great deal of formal market research (rather than zeroing in on what the company thinks will be that one big winner) is that the market decides which products will be successful and which will fail. If the market decides against that one big winner, and it often does, the firm has blown a large market opportunity. But a firm that tries lots of alternatives is likely to have at least a few winners mixed within the pack of losers.

4. PROFITS FROM NEW PRODUCTS

New products are the life-blood of future earnings. A survey of the new product development practices of seven hundred firms by Booz, Allen & Hamilton, the prestigious consulting firm, found that in the 1980s companies expected to earn one-third of their profits from new products, compared with just over one-fifth in the 1970s.[2] In more recent years that trend has accelerated. Firms without a steady flow of new products ultimately face decline. Is it any wonder that during the past decade the flood of new products has increased greatly?

5. SHORTER PRODUCT LIFE CYCLES

Product life cycles seem to be shortening. Whereas market growth used to last for years, it now lasts only months. Long-term growth has been replaced by a series of short-lived fads. That means that firms must get to market before the peak of popularity passes. Otherwise, they miss the majority of profits. That leaves little time for detailed market research. Firms must move, and move fast.

6. MORE COMPETITION IN GROWTH MARKETS

The product life cycle postulates that competition is less intense in high-growth markets. Because demand exceeds supply there are few reasons to cut prices. Profits are thus highest in the growth stage of the product life cycle. That may have been true in the past, but it is no longer the case. Firms now fight vigorously in high-growth markets. As a result, most growth markets are crowded with competitors and are intensely competitive.

7. RAMPANT COPYING

In the 1960s, Proctor & Gamble market-tested Pampers, the first mass-market disposable diaper, for nearly a decade. Today, such extensive testing is all but impossible. It would invite too many copycats. Competitors routinely steal new product ideas in test markets. It is not unusual to find one firm conducting a market test while another speeds a copy of its product directly to market. While one firm is analyzing, the other is acting.

8. GAINING SHELF SPACE EARLY

A growing number of new products must compete for limited retail shelf space. That means that firms must get to market quickly or risk being closed out of the best distribution outlets. In many product categories there is room on the shelf for only a few brands. In the late 1960s and early 1970s, for example, later entrants into the disposable diaper business had a tough time finding shelf space. Retailers had room for only two or three of the bulky brands. Smaller, later entrants into personal computers faced the same dilemma. Retailers already had enough brands to carry.

9. FOSTERING A SENSE OF CREATIVITY AND EXPERIMENTATION

Finally, a fast-moving strategy promotes a culture of doing and trying rather than a culture of bureaucrats and paperwork. The very essence of speed as strategy is that it eschews deep hierarchies of decision making and the multiple approval levels they create. Decisions flow as quickly as the products in a fast-moving firm.

QUICKENING THE PACE OF INNOVATION

One way speed finds its way into strategy is through faster innovation. There are two aspects to this approach. First, firms must move products more quickly from the drawing board to the retailer's shelf. They must quicken the pace of innovation. The second aspect concerns frequency. Not only must firms bring products to market more quickly, they must do so more often.

Speeding new products to market requires that firms replace traditional models of new product planning with alternative approaches that better captures the frantic pace of today's markets. Exhibit 12.1 presents a side-by-side comparison of two popular approaches.

Exhibit 12.1
"New" Versus "Old" New Product Planning

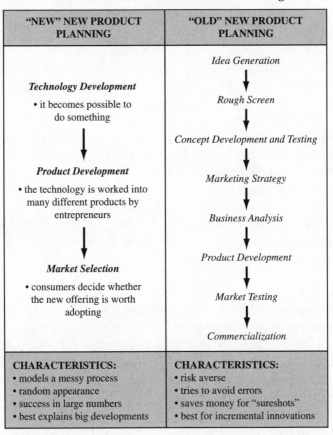

"NEW" NEW PRODUCT PLANNING	"OLD" NEW PRODUCT PLANNING
Technology Development • it becomes possible to do something ↓ *Product Development* • the technology is worked into many different products by entrepreneurs ↓ *Market Selection* • consumers decide whether the new offering is worth adopting	*Idea Generation* ↓ *Rough Screen* ↓ *Concept Development and Testing* ↓ *Marketing Strategy* ↓ *Business Analysis* ↓ *Product Development* ↓ *Market Testing* ↓ *Commercialization*
CHARACTERISTICS: • models a messy process • random appearance • success in large numbers • best explains big developments	**CHARACTERISTICS:** • risk averse • tries to avoid errors • saves money for "sureshots" • best for incremental innovations

"NEW" NEW PRODUCT PLANNING

In recent years there has been a revolution in new product planning. Procedures for bringing new products to market have been overhauled to promote speed. Many of the new procedures copy those used by Japanese firms, such as Panasonic, which have a well-earned reputation for fast response. The model presented in Exhibit 12.1 contains three steps.

1. Technology Development. The first step in a speed strategy focuses on scientific and engineering research. This research is not concerned with producing marketable products. That comes later. At this stage, technology itself is the focus of all actions. The goal is to make discoveries that result in the creation of "technology platforms," which can be incorporated rapidly into new and existing products. An example of a technology platform might be the discovery that lasers can be used to store information on disks. That is not a product, but a technological possibility.

Technological discoveries have two nettlesome problems: they are virtually impossible to predict, and it is never quite clear where they will lead. They usually happen unexpectedly, often by chance, or when a scientist is looking for something completely different. Their ultimate use is also difficult to discern. When Thomas Edison created the phonograph—the ability to store and play back sound on machine—he saw all sorts of uses for his device. Listening to music was not one of the prime candidates.

Consider the case of CD players. Akio Morita, the late chairman of Sony, contends that his firm did not set out to discover the CD player. The process was much messier than that. Instead, Sony was working on laser technology, which later led to a useful product. It would have been impossible, he claims, to have so perfectly predicted the course of events that unfolded as laser research evolved into today's CD player. Flexibility and an openness to new ideas are needed at this stage of the new product planning process.

2. Product Development. Once a technology proves workable, the second stage—product development—proceeds. At this stage the firm seeks to incorporate the technology platform into marketable products. It might use laser technology to store data on computers, for example, or store snapshots from cameras, or produce music for CD players. The product development stage seeks to apply what was discovered in the first stage into useable products.

The focus is on getting the technology into products quickly. No new technological advances are sought. Revisions and product reformulations to incorporate the latest developments are postponed until a later model is introduced. The goal is to move quickly to market.

The focus is also on large numbers of products. Product development seeks to apply the technology platform to as many products as possible. If it is not possible to predict which products will be successful, many products should be tried.

Large-scale market research studies usually play a small role in this type of product development. There is no time for lengthy study. The intent is to try it out and see if it works.

3. Market Development. Speed as strategy substitutes strength in numbers for one "winner-take-all" product. The idea is to pepper the market with products that incorporate many different aspects of the new technology. It is understood that some products will be successful while many others will fail.

Speed as strategy lets the market decides which products have the greatest potential. Extensive market studies and long-term sales projections are avoided. In essence, the market itself is the test market.

A firm must be able to move quickly when a product proves successful. Flexible factories are part of the process. Production is expanded for products that are successful, while unsuccessful products are quickly discontinued. The goal is to concentrate on the products that hit, and quickly withdraw the products that fail to attract customers.

Tonka, the toy maker, follows a speed strategy in an industry where new products come and go quickly. Tonka enters fast with a barrage of new toy products. As chairman Stephen Shank notes: "We don't need home runs, we just need reasonable success, but we also need a logical candidate to hit a home run."[3] Tonka claims to be equally fast at yanking losers. Poor sellers are withdrawn from the market in as little as three months. Before moving to a speed strategy such products would have lingered in product lines much longer.

TRADITIONAL NEW PRODUCT PLANNING

Traditional new product planning follows a completely different path. It embraces extensive market research, long lead times, and a lengthy sequence of steps. The basic philosophy is to go slowly and whittle a large number of potential new product ideas down to a small number of likely-to-be-successful products. The goal is to avoid product failure and postpone heavy spending until it is clear which product will ultimately be a winner.

The most widely cited new product planning formulation was proposed by Booz, Allen & Hamilton in the 1960s and has been updated in subsequent decades. It contains many steps, the most important of which are summarized here.

1. Idea Generation. Before the new product process can proceed, new product ideas are needed. Ideas are generated with brainstorming, making unlikely product connections, and other creative approaches.

2. Idea Screening. New product ideas are then put through a "rough screen," which quickly and inexpensively eliminates those that serve no market, can never make a profit, or are a poor fit for the firm.

3. Concept Development and Testing. Crude ideas that pass the initial screen are refined into product concepts, which describe actual versions of the product. Consumer reactions are sought. Losers are dropped from further consideration.

4. Marketing Strategy. Pricing, distribution, and promotional strategies, as well as how the product should be positioned, are drawn up for each of the products that passes the previous steps. Long-term goals for sales, profits, and market share are also estimated.

5. Business Analysis. An analysis is conducted to assess which proposals are worthwhile. Detailed forecasts of sales, costs, and profits are made. If predictions point to a product that will earn profits, the process moves to the next step.

6. Product Development. Product development follows for attractive proposals. At this stage product prototypes are developed.

7. Market Testing. Market testing is then conducted to estimate actual sales. This includes small-scale consumer tests and, possibly, large-scale test markets. Expenses begin to escalate.

8. Commercialization. Successful tests are "rolled out" to regional, national, and international markets.

A COMPARISON OF THE TWO APPROACHES

The new and traditional approaches to new product planning summarized in Exhibit 12.1 differ in the following five ways.

1. Short Versus Long Lead Times. Traditional product planning is slow. It requires long lead times. It avoids errors but at great cost in terms of time. It trades time for precision. By analogy with riflery, traditional planning spends lots of time aiming. Speeding new products to market aims quickly and then tries to get off as many shots as possible. The target is moving.

2. Experimentation and Adaptability Versus Risk Reduction. In theory, more careful study and longer lead times allow for a reduction in the risk of failure. In fact, market changes and the actions of more nimble competitors often negate the benefits of more lengthy study. Sometimes, by the time the new product is introduced, it is perfectly fitted to a world that no longer exists. Speed is more adaptable. It accepts risk for what it is and tries to capture trends as they occur rather than trying to outguess them.

Support for adaption and experimentation comes from an influential article by Richard Pascale who studied Honda's entry into the American motorcycle market in the mid-1960s.[4] He concluded that Honda's entrance was replete with miscalculations and strategic mistakes, and that success was the result of serendipitous events. Instead of the order implied by formal strategic planning tools, Pascale found that Honda executives really had no plan. They simply responded to the market as it emerged with no real idea as to where sales would ultimately lead. Pascale contrasts Honda's actions with the beliefs of academic theorists. He argues that while many experts prefer theories that stress a rational and orderly progression of events, the reality is much different. The actual way in which most markets evolve is through a series of fits and starts, responses to unforeseen developments, and creative solutions to unexpected problems. Marketing strategy, in short, is a much messier process than presupposed by orderly strategic concepts.

3. The Merits of Market Research. Traditional new product planning relies heavily on market research tools to avoid failures and zero in on the successes. Unfortunately, such tools are notoriously inaccurate for "new-to-the-world" products, with which consumers have little experience. Imagine companies asking consumers about their needs for cellular phones, VCRs, compact disc players, or any other major innovation of the past few decades. Would the results of that survey be indicative of the market's true potential?

4. The Number of New Products Introduced. Traditional new product planning focuses efforts on getting to that one best product idea. It puts all its eggs in one basket. Speed, in contrast, recognizes the impossibility of such foresight. It acknowledges the inherent inability to predict what the market will want. The assumption of speed is more in tune with today's markets.

5. Action Versus Analysis Paralysis. Speed as strategy is action-oriented. It is a reaction to the criticism that planning is encumbered by analysis paralysis.

REQUIREMENTS FOR FASTER NEW PRODUCT DEVELOPMENT

Speeding up the new product development process requires a number of special skills.

Parallel New Product Development. The traditional approach sees new product planning as a relay race. When the design team is finished with the product, they pass it off—like the baton in a relay—to the engineers, who then pass it on to manufacturing. Eventually, marketing ends up with a product they are expected to sell. Events follow in sequence, one after the other.

Speed as strategy takes a different view. It envisions new product development as parallel processing, "a holistic or rugby approach—where a team tries to go the distance as a unit, passing the ball back and forth."[5] Parallel product development overlaps different tasks. Marketing, for example, works on a plan to sell the product while designers are still designing it.

Design for Assembly. Superfast innovation requires that products be designed so that they can be manufactured quickly and easily. Designing products that have fewer parts and fewer assembly steps cuts assembly time. Fewer parts also leads to greater reliability and lower costs—there are fewer parts to break down and less to buy.

A Culture of Speed and Innovation. Firms that introduce a rapid succession of new products often have a reputation for "on-the-edge" innovation. They tend to stay one step ahead of the competition in terms of styling, technology leadership, or quality. Employees at such firms embrace a philosophy of speed and innovation. They abhor bureaucracy and move quickly by making fast decisions on their own. Along with responsibility, speed requires that employees be given increased authority.

AN EXPLOSION OF PRODUCT VARIETY

A consequence of speeding so many new products to market is a much greater variety within each product category. Markets are splintered into ever-finer segments as firms introduce ever more variations on a basic product theme. The result is a product for every conceivable purpose. Whereas a single product used to satisfy a multitude of consumers, a multitude of products now serve ever-smaller segments of users. Mass marketing has given way to extreme segmentation and product proliferation.

The explosion of variety has occurred across a broad range of consumer and industrial products. In soup, for example, Campbell's once sold all its different flavors in red and white cans. Now it offers microwaveable soups, powdered soups, soup for one, low-sodium soups, and a seemingly endless variety of other choices. At least eleven different kinds of soup were introduced by Campbell's in the 1980s alone.

The major soft drink sellers have followed a similar strategy. Whereas Coca-Cola once sold a single cola soft drink—regular Coke—it now sells diet Coke, caffeine-free Coke, caffeine-free diet Coke, and other myriad flavors in two-liter, three-liter, and a multitude of other sizes. Pepsi does the same.

Consumer electronics present an even more bewildering array of merchandise. Even a single branded product such as the Sony Walkman, which was introduced in 1979, now comes in a dozen different styles, each with its own combination of features. There is a children's model, a recording model, a sports model, and so on.

Changes in telephones have been the most profound. Before deregulation, consumers rented a phone from Ma Bell. Choice was limited to a desktop or wall model, in a few different colors and styles. After deregulation, variety exploded as hundreds of different models incorporating dozens of different features, all at different price points, flooded the market. Some contain answering machines, others remember, recall, and redial phone numbers. It would take a week of careful study to fully assess the benefits and drawbacks of each seller's offering.

THE CONSEQUENCES OF EXTREME VARIETY

Product variety has many effects on consumer behavior.

More Choice. Greater variety gives consumers more choice. Instead of a simple, inexpensive pair of sneakers, consumers can now spend more than $100 on a pair of Nikes precisely designed for a particular sport.

Reduced Price Sensitivity. A large number of highly differentiated products reduces price sensitivity. Many consumers willingly pay more for a product precisely designed for their needs.

Difficulty Comparing Prices. In some product categories, such as consumer electronics, the sheer multitude of products makes price comparisons difficult. Most retailers cannot carry every brand and model. They stock only a subset. In personal stereos, for example, the models are identified by long numerical codes. It requires persistence, more persistence than most consumers are willing to put forth, to compare prices among models, or among retailers.

Excitement. A wide variety of new products with many different features builds excitement in the product category. There is always something new for the consumer to see, and salespersons have something interesting to talk about.

Wasteful Variety. Critics contend that such extreme variety is wasteful, resulting in artificially high prices and the creation of artificial needs.

They argue that it is bad to convince poor, inner-city youths that they must have something they cannot afford, like that $100 pair of sneakers. They think it would be better to make one model more efficiently and sell it at lower prices for the masses. Proponents of product variety disagree. They argue that specialization, even extreme specialization, gives consumers what they want. They point to the fact that most markets offer low-priced, more generic goods. Extreme variety allows for that option also.

TRENDS IN PRODUCT VARIETY

The trend toward ever finer gradations of demand has slowed in recent years, and may even be turning back. Some firms in these cost-conscious times are pruning product lines to increase efficiencies. That allows them to reduce prices. That does not mean the trend to greater variety has stopped. It merely means that it has gone so far, so fast that countervailing economic factors are pushing back in some firms, in some markets. Others markets continue to race ahead.

QUICK RESPONSE SYSTEMS

Quick response is a different concept than superfast innovation. Quick response concentrates on lessening the time it takes to get *existing* goods to consumers. It speeds up the transmission of marketing information, improves communication between those who make the product and those who sell it, improves manufacturing responsiveness, and quickens the distribution of goods. The goal is to make sure that the seller has the right product in the right place, at the right time. If, for example, large numbers of customers suddenly start to buy a particular style of jeans, in a particular color, in size 10, the retailer and suppliers farther up the channel of distribution all want to make sure that more of that style and color are available for sale quickly, not in eight months. To do so requires a quick response system.

There are four parts to any quick response system: (1) getting close to customers, (2) improving communication among channel members, (3) superfast production, and (4) speedier distribution.

GETTING CLOSE TO CUSTOMERS

Before a firm can respond quickly to changes in consumer preferences it must know what those preferences are. That requires a mechanism for systematically listening to customers. In that sense, quick response systems are a market research tool, but they collect information electronically from point-of-sale cash registers, rather than from lengthy marketing research questionnaires. A typical system tallies consumer purchases at the point of sale. Data is instantaneously fed back to a central location where it is analyzed to see which items are selling briskly and which are not. An added benefit of quick response systems is that they speed customers through checkout lines.

Quick response systems started in the textile and apparel industries, which have been heavily battered by imports. Levi Strauss, the blue jeans manufacturer, was an early innovator of a manufacturer-sponsored quick response system. The Levi system requires close contact between Levi and retailers. Levi affixes barcodes to goods at the factory and provides elaborate software to track the flow of jeans through the distribution channel. Levi's computers communicate directly with retailer's computers. When an item sells at retail, the information is instantly passed to Levi, which automatically reorders and ships a replacement. The benefits of staying close to customers have been clear. Whereas ten years ago it used to take forty days between the time an order was placed and the receipt of shipment, it now takes less than ten days. Costs have also fallen dramatically.

COMMUNICATION AMONG CHANNEL MEMBERS

A good quick response system requires extensive communication among channel of distribution members. Buyers and sellers must coordinate their efforts to serve customers faster, and at less expense. The textile and apparel industries were the first to form voluntary organizations to promote such coordination. The system they created in 1986 has four key linkages as shown in Exhibit 12.2.

Apparel Manufacturers and Retailers. The first link in the chain is VICS—Voluntary Interindustry Communication Standards—which connects apparel manufacturers and retailers. VICS sets communication standards between computers in order to capture information concerning consumer purchases.

Textile Manufacturers and Apparel Makers. The second link in the chain is TALC—the Textile and Apparel Linkage Council. It promotes cooperation between textile manufacturers and apparel makers. TALC sets electronic standards for labeling rolls of fabrics with barcodes and transmitting orders between buyers and sellers to speed customer ser-

Exhibit 12.2
Quick Response in the Textile and Apparel Industries

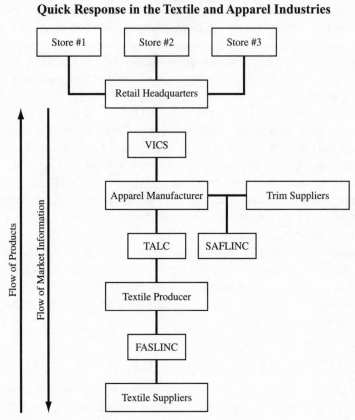

vice. TALC also sets standards for product quality. That speeds the movement of fabrics to garment makers.

Suppliers to the Textile Industry and Textile Producers. The third link is FASLINC—the Fabric and Suppliers Linkage Council—which promotes cooperation between textile suppliers and textile producers. FASLINC sets uniform quality ratings and seeks to eliminate the cost, time, and need for duplicate quality tests. In the past, buyers up and down the channel had to check goods to see if they met that firm's unique definition of quality. Firms spent more time checking up on each other than they did on serving customers. Agreement as to what constitutes quality means less need for multiple checking and faster, less expensive, customer service.

Apparel Manufacturers and Makers of Trim for Apparel. The final link in the industry chain is SAFLINC—the Sundries and Apparel Findings Council. It promotes cooperation between apparel manufacturers and makers of trim for apparel. The goal is to get the industry to respond quicker to fashion changes and become more competitive against lower-cost imports.

Those four linkage organizations work closely together to coordinate the sending of orders throughout the chain of distribution, forecasting demand at various stages within the chain, and tracing inventory and shipments along the way. The ties are meant to promote quick response. They are also meant to take maximum advantage of the competitive edge of American textile and apparel firms against imports. As products flow up the diagram in Exhibit 12.2, information flows upward and downward, to and from the retailer and supplier.

Quick response systems have been so successful in textiles, apparel, and retailing that supermarkets are now starting to set up a similar sort of system. Their system, called Efficient Consumer Response, links supermarkets, wholesalers, and suppliers for the purposes of reducing costs and quickening the flow of goods through channels of distribution.

"SUPERFAST" PRODUCTION

The third step in a quick response system is superfast production. Once customer needs have been ascertained, and communications sent back through the channel of distribution, firms must be able to switch production rapidly to the models now in demand. This requires flexible factories, which can act as superfast producers. The introduction of automation and just-in-time inventory methods into U.S. factories cut costs and sped up production in the early 1980s.

QUICKENING DISTRIBUTION

Distribution is where most of the emphasis is being placed in the 1990s. Sellers realize that chronically slow orders and wrong shipments create ill-will among customers. A quick response system can cut delivery times from months to weeks, or even days.

Wal-Mart established one of the first retailer-sponsored, state-of-the-art quick response systems. It requires all vendors to connect to its computer system. Sales data is sent instantaneously straight from the selling floor to the manufacturer's factory, where a repurchase order is immediately processed. In addition, manufacturers are often required to pre-tag items and place them on racks ready for sale. That allows Wal-Mart to cut back on distribution space. It allocates less than half as much store space for inventory as the average retailer with which it competes.

THE BENEFITS OF QUICK RESPONSE

In addition to putting more speed in the system, there are numerous other benefits that arise from a quick response.

Lower Costs. Quick response is not only faster but less expensive. In fact, what started as a system to increase speed has now turned largely into a system to cut costs. This is especially true in distribution, which in the restructuring-mad 1990s is the largest controllable cost in a product's price. Often, distribution makes up 35 percent of that price. Cutting distribution costs not only speeds up the system but leads to lower costs.

Some retailers, such as Wal-Mart, have sought to cut out the middleman, dealing directly with manufacturers. Other efficient retailers, such as the off-price warehouse clubs, deal mostly with manufacturers. There is no stock room at the Price Club. Deliveries go straight to the sales floor.

Some sellers are "outsourcing" distribution to companies such as Federal Express. That increases the speed of delivery but, equally important, makes distribution a variable rather than a fixed cost.

Quick response systems also result in fewer markdowns. Markdowns result from errors in forecasting consumer demand. Orders for clothing, for example, used to be made a year in advance. If the fashion proved less popular than expected, markdowns were required to move the merchandise off retailers' racks. Quick response makes it possible to reduce initial order time from one year to two or three months. That, in turn, moves the time horizon closer to actual consumer demand.

Quick response also results in fewer stockouts, which occur when a consumer wants an item and it is not available in the store. Quick response systems allow stores to reorder in smaller quantities, and receive their order quickly, avoiding stockouts. Wal-Mart cut stockouts by 50 percent with quick response.

Quick response also results in smaller inventories. Smaller orders, sent more frequently, keeps inventory moving quickly through the channel of distribution. That, in turn, reduces costs. Twenty years ago in the textile industry it was not unusual for a garment to take sixty-five weeks to reach a customer. The material was processed for only fifteen of those weeks. It sat in inventory for the other fifty weeks. That is why inventory costs averaged 6.4 percent of sales. Quick response systems lowered those costs substantially.

Better Service. Speeding orders to customers inevitably results in customers being served more promptly, delays in delivery being minimized, and merchandise in demand being readily available.

Stronger Ties Between Buyer and Seller. Computer linkages aid communication among channel members but have the added effect of creating a relationship between a buyer and seller. There is an incentive for both parties to remain loyal. The bond can be broken but is more likely to be continued as long as the relationship satisfies both partners.

QUESTIONS RAISED BY SPEED AS STRATEGY

The aspect of speed as strategy that proposes rushing new products to market quickly and without sufficient testing has been heavily criticized. Many troubling questions remain unanswered.

ARE THERE BENEFITS TO MOVING SLOWLY?

The race may not be over. The hare may now be ahead but the tortoise may ultimately win the race. There are, in fact, benefits to moving slowly and deliberately. McDonald's, for example, moves slowly into new food products. It is known for exhaustive product testing. Salads, which now contribute substantially to store sales and profits, took twelve years to reach their 1987 premiere.

Burger King, in contrast, moved too quickly, speeding new products and new ad campaigns to market. Its menu changed so often that consumers were confused and unsure of what products would be for sale when they next visited. While Burger King sped a perpetual stream of new products to market, McDonalds' stayed a steady pace, and won the race.

In products where safety is a key concern, rushing a new product to market could be catastrophic in today's hyper-litigious society. Rushing to market can shortchange the testing procedures necessary to foresee potential problems with new products.

Rushing to market with an unsafe and not fully ready product can also tarnish a firm's image irreparably. Consider the case of Britain's deHavilland, which introduced the first commercial jet airliner in 1952. The deHavilland Comet was a resounding success. Airlines lined up to buy them. For a while it seemed as though the firm would dominate the world's aircraft industry because of its quick entry. Then came the crashes. The most serious occurred in 1954 when a Comet broke up in mid-air after taking off from Rome's airport, killing all on board. Structural failure was deemed the cause. The remaining planes were grounded and quality bugs were worked out by 1958. But it was too late. Boeing had entered with the 707. None of the world's airlines wanted a jet from a company with a history of frequent crashes.

DOES SPEED WORK FOR ALL PRODUCTS?

Rushing new products to market is not appropriate for all kinds of products. One of the few studies that criticizes the speed-as-strategy movement advises that moving quickly works best on "incremental innovations" that are no more than simple extensions of current markets.[6] These are typically the minor kinds of product modifications found in supermarkets and other mass merchandisers. They are incidental innovations. The authors advise that it is better to go slow when radically new product innovations are at stake, especially when those products are based on new core technologies.

The use of speed as strategy is not that simple, however. Market research usually works well on incidental kinds of innovations with which consumers are familiar. It fails more often when assessing the potential of radical innovations. That suggests that market research, and the time it takes to conduct it, are more appropriate for incidental innovations. For major innovations a firm may have no choice but to test the marketplace.

Many of the examples used to illustrate the idea of rushing product to market come from high-technology businesses, where change is fast and competition is fierce. Developments in computers, for example, move much too quickly for lengthy deliberation. The market rewards action over analysis. To date, it is unclear just when moving quickly is superior to moving more cautiously.

HAS THE FLOOD OF NEW PRODUCT GONE TOO FAR?

Some marketers contend that the pace of new product introductions is now slowing. Supermarkets, which were at the end of that flood of new products, now routinely charge "slotting fees" to accept untested new products, and in some cases even assess penalties on new products that fail. There is a growing recognition that a dozen variations of a single minor product is wasteful and too costly. But so far, there has been no major trend away from overwhelming product variety. The flood of new products continues.

IS SPEED A SHORT-TERM PERSPECTIVE?

In recent decades, American managers have been castigated for focusing too intently on next quarter's results. While foreign competitors take the long view, American firms pursue short-term goals. Critics argue that speeding new products to market is yet another short-term fix. It concentrate a firm's attention on fads at the expense of more long-lived opportunities. Fast-moving firms are forced to switch from one fad to another as growth advances then recedes.

In a related issue, rushing a large number of new products to market means that those that do not succeed immediately are quickly withdrawn and replaced with other new products. But most major new products take time to incubate. Pulling and pushing them on and off the market may not give new products enough time to prove themselves.

TIME COMPRESSION MANAGEMENT

The scope of speed as strategy is still expanding. In the early 1980s it was manifested only in just-in-time inventory methods. By the early 1990s, it had expanded into distribution, product innovation, and the flow of information among industry members. But it remained a function-by-function area of study until the mid-1990s when it was renamed time compression management. Speed as strategy is now envisioned as a company-wide action the purpose of which is to eliminate all business activities not directly concerned with "adding value" to the firm's products. That includes purchasing, design, and even customer service. Akin to the restructuring craze that has raged during much of the 1990s, time compression management seeks to cut, cut, cut to be faster and more flexible. In many respects, the cost-cutting part of the time compression concept has eclipsed the time-saving part. An added benefit is cutting response time to market. Critics argue that the expanded version of speed as strategy is merely a more palatable way to pare payrolls and outsource once indispensable in-house functions. Whatever the reason, speed as strategy is an important and growing component of any marketing strategy.

NOTES

[1]Amar Bhide, "Hustle as Strategy," *Harvard Business Review,* September–October 1986, p. 59.

[2]Susan Fraker, "High-Speed Management for the High-Tech Age," *Fortune,* March 5, 1984, pp. 62–68.

[3]Steve Weiner, "Keep on Truckin'," *Forbes,* October 16, 1989, pp. 220–21.

[4]Richard Pascale, "Perspectives on Strategy: The Real Story Behind Honda's Success," *California Management Review,* Spring 1984, pp. 47–72.

[5]Hirotaka Takeuchi and Ikujiro Nonaka, "The New New Product Development Game," *Harvard Business Review,* January–February 1986, p. 137.

[6]James Utterback, et al., "When Speeding Concepts to Market Can Be a Mistake," *Interfaces,* July–August 1992, pp. 24–37.

CHAPTER 13

CUSTOMER SATISFACTION

Starting in the late 1980s, customer satisfaction turned from a backwater curiosity into a mainstream craze. Companies in virtually every industry recognized that they could gain competitive advantage by keeping customers happy, or even "delighted." They embraced the idea that satisfied customers are more loyal, less likely to switch to a competitor who offers lower prices, and can spread favorable word-of-mouth communications. Companies as diverse as Nordstrom, Four Seasons Hotels, and L. L. Bean will do virtually anything to keep customers satisfied and, they hope, loyal. They rarely sell at the lowest prices but usually provide the most rewarding overall purchase experience.

The craze for customer satisfaction grew out of the total quality management (TQM) movement of the 1980s. As the 1980s faded, it became clear that merely providing customers with products that were reliable and durable was not enough. The search for quality evolved into the search for total customer satisfaction.

The customer satisfaction movement expands upon the central tenets of the marketing concept first espoused in the 1950s. Not only do firms seek to find out and then give customers what they want—as advised by the marketing concept—they strive to completely satisfy those customers, by whatever means necessary. This chapter is about the newfound interest in getting close to customers.

WHY CUSTOMER SATISFACTION IS IMPORTANT

There are clear strategic benefits to customer satisfaction, some of which are described below.

A REACTION TO LOW-COST PRODUCERS

Competition in many industries is characterized by overcapacity and oversupply. That has led, in some cases, to sheer price cutting as a means to gain market share. The recent interest in customer satisfaction is large-ly an attempt to defend against low-cost producers. Firms find that many customers are willing to pay higher prices for better service and higher quality.

There is also a macro-economic effect. Countries that have higher cost structures have embraced customer satisfaction as a means to com-pete globally. They offer higher-priced, but better-quality merchandise, along with superior service as an antidote to low-cost producers.

THE ECONOMIC BENEFITS OF CUSTOMER RETENTION VERSUS PERPETUAL PROSPECTING

There are sound economic reasons for keeping customers satisfied, even if doing so costs money in the short run. Numerous economic studies have shown that it is cheaper to keep current customers satis-fied than to prospect continually for new customers. Current customers have no acquisition costs. Keeping them happy, and hopefully loyal, can boost profits compared to a firm that must perpetually replace the 10 to 20 percent of its customer base that the average firm loses every year.

THE CUMULATIVE VALUE OF CONTINUED RELATIONSHIPS

In recent years, there has been a growing recognition of the lifetime value of customer relationships. Keeping a customer loyal to the firm's products and services for an extended period of time creates an annuity that dwarfs the value of an individual purchase. Consider, for example, the case of a customer who spends only $10 a week on the firm's prod-ucts. After a year that consumer has spent $520, after a decade $5,200, and so on. For higher ticket items the lifetime value of a customer rela-tionship is even more pronounced.

THE POWER OF WORD OF MOUTH

The persuasiveness of opinion leadership is well documented. Many companies have found that the opinions of friends and family are far more persuasive than advertisements. For that reason many firms track not only overall satisfaction but how willing a customer is to recommend the firm's products to others. It is an especially popular practice in indus-tries such as cars and appliances, where consumers purchase once and are then out of the market for years. In such instances, recommendations can mean more than satisfaction ratings.

Recommendations are especially important in business where every firm is given a high customer satisfaction rating. A firm that earns high ratings but low recommendation scores has a problem.

Negative word of mouth can be as devastating to a company as positive word of mouth is beneficial. Dissatisfied customers infect others with a strong, negative predisposition toward a firm's products and services even though the recipients of that advice have no direct experience with the firm. The problem grows exponentially as the number of dissatisfied customers increases. If the firm creates enough dissatisfied customers, negative word-of-mouth communications dominate, and even define, the firm's public image. That is why dissatisfied customers can be "terrorists" to a firm's reputation.

Equally troublesome is the tendency for negative word of mouth to spread faster and farther than positive word of mouth. Dissatisfied customers are more likely to tell others about their bad experiences than satisfied consumers are likely to relate good experiences. That alone is a potent reason for firms to adopt a customer satisfaction program.

REDUCTION IN PRICE SENSITIVITY

There is evidence that satisfied customers with long-term ties to a company are less likely to bargain for lower prices on every individual purchase. In many instances, customer satisfaction takes the emphasis off price and puts it on service and quality.

CONSUMER SATISFACTION AS A FORWARD-LOOKING INDICATOR OF BUSINESS SUCCESS

Consumer satisfaction is a long-term strategy. It takes time to cultivate a reputation for superior service, and requires that a firm invest heavily in a wide range of activities meant to please present and future customers. Customer satisfaction programs are expensive propositions that add nothing to the immediate "bottom line." The payoff comes long after. But the benefits persist long-term. As such, consumer satisfaction is a forward-looking indicator of business success that measures how well consumers *will* respond to the company in the future. Other measures of market performance, such as sales and market share, are backward-looking measures of success. They tell how well the firm has done in the past, not how well it will do in the future. A firm might sport fine financials but if it is sowing dissent and dissatisfaction among its customer base those financials will not last. Customer satisfaction measures can be more predictive of future performance than current accounting data.

SEVEN ELEMENTS OF A SUCCESSFUL CUSTOMER SATISFACTION PROGRAM

Customer satisfaction programs usually include some combination of the following elements: (1) quality products and services, (2) relationship marketing, (3) loyalty promotion programs, (4) a focus on the best customers, (5) efficient complaint handling, (6) unconditional guarantees, and (7) pay-for-performance packages.

1. QUALITY PRODUCTS AND SUPERIOR SERVICE

Before a firm can even hope to implement a customer satisfaction program it must have a quality product and good service. At the very least, standards must meet those of major industry players. A product that does not work, is unreliable, backed by poor service, or deficient in any other important respect does not even meet the prerequisites for customer satisfaction. Quality comes first, satisfaction programs follow.

High customer satisfaction firms also tend to provide high levels of customer service. That is often how they justify their higher prices. On average, high-service firms charge 10 percent more than lower-service firms.

2. RELATIONSHIP MARKETING

A key ingredient to any loyalty promotion program is the building of long-term relationships with customers. The assumption is that strong, mutually beneficial relationships between buyers and sellers build repeat business and promote customer loyalty. Examples of relationship marketing can be found in every sector of the economy and the trend toward more and stronger relationships is growing. Today, an increasing number of economic transactions take place between buyers and sellers who are working together.

The differences between single-transaction and relationship marketing are many. Single-transaction marketing focuses on a discrete, individual sale. Like a one-night stand, the relationship ends once the sale is consummated. Relationship marketing assumes a different kind of courtship. It proposes a veritable marriage between the buyer and the seller that starts once the first sale is transacted.

Relationship marketing differs from single-transaction marketing in other respects as well. While the latter focuses almost solely on price the former shifts the emphasis to noneconomic satisfactions, such as service, delivery time, and the certainty of continued supply.

Relationship marketing presupposes the opportunity for shared benefit. It works only if the buyer and seller can agree on a relationship that satisfies both partners. Single-transaction marketing works on a model of contradictory needs—the buyer wants a good price; the seller wants a high profit.

Single-transaction sellers are sometimes part of the seedier side of marketing. New York City electronics retailers, for example, often run afoul of the authorities for advertising unrealistically low prices, then once the consumer is in the store, engaging in "bait-and-switch" and other less savory sales tactics. They can get away with it because of the steady flow of tourists and the almost complete lack of repeat business. Their goal is not to build lasting relationships with customers but to make a continuous series of first-time purchases. Other merchants, with a greater incidence of repeat business, would not last long with such practices.

Some relationships are forced. Firms that engineer switching costs into their transactions tie the customer to the seller but do so in a way that denies the buyer a real choice. Buyers can leave the relationship but will incur costs for doing so. Firms that rely on proprietary technologies and patented parts also form forced relationships. Long-term contracts do the same. In each of these cases the seller may bolt given the opportunity to do so.

There are risks to relationship marketing. A firm that builds a relationship with its customers usually charges a premium price for the increased service. That leaves the firm vulnerable to price competition from low-price sellers, who offer less service but also charge less.

More insidious, the defection may be partial. Customers may switch their large, easy-to-fill orders to lower-priced competitors who specialize in such transactions, and leave the smaller, more difficult orders to the high-service firm. That is a bad relationship for the seller that must be fixed or ended.

Attempts to build relationships with customers may fail for other reasons as well. First, some customers may refuse to become dependent on a single supplier. In other cases, there may be no mutual benefit for buyer and seller. Third, some customers may prefer a short-term focus based solely on low prices. Relationship marketing is often, but not always, successful.

3. LOYALTY PROMOTION PROGRAMS

Loyalty promotion programs have become a widely used way to build buyer-seller relationships. Typically, they reward heavy users for staying loyal to a single seller's product. The airline industry was the first to exploit this concept, implementing frequent flier programs on a grand scale. In the cutthroat competition of the early 1980s, the large, full-service carriers began rewarding frequent fliers with free trips if they used a single carrier. The frequent business traveler is the most coveted airline customer. Since the company pays for the ticket, and the traveler gets the frequent flier miles, the airlines are able to steer price insensitive customers to their high-priced, commodity product (most airlines provide basically the same service) and build customer loyalty.

Similar loyalty promotion programs have spread to virtually every other industry. Hotels and car rental companies have adopted almost identical programs. Long distance phone companies and mail-order catalogs have club programs. Partnerships among sellers have also spread widely. Hotels team up with airlines and car rental companies to form a network of binding ties. Such systems are now so pervasive, and often so complicated, that it is difficult to understand the specifics of each plan.

4. A FOCUS ON THE BEST CUSTOMERS

Although loyalty promotion programs vary greatly, what all have in common is that they target the most valued customers. They almost always focus on the 20 percent of customers that routinely consume 80 percent of sales. But the best customers are more than merely heavy users. Of course, they spend more, but they also pay their bills promptly, require less service (they already know how to interact with the firm), and are sometimes less price sensitive—preferring stability over perpetually changing to the vendor that currently offers the lowest price.

Inherent in a focus on the best customers must be a willingness to let bad customers go. Studies have shown that many small customers not only do not generate enough sales volume to make their business worthwhile but they often take up a disproportionate amount of the seller's service time. Sometimes the seller loses money on each such transaction. Just as loyalty promotion programs reward heavy users, so too do additional fees and annoying surcharges discourage continued patronage of small, unprofitable buyers.

MINI-CASE: BANKS AND SMALL CUSTOMERS

In recent years, as competition among retail banks and mutual funds has increased there has been a growing recognition that small customers are unprofitable. As a result, banks have raised "nuisance" fees to discourage continued patronage by small savers or to make them pay for the services they demand. This has created a controversy. Many banks now require high minimum balances for free checking, and charge heavily for bounced checks. Some banks are even starting to calculate how much they actually make from each customer—including interest on loans and credit card balance finance charges—and rate those customers on a scale. A computer terminal instantly lets a teller know whether someone is a one-star or a four-star customer, and services and fees are tailored accordingly. The banks contend that they must do this to remain competitive. They argue that mutual funds do the same and are stealing their customers. Critics argue otherwise. They contend that large numbers of people will be shut out of the banking system by such practices. What do you think? Should banks be forced to cater to small customers? Do they have a social responsibility to do so? Or should the market be allowed to operate as it will?

5. EFFECTIVE COMPLAINT HANDLING

Complaint handling is tied tightly to product quality. A firm must make products that work right the first time before it even considers installing a complaint handling system. Only then, if something goes wrong, does the firm move quickly to fix the problem. Quality assurance must precede complaint handling.

There are strong economic arguments for installing a complaint handling system. While estimates vary wildly, it is clear that most consumers have experienced problems with at least some products, delivery

Exhibit 13.1
The Complaint-Handling Process

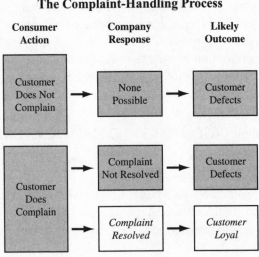

times, or service in the past year. The question is what happens once they have a problem. Exhibit 13.1 illustrates the three-step process.

The dissatisfied consumer typically makes a decision either *to complain* or *not to complain.* An absence of complaints is not necessarily a good thing. Upwards of 70 percent of all consumers experiencing a problem with a product or service do not complain. Most do not have the time or do not think it will do any good. These dissatisfied customers take an easier action—they simply defect to another seller, then tell others about their bad experience. The firm that lost the customer has no idea what happened.

Complaining customers represent the "tip of the iceberg." They give the *firm a chance to resolve the complaint* to the satisfaction of the customer.

Speed of response is important. There is only a short period of time when the dissatisfied customer can be turned back into a loyal patron. A consumer whose complaint is not resolved quickly may become permanently dissatisfied with the sponsor and defect to other sellers. Front-line employees must be empowered to act quickly on consumer complaints without having to obtain myriad signatures and approvals.

It must also be easy to contact the firm. The 800 numbers that have proliferated in recent years make it easy for customers to contact the company with comments, questions, and complaints. A firm that allows for easy access stands in stark contrast to a firm that passes consumers from one person to another in the organization until they give up and shop elsewhere.

It is also important to have empathy with the irate customer. The firm's representatives must view the problem from the consumer's perspective. If, for example, a customer is angry because her plane is delayed it is not enough simply to state the facts—that bad weather is beyond the company's control. That will only make the customer more angry. Instead, the representative must put himself in the customer's situation. Contrast the response style of Pan Am with that of British Airways. When a Pan Am flight delayed by bad weather made customers angry, Pan Am compounded the problem by giving disgruntled consumers the wrong information on who to complain to. Eventually, the dissatisfied consumers were told Pan Am was not responsible for the weather. British Airways responded differently when a mechanical problem grounded their Concorde. Angry customers were given a full refund and a letter of apology, and planes were chartered specifically to fly them to their destinations. As one executive noted: "We'd rather spend money and keep customers satisfied than initiate five or six complaints."[1] That is a key reason why British Airways continues to earn accolades for customer satisfaction into the mid-1990s while Pan Am no longer exists.

Complaint resolution is the only path that leads to *continued brand loyalty*. Customers who do not complain and customers who complain but whose complaints are not resolved are both likely to defect to another seller. Furthermore, they are likely to avoid not only the product with the problem, but the firm's entire product line. Again, statistics vary but between one-half and three-quarters of consumers whose complaints are resolved report that they intend to repurchase from the same firm. That is why effective complaint handling is so important.

6. UNCONDITIONAL GUARANTEES

Unconditional guarantees are required for any customer satisfaction program. They reduce the risk of consumer purchase, signal product quality, and unequivocally state that the company stands behind its product. The best guarantee is one that the consumer will never have to act on.

A good guarantee must contain the following characteristics:

- It must be unconditional. There can be no caveats or conditions that restrict the return policy. If the customer is unhappy, the product can be returned with no questions asked.
- It must be specific. It is not enough to state that service will be fast. It is necessary to state that the customer's muffler will be installed in one hour or less, or the job is free. Federal Express promises delivery by 10:30 the next morning, not sometime the next morning.
- It must be realistic. A guarantee that offers too much smacks of gimmickry. Pre–World War II fountain pen manufacturers, for example, offered lifetime guarantees. (It was never clear whose lifetime.) Waterman even introduced a one-hundred-year guarantee for pens it produced in the 1940s. The length of these guarantees brought government requests to moderate the promotions. A gimmick will be recognized for what it is—an attempt to promote products rather than satisfy consumers. Still, some companies such as L. L. Bean have return policies that allow the customer to return the product for repair or replacement at any time.
- It must be stated in simple, easy-to-understand language, not the language of lawyers. The guarantee must clearly state the terms of the offer.
- It must be easy to collect on. It cannot require that consumers obtain advance clearances, send the product insured to distant places at their own expense, or retain extensive documentation. Imagine invoking the guarantee on the one-hundred-year pen, only to be told that proof of purchase was necessary.

One of the risks of unconditional guarantees is that fraud will be pervasive. Consumers will take advantage of the return policy. Most consumers have heard stories of a friend, relative, or neighbor who obtained a refund unfairly. That consumer may have returned a dress that was worn to a party, or a gift that was bought from a different merchant at a different price. Such rip-offs are inevitable and cannot be allowed to run amok. But, fortunately for the firm, the vast majority of consumers invoke guarantees only when they are truly dissatisfied. More important, the goodwill and positive word of mouth that is created by the guarantee usually far outweighs the inevitable rip-offs.

7. PERFORMANCE-RELATED PAY

A customer satisfaction program cannot work without people. Specifically, employees must be rewarded for helping increase customer satisfaction. That is why many firms moved to install performance-related pay in the 1990s. In fact, a recent study found that 26 percent of all sampled companies had sales compensation programs tied to customer satisfaction and quality measures.[2] Most typically, such programs provide incentive bonuses to those employees who earn outstanding customer satisfaction ratings. In the auto industry, for example, dealership employees—including salespersons and repair shop personnel—earn substantial proportions of their salaries based on the results of customer satisfaction surveys. Proponents claim this has helped increase service and build repeat business. Critics argue that, as with other such schemes, employees merely manipulate the process to boost ratings.

MEASURING CUSTOMER SATISFACTION

Spending on customer satisfaction measurement soared during the first few years of the 1990s.[3] In fact, a review of the top fifty market research firms, advertising agencies, and opinion research organizations revealed that customer satisfaction measurement was responsible for much of the growth in research industry revenues.[4] The "1993 Directory of Customer Satisfaction Measurement Firms" published in *Marketing News* (October 25, 1993) lists more than ninety companies that offer services in more than forty different sub-areas within customer satisfaction—ranging from customer retention to quantified measurement. Spending for customer satisfaction measurement is now slowing, but the growing interest in other countries means demand should remain high in the years ahead.

WHAT TO MEASURE

There is no one universally accepted "best" measure of customer satisfaction. Instead, there are as many ways to measure it as there are measurers. Most measures, however, focus on the same core concepts.

1. *Overall customer satisfaction.* The most straightforward way to measure customer satisfaction is to simply ask consumers how satisfied they are with a particular product or service. Typically, there are two parts to the process—the first measures rates of satisfaction with a *client* firm's products and/or services, the second asks how *competitors* rank in terms of overall customer satisfaction.
2. *Dimensions of customer satisfaction.* Some studies break the problem down into its component parts. Typically, there are four steps in the process. First, they identify the *key dimensions* of customer satisfaction. Then, they ask consumers to *rate the client's product* and/or services on specific items such as speed of service or friendliness of service personnel. The third step entails doing the same for *competitors'* products. Finally, consumers are asked which dimensions are *most important* in judging overall customer satisfaction.
3. *Confirmation of expectations.* Still other studies infer satisfaction based on whether the firm's product and service met or exceeded consumers' expectations.
4. *Repurchase intent.* Some researchers attempt to measure customer satisfaction behaviorally by asking consumers whether they would patronize the seller again.
5. *Willingness to recommend.* In durable good purchases, such as cars and appliances, consumers are unlikely to repurchase for years. As a result, some firms measure how likely those consumers are to recommend the product to a friend or family member. Such measures also get around the problem of all firms getting high ratings but low recommendation scores.
6. *Customer dissatisfaction.* Finally, some firms monitor (a) complaints, (b) returns, (c) recalls, (d) warranty costs, (e) negative word of mouth, and (f) defections.

Most marketing research firms then propose ways to *improve* customer satisfaction ratings, and offer a continuous *tracking study* to monitor changes in customer satisfaction over time.

MEASUREMENT SCALES

Numerous scales have been proposed on which to measure customer satisfaction. Exhibit 13.2 presents some of the more popular options as described by Mack Hanan of the Wellspring Group and Peter Karp of Business Science International.[5]

MYSTERY SHOPPERS

In recent years there has been a surge in interest in measuring customer satisfaction using observational methods. "Mystery shoppers" are sent into retail stores to see if employees meet or exceed service standards set by the firm. It is not a new idea. For decades, mystery shoppers monitored employee theft and change-making. But now the approach is used to measure service quality. "Mystery callers" are also common. Research firms telephone client firms to see how quickly the call is answered, the

Exhibit 13.2
A Sample of Customer Satisfaction Measurement Scales

2-point scale: (used by Gordon S. Black, who claims it eases interpretation)	Was the product delivered as promised? Yes No			

4-point scale: (used by Louis Harris and Associates)	Overall, how would you rate the quality of the service provided for you by _____ within the past three [six] months?			
	1	2	3	4
	Very Satisfied	Satisfied	Dissatisfied	Very Dissatisfied

5-point scales: (used by IBM)	1	2	3	4	5
	Very Satisfied	Satisfied	Neutral	Dissatisfied	Very Dissatisfied
(used by Cablevision)	1	2	3	4	5
	Excellent	Good	Satisfactory	Not Too Satisfactory	Poor
(used by Louis Harris and Associates)	1	2	3	4	5
	Excellent	More than Satisfactory	Satisfactory	Less than Satisfactory	Un- Acceptable
(a competitive measure used by General Foods in dry cereals and Procter & Gamble in detergents)	1	2	3	4	5
	Much Better	Better	About the Same	Not as Good	Much Worse

(continued)

Exhibit 13.2 *(continued)*

7-point scale:	How do you feel about _____? I feel:

Delighted-Terrible Scale by Robert Westbrook, "A Rating Scale for Measuring Product/Service Satisfaction," *Journal of Marketing*, Fall 1980, pp. 68–72.	7 6 5 4 3 2 1
	
	De- Pleased Mostly Mixed Mostly Unhappy Terrible
	lighted Satisfied (about Dis-
	                      equally satisfied
	                      satisfied
	                      and dis-
	                      satisfied)

10-point scales:	Given all your experiences as a _____ owner, how satisfied or dissatisfied are you with your _____ ?
(used by the Swedish National Customer Satisfaction Barometer)	1 _____ 10 Very Dissatisfied Very Satisfied
(used by General Electric)	1 _____ 10 Poor Excellent

101-point scale:	Overall, how satisfied have you been with this _____ ?
(used by Federal Express)	0% _____ 100% Complete Complete Dissatisfaction Satisfaction

extent of product knowledge demonstrated by employees, how problems are resolved, and other customer satisfaction-related issues.

CONTINUOUS TRACKING STUDIES VERSUS ONE-TIME SURVEYS

The earliest and crudest measures of customer satisfaction relied on one-time, single-shot studies aimed at assessing whether consumers were satisfied with a particular purchase. For the most part, that approach has been replaced by tracking studies, which measure customer satisfaction at regular intervals and assess temporal changes in an ongoing relationship with the customer.

Research firms like tracking studies because they provide a continued source of revenues, but they run the risk that once they set up a customer satisfaction tracking system the client will move it "in-house" and cease, or least reduce, its relationship with the research firm. The client may be willing to pay for the initial setup but may be unwilling to fund a continuous tracking study.

Consider the case of J. D. Power and Associates, which signed up Toyota as its first big customer shortly after the research firm was founded in 1968. Within a few years, Toyota's business provided 75 percent of Power's revenues. After a few years, however, Toyota moved that market research function in-house, cutting J. D. Power out of the picture.

COMPARATIVE VERSUS MONADIC MEASURES

Customer satisfaction is a relative measure. As all firms increase their level of customer satisfaction, any individual firm must increase its rating just to remain constant in terms of competitor rankings. As a result, most customer satisfaction studies measure perceptions of competitors' satisfaction as well as those of the client firm.

CUSTOMIZED VERSUS SYNDICATED SERVICES

As with most other marketing research services, some customer satisfaction research firms offer customized measurement services, designed specifically for an individual firm. Others, such as J. D. Power, sell their standardized service to all members of a particular industry.

J. D. Power and Associates is one of the most influential firms measuring customer satisfaction. Founded in 1968, it is best known for three customer satisfaction studies in the auto industry (in addition to its Initial Quality Study, which measures the incidence of repairs during the first three months of car ownership).

1. *Sales Satisfaction Study.* This annual survey of 40,000 new vehicle buyers provides manufacturers and dealers with feedback on three aspects of customer satisfaction: (1) the sales experience, (2) delivery of the vehicle, and (3) initial product condition. It measures overall customer satisfaction at the time of purchase and provides an index score that allows sellers to compare one manufacturer's model with another.

2. *Customer Satisfaction with Product Quality and Dealer Service Study.* Started in 1981, 80,000 questionnaires are mailed (typically, 30,000 respond) to new vehicle owners after one year of ownership. The survey evaluates the manufacturer and the dealer, and measures the intention to repurchase as well as overall satisfaction. Clients pay up to $130,000 for the results based on a sliding scale of their ability to pay.

3. *Vehicle Performance Index.* Started in 1991, this study surveys 20,000 customers after two to three years of ownership. The survey measures product performance and service quality.

Questionnaires are sent to registered automobile owners on a list purchased from R. L. Polk, which obtains the data from motor vehicle records. Owners are sent a six- to eight-page questionnaire that contains up to ninety questions and takes thirty to forty minutes to complete. A crisp, new one dollar bill is included with the mailed questionnaire to gain cooperation. A minimum of 150 completed questionnaires is needed to analyze the data for a specific car model. Power claims a response rate of between 38 and 50 percent.

The company earns money from customer satisfaction surveys in two ways. First, it charges clients to see the results of its studies. To rank near the top is a prestigious achievement. Interestingly, unlike *Consumer Reports,* J. D. Power only reports "winners" to the public. Results on poor performers are not released. Second, Power controls and charges for the right to use its ratings in client advertising, charging about $10,000 for each ad, with an additional $2,000 to $3,000 levied when an ad is created. A favorable J. D. Power rating is so coveted that consultants now offer services to help clients improve scores.

Power's success with customer satisfaction in automobiles has led to an expansion into similar services for computers and airlines, with its newest and grandest proposal for a brand-based "Customer Satisfaction in America" study, which will survey five thousand consumers of nearly three hundred products, including public services such as the post office, education, and police services.

A CONCEPTUAL MODEL OF
CUSTOMER SATISFACTION

According to the "expectancy/disconfirmation paradigm," customer satisfaction ratings emerge from a comparison between prior expectations and actual product performance. The result of that comparison then leads to either confirmation or disconfirmation of those prior expectations, which, in turn, leads to customer satisfaction or dissatisfaction. The benefit of customer satisfaction to firms comes only when customers stay loyal to their products. A customer who is satisfied but defects to another seller's wares is of no economic value to the firm that has undertaken a customer satisfaction building program. That four-step process is illustrated graphically in Exhibit 13.3.

Exhibit 13.3
A Conceptual Model of Customer Satisfaction

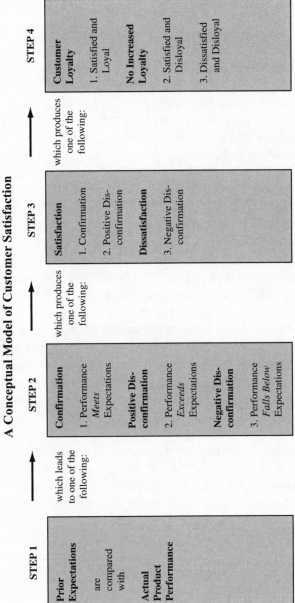

STEP 1

Prior Expectations

are compared with

Actual Product Performance

which leads to one of the following:

STEP 2

Confirmation

1. Performance *Meets* Expectations

Positive Disconfirmation

2. Performance *Exceeds* Expectations

Negative Disconfirmation

3. Performance *Falls Below* Expectations

which produces one of the following:

STEP 3

Satisfaction

1. Confirmation
2. Positive Disconfirmation

Dissatisfaction

3. Negative Disconfirmation

which produces one of the following:

STEP 4

Customer Loyalty

1. Satisfied and Loyal

No Increased Loyalty

2. Satisfied and Disloyal
3. Dissatisfied and Disloyal

1. EXPECTATIONS VERSUS ACTUAL PRODUCT PERFORMANCE

Expectations are anticipations about how brands or products will perform. Consumers may expect products to be easy to use, reliable, stylish, inexpensive, indicative of good taste to their friends, or laden with features.

Expectations are formed prior to purchase based on previous experience with similar products, word-of-mouth communications with others, and the promotional efforts of the firm. Advertisements can make claims that overstate, understate, or realistically portray the product's benefits.

Expectations influence perceptions of product performance. Two explanations have been offered based on two prominent theories: (1) consistency theory, and (2) assimilation-contrast.

Consistency theory predicts that consumers will avoid inconsistencies in their beliefs whenever possible. They will bend their perceptions of product performance to match their prior expectations for that product. Consumers with high expectations for a product will be more satisfied with a product than consumers with low expectations. Consider, for example, product evaluations of automobiles. Consistency theory predicts that consumers with low expectations for American-made cars will, in fact, judge those cars to be of low quality, even if actual product quality has been improved. Likewise, high expectations for Japanese cars will result in judgments of higher quality, even if the consumers' actual performance is less than expected. Consistency theory argues that those consumers will maintain psychological consistency at all costs. Their expectations will color their judgments of product performance and their ultimate satisfaction with the product.

Assimilation contrast theory argues otherwise. It contends that if expectations are set unrealistically high, and actual performance falls short, consumers will experience a contrast effect with prior expectations. They will perceive the product as worse than it actually is. If, on the other hand, the original claim sets up an expectation that stretches the truth just a little, consumers will assimilate the difference and perceive the product to be better than it actually is. Involvement with the product category determines their latitude of their acceptance. High involvement leads to a narrower latitude of acceptance and a greater likelihood of a contrast effect.

Which theory is right? Over the years, research into the relative importance of prior expectations, product performance, and confirmation/disconfirmation on customer satisfaction has produced mixed results. Some studies have found that prior expectations are more important than actual product performance, while others have found product performance to be more important. Still others have found that both constructs are important.

Customer satisfaction also depends on actual product performance, or how well a product works. Unlike expectations, performance can be engineered into a product. When measured objectively, some products simply offer higher levels of performance than others.

Higher levels of performance directly affect perceptions of satisfaction and lead to higher consumer satisfaction. One study found that the actual performance of the product was a more important predictor of customer satisfaction than the other psychological constructs.

2. CONFIRMATION/DISCONFIRMATION

Consumer satisfaction results from a comparison of prior expectations and actual product performance. Expectations are either confirmed or disconfirmed when compared with actual product performance. Three outcomes are possible: confirmation or two variants of disconfirmation of prior expectations.

1. *Confirmation of expectations.* A product can perform as expected. What consumers thought the product would do, it did. A product expected to perform well does. A product expected to perform poorly performs poorly.
2. *Positive disconfirmation.* A product may work better than expected—a pleasant disconfirmation of prior expectations. Expectations may have been too low or product performance exceptionally high.
3. *Negative disconfirmation.* Least fortunate for the seller, the product may turn out to perform worse than expected. Expectations may have been set too high, or product performance may be too low. Negative disconfirmation leads to lower customer satisfaction.

3. CONSUMER SATISFACTION/DISSATISFACTION

The third step in the model is customer satisfaction, or dissatisfaction, itself. Three paths are possible.

1. A product that meets or exceeds expectations produces a confirmation of expectations, which results in customer satisfaction.
2. A product that exceeds expectations also produces satisfaction, but disconfirms prior expectations.
3. A product that performs worse than expected produces consumer dissatisfaction and disconfirms prior expectations.

Exhibit 13.4
The Satisfaction/Loyalty Relationship

LOYALTY

		Low	High
	Low	*Failures* *dissatisfied and not loyal*	*Forced Loyalty* *dissatisfied but tied to the firm by loyalty promotion program*
CUSTOMER SATISFACTION			
	High	*Defectors* *satisfied but not loyal*	*Successes* *satisfied, loyal, and most likely to engage in positive word of mouth*

4. THE CONSEQUENCES OF CUSTOMER SATISFACTION

The fourth and final step in the model recognizes that higher levels of customer satisfaction do not always lead to increased levels of brand loyalty. As Exhibit 13.4 illustrates, four outcomes are possible.

1. Sometimes consumers are satisfied and remain loyal to the firm's offerings.
2. At other times, consumers are satisfied but defect to another firm when given the chance. Satisfaction is high but the strategic benefits of customer loyalty to the seller are not realized.
3. Still other consumers would defect if they could, but some loyalty promotion program such as frequent flyer miles forces them to remain loyal. They are stuck with the firm even though they are not completely satisfied with its products and services.
4. Finally, there are consumers who are neither satisfied nor loyal to the firm's offerings.

DEALING WITH CUSTOMER DEFECTIONS

In recent years, there have been considerable criticisms leveled at the entire customer satisfaction movement. The essence of the argument is that while 90 percent of a firm's customers routinely rate themselves as "satisfied" or "very satisfied" with the firm's products and service, only 30 to 40 percent of those same customers actually repurchase from the firm. The rest defect to another seller. In fact, it has been observed that more than 50 percent of all defectors reported just prior to defecting that they were either "satisfied" or "very satisfied" with the firm's products and services. Critics claim that that is because customer satisfaction is the wrong thing to measure. It is the bond between satisfaction and loyalty to the firm's brand that is most important. Consequently, firms should study ways in which to ensure that satisfied consumers stay loyal to the firm.

CREATING "COMPLETELY SATISFIED" CUSTOMERS

A recent article by Jones and Sasser argues that the difference between customers who are "satisfied" and those who are "completely satisfied" is huge.[6] It argues that only "completely satisfied" customers are loyal. Customers who report being merely "satisfied" are ripe for defection. Since a large percentage of respondents to customer satisfaction surveys report they are either "satisfied" or "completely satisfied," the cut is not between satisfied and dissatisfied but between the two degrees of satisfaction. Firms may think they are doing well, the authors argue, by achieving a high customer satisfaction rating, but unless they are creating a steady stream of completely satisfied customers they are likely to experience defections.

The numbers are staggering. The authors report that "totally satisfied customers were six times more likely to repurchase Xerox products over the next eighteen months than its satisfied customers." The strategic advice is clear. Companies should spend heavily to create hordes of "completely satisfied" customers. It is a tough sell for the consultant. Companies are reluctant to spend the large amounts of money necessary to boost ratings that one extra notch. According to Jones and Sasser, this is why customers continue to defect.

STUDYING CUSTOMER DEFECTIONS

Estimates vary, but the average firm loses between 10 and 20 percent of its customer base each year. That means that unless something is done to stop customer defections, firms must perpetually prospect for new customers, an expensive option with an uncertain outcome. A recent article by Frederick Reichheld argues that firms can learn much by studying failure.[7] Specifically, they should find out why customers defect and then try to root out the causes. Executives should spend time talking to customers who have defected to other sellers so that they can understand first-hand the nature of the problem.

Reichheld believes that failure analysis is far more fruitful than superfluous satisfaction surveys. He contends that customers are "over-surveyed" and find it easier to be nice than to be truthful. Furthermore, when cash incentives are at stake, employees can easily manipulate the entire process, learning how to get good customer satisfaction scores without actually improving deep-felt satisfaction. He argues that that is why only 30 to 40 percent of customers repurchase even though 90 percent are satisfied. Studying the *causes* of defection, he suggests, is of much greater value.

Whatever the case, customer satisfaction is a key consideration in any firm's strategic position. It provides a unified purpose for the firm based on the principle that customers stand at the center of all the firm's activities. It is the embodiment of the age-old statement that the "Customer is King," or is it "Queen"?

NOTES

[1]Patricia Sellers, "How to Handle Customers' Gripes," *Fortune,* October 24, 1988, p. 92.

[2]Catherine Romano, "Pay for Satisfaction," *Management Review,* December 1995, p. 16.

[3]Jack Honomichl, "Spending on Satisfaction Measurement Continues to Rise," *Marketing News,* April 12, 1993, pp. 17–18.

[4]Jack Honomichl, "Three Factors Drive Growth of the Top 50 Research Firms," *Marketing News,* January 7, 1993, pp. H2, H18.

[5]Mack Hanan and Peter Karp, *Customer Satisfaction: How to Maximize, Measure, and Market Your Company's "Ultimate Product,"* New York: Amacom (American Management Association), 1989.

[6]Thomas Jones and Earl Sasser, "Why Satisfied Customers Defect," *Harvard Business Review,* November–December 1995, pp. 88–99.

[7]Frederick Reichheld, "Learning from Customer Defections," *Harvard Business Review,* March–April 1996, pp. 56–69.

NAME INDEX

SUBJECT INDEX

ABOUT THE AUTHOR

STEVEN P. SCHNAARS is currently Professor and Department Chair in the Department of Marketing at Baruch College, New York, where he has taught since 1979. His research focuses on how new technological products evolve from inception to market acceptance and how firms compete strategically in hypercompetitive markets. His published books include *Managing Imitation Strategies* and *Megamistakes* (both published by The Free Press). When not working, he runs serious long-distance races. He lives in Huntington, New York.